Conversations with Toni Morris

Literary Conversations Series

Peggy Whitman Prenshaw
General Editor

Conversations with Toni Morrison

Edited by
Danille Taylor-Guthrie

University Press of Mississippi
Jackson

Books by Toni Morrison

The Bluest Eye. New York: Holt, Rinehart, & Winston, 1970.

Sula. New York: Knopf, 1973.

The Black Book. Compiled by Middleton Harris, with the assistance of Morris Levitt, Roger Furman, Ernest Smith. Edited by Toni Morrison. New York: Random House, 1974

Song of Solomon. New York: Knopf, 1977.

Tar Baby. New York: Knopf, 1981.

Beloved. New York: Knopf, 1987.

Jazz. New York: Knopf, 1992.

Playing in the Dark: Whiteness and the Literary Imagination. Cambridge, Mass.: Harvard University Press, 1992.

Race-ing Justice, En-gendering Power: Essays on Anita Hill, Clarence Thomas, and the Construction of Social Reality. Edited by Toni Morrison. New York: Pantheon, 1992.

Copyright © 1994 by the University Press of Mississippi
All rights reserved
Manufactured in the United States of America

05 04 03 02   8 7 6 5

The paper in this book meets the guidelines for permanence and durability of the Committee on Production Guidelines for Book Longevity of the Council on Library Resources.

Library of Congress Cataloging-in-Publication Data

Morrison, Toni.
    Conversations with Toni Morrison / edited by Danille Taylor-Guthrie.
        p.   cm. — (Literary conversations series)
    Includes index.
    ISBN 0-87805-691-2. — ISBN 0-87805-692-0 (paper)
    1. Morrison, Toni—Interviews.   2. Afro-American women novelists—20th century—Interviews.   I. Taylor-Guthrie, Danille Kathleen, 1952–   II. Title.   III. Series.
PS3563.08749Z464   1994
813'.54—dc20   93-44738
                                                CIP

British Library Cataloging-in-Publication data available

Contents

Introduction

Toni Morrison being awarded the 1993 Nobel Prize for literature makes her the first African American to be so honored and marks not only a personal triumph but also the recognition of the artistry of African American fiction and the validity of the black woman's voice.

Born Chloe Anthony Wofford, in 1931 in Lorain, Ohio, the author Toni Morrison as a writer has evolved with each new work. For her there was no immediate realization that she was a "writer" until after the 1977 publication of her third book *Song of Solomon*. What she did feel, however, after she completed her first novel, *The Bluest Eye*, was that writing was a "way of thinking" she never planned to live without, even if her subsequent works were never published. In the interviews collected here, Morrison gives thoughtful and engaging responses, frequently charming her interviewers. Nearly all begin by asking about *The Bluest Eye*. The impact of her story of a young battered African American girl who sought love and acceptance through the miracle/nightmare of blue eyes would have been impossible for any to predict. As a result Morrison became an integral part of a nascent group of black women writers who would alter the course of African American, American, and world literature. Alice Walker, Paule Marshall, Audre Lorde, Toni Cade Bambara, Maya Angelou, Sonia Sanchez, Nikki Giovanni, Gayl Jones, and Morrison all directed their unwavering gazes on subject matters previously marginalized in literature—black women and their worlds.

Morrison's writing is distinctive for it probes and fleshes out within narrative and characterization ideas about which she is curious. She is an intellectual who via the craft of writing and art of storytelling seeks to discover the consequences of choices and actions. Her readers are not handed ready answers but rather must become part of a tale's resolution. Her fiction emerges from within the universe of her mind, which has been shaped by the African American culture of her childhood, expanded by a formal education in English and the Classics at Howard and Cornell Universities, and forged by her experiences as an African American woman. Her intellectual and imaginative sensibilities are unromantic and unsentimental like those of her literary foremother Zora Neale Hurston. Hurston viewing herself as "nontragically Black" knew that there was far too much spirituality, humor, and wisdom in the folk to view them as mere tragic victims. In a similar vein Morrison, in her fiction, retrieves the past, historically and mythically engaging her characters to fully participate in their lives through the prism of African American culture.

The interviews gathered here range from conversations with academics to a television appearance. They provide the opportunity to chart not only her career as an artist but also her role as an African American artistic celebrity. Few African American authors gain recognition in mainstream magazines and newspapers so Morrison being featured on the cover of *Newsweek* in 1981 was a major occurrence. Morrison always proudly presents herself as a branch on the ancient tree of black assertiveness and self-definition that is richly and deeply rooted in the folk culture. She unapologetically declares herself to be a "black woman writer" but beyond that chafes at categorization. She is frequently noted as being almost mesmerizing and as having a powerful presence despite her small stature. Her lyrical voice matches her fiction. She can be intolerant of foolishness yet ready to share her gregarious laugh. In her interviews Morrison is open about her art, and this helps one to distinguish between the artist and the product, the mind and the artifact— to appreciate the power of her imagination.

In scanning Morrison's interviews her honest aim as an artist is evident. The "call" to write is not only a personal vocation; it also serves her community. There is no tension between function and aesthetics for Morrison. Her fiction, like all art she says, is inherently political and should be "beautiful." She does not sacrifice aesthetics for polemics. She notes that it is her challenge to craft with language a distinct cosmology and historical perspective that too often have been ignored and forgotten. Morrison retrieves for the "village" its past and its ancestors. In other words, as in traditional black music, new experiences are synthesized or interpreted according to the logic of the community via an art form. She believes that black music, because of commercial forces and the need to be widely accessible, has lost this ability but that contemporary African American fiction in innovative forms is in a position to fill this cultural void. It is an intriguing idea whose validity might be found in the 1992 phenomena of three works by African American women appearing on the *New York Times*'s best seller list simultaneously: Terry McMillan's *Waiting to Exhale*, Alice Walker's *Possessing the Secret of Joy*, and Morrison's *Jazz*. Morrison's book of critical essays, *Playing in the Dark*, concurrently appeared on the nonfiction list.

Morrison talks frequently of her twenty-year career as an editor and her struggle to make publishers acknowledge and accept African American writing. Morrison is one of the few who understands creative writing and the business of publishing, and she has never seen them as intellectually competitive. For her publishing, as well as teaching, were sources of income and stimulation. Morrison's responsibilities as a single parent mandated that she provide food and shelter for her two sons, obligations she readily fulfilled. For her a career is a major component of the African American woman's self-concept. Further, she considers herself representative of the societal and historic roles African American women have held in a nation that imported African women first and foremost as laborers. Despite the oppressive nature of this definition African women, who also worked in traditional Africa, continued to expand and improvise upon what they knew and came to know about life as it became constructed in America. Not surprisingly they were the economic equals of black men and were, as Morrison states, the "comrades" of their men in the important task of ensuring family survival against almost overwhelming odds. Though she was the first in her family to attend college, she went there with the assumption that she would have to, perhaps would even want to, work and utilized her education as a teacher while married. She started in publishing and continued to teach after the dissolution of her marriage and birth of her children.

In 1987 Morrison says she realized that a "renaissance" had taken place and its impetus was black women writers like herself. "This one is interesting because it may have started out as a fashionable thing to do because of the Civil Rights Movement and so on, but it ended up as . . . we snatched it! So maybe this is really *our* renaissance for the moment, rather than entertaining or being interested in the Other." The "other" here are Anglo American men and the

standards they have promulgated. She consistently insists that
women should not be asked to choose between working and nurturing because African American women have always done both. This
illustrates the impact of race upon black women's lives versus that of
gender alone and distinguishes their issues from those of Anglo
American women. It is noteworthy that there is no articulation of a
feminist perspective evident in her interviews. She might be classified
more as a nationalist, though she says she finds political philosophies
as such, including Black Nationalism, to be confining. The artist's
responsibility is toward truth and clarity. Similarly, an audience can
critique but must never censor an artist. There is no contradiction in
her belief that art is political, that it must have aesthetic qualities,
and that ideally it must be committed to its people.

Morrison has sought to delineate the defining qualities of writing
by African Americans. In the more than twenty years she has been a
writer there are certain characteristics that she has identified as
authenticating a piece as "black": a participatory quality between a
book and reader; an aural quality in the writing; an open-endedness
in the finale that is agitating; an acceptance of and keen ability to
detect differences versus a thrust toward homogenization; acknowl-
edgement of a broader cosmology and system of logic in touch
with magic, mystery, and the body; a functional as well as aesthetic
quality; an obligation to bear witness; service as a conduit for the
"ancestor"; uses of humor that are frequently ironic; an achieved
clarity or epiphany and thus a tendency to be prophetic; and an
ability to take the "tribe" via art through the pain of a historical
experience that has been haunted by race to a healing zone.

These interviews are arranged chronologically by the date when
they were conducted rather than published, and all primary printings
have been noted. The first interview located occurs in 1974 after the
publication of *Sula* begins to draw attention to her as a writer of
note. In that first interview with Alice Childress, Morrison defines
the role of the writer as "witness bearer"—an idea that will be
repeated throughout her career. The ability to bear witness is closely
tied to her concept of prophecy that if not religious, certainly has
sacred undertones. It is tied to what will be her evolving concept of
language where she attempts to recapture the "parabolic" tones of
African American speech. This prophecy, or bearing witness, in her

fiction is essential to her belief that the future is inextricably tied to
the past. There has been a consistency to Morrison's articulation of
these concepts over the years. They expand rather than oppose
earlier statements.

The 1977 release of *Song of Solomon*, for which she received the
National Book Award and which was a main selection of the Book-
of-the-Month Club, marks an upswing in her renown as a novelist.
The irony of her fame at this point is that, though known for her
books about African American women, *Song of Solomon*'s central
character is a man, Milkman Dead. Morrison's focus in the third
novel becomes more externally directed, moving beyond the intimacy of the enclosed communities found in her first two novels.

In the Watkins interview she discusses two related major concepts.
For her writing is a "way of thinking," a process. Through fiction
she answers questions and explores unchartered waters. "It (writing)
stretches you, makes you think the unthinkable, project yourself
into people you even dislike, people I couldn't stay in a room with
for 20 minutes. It makes you stay in touch with yourself; I guess it's
like going under water for me, the danger, yet I'm certain I'm going
to come up." The submersion of the self is the thrill for Morrison.

The other concept is the influence of painters on her work. She is a
writer who works from images. She must have an image of a scene in
her mind before she can write it. Thus the techniques of painters,
their ability to re-create interpreted mental images to visual forms,
fascinate her. It is her goal as a writer to transform the visual to the
aural via language so readers can create pictures in their own mind.

With Bakerman in 1978 Morrison discusses craft and her love of
the work of writing—she writes and rewrites and rewrites and, if
need be, rewrites again and again until the language achieves a high
level of exactness. It is this labor that she enjoys the most. "It must
appear effortless! No matter what the style, it must have that. I mean
the seams can't show!" For her the issues and idea she wants to
explore within characterization become characters who are forced to
the extremes of life, and this literary strategy leaves no space in her
fiction for cumbersome self-explication. Her declaration is similar to
Langston Hughes's proclamation of the African American artist's
independence in his essay "The Negro Artist and the Racial Moun-
tain" of 1926. In addition the recurring theme that is found in all her

fiction is identified early—"I'm writing about love or its absence."
Love as the source of creation and destruction is a perspective
important in her fiction.

In the 1981 Thomas LeClair interview the role literature plays in
society is explored. Morrison envisions herself writing "village"
literature. The function of novels in this literature is to "clarify the
roles that have become obscured; they ought to identify those elements from the past that are useful and those things that are not; and
they ought to give nourishment." These functions were once culturally performed by black music but are no longer. To accomplish
this Morrison offers a solution that though perhaps not new is culturally consistent. It is her desire to restore the power of African
American language to the people—the "nommo" or power that
exists in language and that has the potential to reshape reality. She
thus hopes to aid the survival of the tribe whose longevity is not
insured.

Morrison in her 1981 novel *Tar Baby* revealed her belief in the
importance of the need for African Americans to be informed of the
danger of killing their "ancestors." The retention of the ancestor
requires the reconciliation of village responsibilities with individual
freedom for a people that can now *choose* whether or not they wish
to be "black." In addition, she considers the unique roles African
American women play. They are not merely the glue that binds the
people together; they are the tar—a holy element. They must be the
"ship and the safe harbor" in the voyage of life. Morrison speaks
to these ideas in nearly all interviews given after 1981.

When Morrison discusses literature with critics/scholars (Stepto,
McKay, Tate, etc.), other nuances and subject matter project themselves. With them she demands that a critical audience be established
that meets the literature on its own terms—out of the context from
which the literature is created rather than through theories forced
upon it, especially theories cultivated to address the artistic needs
and interests of male Euro-centric art. This sentiment rejects her
identification with "magic realism," because she thinks that it was
used to negate the ability of art to reflect other ontologies, to be
political, and to possess aesthetic qualities, thereby trivializing the
fiction.

When Morrison began to write *Beloved*, by at least 1985, she began to think more specifically about history and its uses for the writer. With Charles Ruas it becomes articulated as a seeking for "truth." The truth she recovers becomes prophetic and closely tied with Christian theology as formulated by African Americans. In typical Morrison fashion the macro becomes condensed to the micro, or the individual, and is manifested in the self-image of African Americans. As she states to Naylor, "And I thought, it's interesting because the best thing that is in us is also the thing that makes us sabotage ourselves." Thus love, or its deprivation, and its impact on self-image is played across time in her "trilogy"—*Beloved*, *Jazz*, and a third novel yet to be published.

Culturally Morrison draws from African and African American sources as she states in the Marsha Darling interview. This knowledge and mode of perception are perhaps most subtly used in *Beloved* which assumes the African cosmological view of the world of the living and parallel existence and reality of the dead. Language—how she conceives it and manipulates it—is also a focal point of discussion in many interviews. To her it is the source of cultural abuse in the way it has been distorted and maligned. In several conversations she states its uniqueness cannot be captured by changing the spelling of words. "It's the rhythm and where you place the metaphors"—a concept of African American language that places her at the vanguard of the literature.

This volume in the Literary Conversation series contains the interviews in chronological order by the date when they were conducted. Newspaper paragraph breaks have been omitted and all book titles have been italicized. Transcripts have been printed unedited and where transcripts had to be created editing was only done for readability. The interviews are reproduced in their entirety. Though this inevitably leads to repetition, there are nuances in the answers to similar questions that readers should note. Thus the evolution from the *Bluest Eye* to *Jazz* is really one of maturation and clarification rather than revolution. Morrison has come to understand the power of the written word, has studied and practiced her craft, as all masters must, and has thus gained the wisdom of an elder. "I know I can't change the future but I can change the past. It is the past, not the future, which is infinite. Our past was appropriated. I am one of the people who has to reappropriate it.'' As one called and compelled to tell the stories of African Americans through the telescope of myth and truth she underestimates her impact on reshaping the future.

I would like to thank Carla Cannon for her hours of work on typing and transcribing as we worked together to finish this volume; the librarians at Indiana University Northwest who assisted me in locating materials that were often widely scattered; and Leon Forrest for his collegial support. I also want to thank those publications and authors who agreed that this is an important project and gave the rights to reprint the materials contained here; my family (Carlton, Carille and Adam), which has been supportive of what must have been a distracting project; and finally Professor Morrison for her support of this volume which enables all of us to study the ideas contained in her interviews as a coherent whole. Her conversations have been as intriguing and enjoyable for me as her fiction.

Chronology

1931	On Feb. 18th Chloe Anthony Wofford is born in Lorain, Ohio, to Ramah (Willis) and George Wofford.
1949	Goes to Washington, D. C., to attend Howard University; joins the Howard University Players.
1953	Receives a B. A. in English and minors in Classics; goes to Cornell University for graduate studies in English literature.
1955	Receives M. A. from Cornell University; goes to Texas Southern University in Houston to teach English and the Humanities.
1957	Returns to Howard University to teach
1958	Marries Harold Morrison a Jamaican architect
1961	Son Harold Ford is born.
1962	While teaching at Howard University one of her students is Stokely Carmichael; joins a writing group with Claude Browne in it; writes a short story that will later become *The Bluest Eye*.
1964	The family travels to Europe and she divorces when they return. Son Slade Kevin is born in Ohio.
1965	Goes to Syracuse, New York, to work as a text book editor for L. W. Singer, a division of Random House; starts to write *The Bluest Eye*.
1968	Moves to New York City where she becomes a Senior Editor for Random House; publishes many African American writers: Leon Forrest, Gayl Jones, Toni Cade Bambara, Angela Davis, Muhammad Ali, Ivan Van Sertima, Andrew Young, Henry Dumas and John McCluskey.
1970	*The Bluest Eye* is published.

1971   Teaches English at University of New York at Purchase
          through 1972

1973   *Sula* is published.

1974   *The Black Book* is edited and published.

1976–78   Teaches at Yale University

1977   *Song of Solomon* is published and is main selection of
          Book-of-the-Month-Club, the first book by an African
          American to be so selected since Richard Wright's *Native
          Son* in 1940. Becomes a lecturer at Yale. Wins the
          National Book Critics Circle Award.

1978   Named Distinguished Writer of 1978 by the American
          Academy of Arts and Letters

1979   Moves to a boat house on the Hudson River

1980   Appointed by President Carter to the National Council on
          the Arts

1981   *Tar Baby* is published. Teaches at Bard College. Elected to
          the American Academy and Institute of Arts and Letters,
          the Writer's Guild, and the Author's League; featured on
          the cover of *Newsweek*, first African American woman
          since Zora Neale Hurston in 1943.

1983   The musical *New Orleans* goes into limited production
          starring Odetta in New York.

1984   Leaves publishing and accepts the Albert Schweitzer
          Professorship of the Humanities at the State University of
          New York at Albany.

1986   *Dreaming Emmett*, a play commissioned by the New York
          State Writers Institute at SUNY-Albany, is performed;
          the play is directed by Gilbert Moses and produced by the
          Capital Repertory Company of Albany. Wins New York
          State Governor's Art Award.

1987   *Beloved* is published. Named as a member of the Helsinki
          Watch Committee and the Board of Trustees of the New
          York Public Library; is chairperson of the New York State
          Education Department's Committee on Adult Literacy.
          Becomes Regent's Lecturer at the University of
          California, Berkeley.

1988   *Beloved* wins the Pulitzer Prize for Fiction, the Robert F. Kennedy Book Award and the Melcher Book Award from the Unitarian Universalist Association.

1989   Assumes the Robert Goheen Professorship in the Humanities Council at Princeton University; holds a joint appointment in African American Studies and Creative Writing. Wins the Modern Language Association of America's Commonwealth Award in Literature.

1990   Awarded the Chianti Ruffino Antico Fattore International Award in Literature

1992   *Jazz*, her sixth novel, and *Playing in the Dark: Whiteness and the Literary Imagination*, essays, are published, and both appear on the *New York Times* best seller's list. Edits an anthology of essays on the Clarence Thomas-Anita Hill controversy, *Re-Racing Justice, Engendering Power*.

1993   *Honey and Rue*, a song cycle performed by Kathleen Battle, with music by Andre Previn premiers in Chicago, Ill. Morrison wins the Nobel Prize for Literature.

Conversations with Toni Morrison

Conversation with Alice Childress and Toni Morrison

Black Creation Annual / 1974

From the *Black Creation Annual 1974–1975*: 90–92.

The co-editors of *Black Creation* invited Alice Childress and Toni Morrison to share their ideas on contemporary Black literature with our readers. What followed was a free-wheeling, wide-ranging discussion that reveals not only the depth and dedication of these two fine artists, but serves as an excellent overview of major themes and ideas in Black writing today. Playwright Alice Childress is the author of numerous plays, including *Trouble in Mind* and probably her most famous, *Wedding Band*. Toni Morrison is a senior editor at Random House and author of two important novels, *The Bluest Eye* and *Sula*.

BC: We thought we'd start off with a question that might get us into a philosophical frame of mind. In the mid sixties Larry Neal in his essay "The Black Arts Movement" asserted that art equals politics and that politics equals art and that art must serve some political and some consciousness-raising end. Where do you think that concept is today?

Morrison: I think all good art has always been political. None of the best writing, the best thoughts have been anything other than that. I think he was really making two points in that article. One is that Black people who are writing must concentrate on the political plight of Black people. Second, he was trying to forestall a movement towards art for art's sake.

BC: Do you think though that an artist can become too politicized and that his message merely become soap-box rhetoric rather than art?

Morrison: Art becomes mere soap-box not because it's too political but because the artist isn't any good at what he's doing. Now what has happened is that critics have become more sensitive to the political issues themselves. But in many instances their criticism has become increasingly bad because they sway from one topic to the-next saying, "This is a dumb book but it has a wonderful sociological message," etc. They can't seem to put the whole thing together— put together the inseparable qualities of greatness and politics.

Childress: I think very often too that the critic is not as serious about his criticism as the artist is about the work he is creating. I think a critic wants to be relieved of analyzing certain things and discussing certain topics. Very often we have seen poorly done things that are saying little or nothing that have been embraced by critics.

Morrison: I don't believe any real artists have ever been non-political. They may have been insensitive to this particular plight or insensitive to that, but they were political because that's what an artist is—a politician.

BC: A message bringer?

Morrison: Right, right. He bears witness.

Childress: As far as being too political, I know what Jim is talking about. Suppose someone wants to write a play, say, on a period in American history when Blacks were not allowed to vote. You will find that different critics will criticize that play in different ways. One feels you shouldn't vote anyway, you know. He'll comment on how poorly done it was and wonder why it is so political and so forth. Another feels that we should forget about past issues. But you will find other critics who are talented enough to be able to analyze the work and the questions in the work—the subject and the premise of it—and ask if the work is successful on its own terms. I think we're very fortunate that sometimes we have writers who are too political, if we want to put it that way, because of what they bring to our minds and whether they make us quarrel about their topics or reject them or put them down.

BC: When you talk about critics and criticism you raise the entire question of the differences between what a critic does and what an artist does—between the critical faculty and the creative faculty. It seems that these two faculties are really quite distinct and very rarely come together in one person.

Childress: I agree with you. Artists are notoriously bad critics. I do believe a critic has a very special craft and field of writing and that more care should be given to writing criticism. It used to be when more was expected of critics. Now, I wonder if mass media and

television haven't interefered with good criticism and helped deterio-
rate the whole area and . . .

BC: . . . make it circus-like?

Childress: Yes.

BC: As artists, how much attention do you pay to the critic?

Morrison: A great deal.

Childress: I agree.

Morrison: However, I make a distinction between critics and
reviewers; but they are altogether different people. But I pay them
both a great deal of attention for several reasons. One, as a publisher,
I look at them from a publisher's point of view. That is, I try to find
out what they have said that is useful in terms of advertising and so
on. Secondly, I want to know whether they know what they're
talking about and whether they know what I'm talking about. A very
good critical piece is extremely useful for a writer. A critic should
be a conduit, a bridge, but not a law. But if the critic is talking about
himself more than about the work, then his criticism is not so useful.
If he's talking about the book it is useful. If the critic says this part or
this aspect of the work isn't any good and gives valid reasons I'm
very objective about that.

   Childress: I pay attention to critics but it's often very, confusing. If
someone really cares about something you did you tend to be extra
appreciative and if they didn't care about it you just may reject their
criticism more than you should. However, I think you can tell,
especially in theater evaluation, if the critic knows his craft. And
when you come across a person who knows and pays attention and
has respect for his craft, you read his criticism with a deeper interest
in what you can get out of it. Every once in a while you come across
the critic, say, in some little town in the Midwest—somewhere that
you've never heard of—who knows exactly what you meant right on
down the line who offers criticism on the places, perhaps, that you
were worried about or that didn't quite jell for you. That's a good
experience when you come across a critic like that. It's too bad that
economics are so important in the making of things and in the putting
of the creative work out there. A critic is in a very important position
and sometimes newspapers just throw anyone who isn't doing something during a particular week to cover this book or listen to that

music concert or review this play. Well, he may very well be shutting down something without good reason, and then he might enjoy that role if he's masochistic enough.

Morrison: Yes, there's a very strong element of power play in criticism, you know. Critics have vested interests in the survival of art as economics—have vested interest in making art into whatever fad that happens to be needed at the time.

Childress: Right.

Morrison: It's very easy to dislike. It's a very safe position. But Black people must be the only people who set out our criteria in criticism. White people can't do it for us. That's our responsibility and in some way we have to do it. I say you must always tell the truth. And I tell you that we are not weak people and we can stand it. I can take it. I've come many years and if some honest person tells me something I've written is crap, I can take it. We have always taken it. We have taken it from each other. Black people are the most critical people in the world with each other. The most critical. My ego is not so flimsy that if you say something about my work I'm going to faint. I'm going to do better or do more or ignore you or what have you. And I do not think that we should run around and just strike each other's backs. We can say what is good and what is not good. We have to do that because there's a lot of mediocre stuff out here. You know that as well as I do. But Black people just don't want to say it in the public before the man, you know. *Black Creation* published a beautiful essay a few years ago. I forget the author's name just now. I think it won a prize in your literary contest.

BC: Are you talking about Reginald Berry's essay "About Criticism?"

Morrison: Yes. Now, Berry was making a very important point in that essay. He was saying that we must not patronize each other. We must tell the truth as we see it. I believe we have to say that that's not viciousness, careerism or any of that.

Childress: And as long as you have the right spirit and feeling about it—so long as you're not vicious. Viciousness is another thing. Some of the best-known critics in this country make their money on viciousness. Take John Simon in *New York* magazine. He has followers who say, "Let's see who Simon got this time." They'd be disappointed if he did otherwise. It's a style. It's a thing that he does, and I don't think we need to do that.

BC: Here's a question that's a bit different and it's not meant to categorize you as "experts" on Black women writers. Do you see any legitimacy in talking about a separate Black woman's artistic consciousness in writing as opposed to a Black man's artistic consciousness in writing?

Childress: It's there. It just happens.

Morrison: We are different. There's a male consciousness and there's a female consciousness. I think there are different things operating on each of the sexes. Black men—and this may be way off the wall because I haven't had time to fully reflect about this—frequently are reacting to a lot more external pressures than Black women are. For one thing they have an enormous responsibility to be *men*. There's something very large in that word. Men define their masculinity by other men, and they're keenly aware of this in much of their writing. They're so busy quote "proving something" unquote to some . . .

BC: . . . audience or group?

Childress: And frequently they are writing for the very group they are proving something to, which means they're not always writing for me.

BC: Would you agree with the often asserted opinion that men can't create a successful woman character? Is that what is being talked about here?

Childress: Let me answer. I don't think you can say that due to the sex of a person he cannot (or she cannot) create a character of the opposite sex. I think it is due to his experience, his outlook, his philosophy in life whether he can or not.

Morrison: I don't think it impossible for men to do what you ask. All I'm saying is that the root of a man's sensibilities are different from a woman's. Not better, but different.

BC: We're coming close to the end of our time, but there is one particular question that both of you should be asked. It's very broad, but perhaps you can find some response in the broadness of the question. What are some of the main thematic trends in the writing of the seventies? What, if anything, do writers seem to be coalescing around?

Morrison: I was recently reading a most interesting critic who said—and this might apply to other writers as well—that Black

writers seem to be focusing on a very different concept of evil, one
that is unlike normal concepts of evil. They are focusing on a peculiar way in which Black people experience evil and deal with evil.
Now I was certainly very much interested in the question of evil in
Sula—in fact, that's what it was all about. I know evil preoccupied
me in *Sula* and perhaps other writers are preoccupied with it also. It
never occurs to those people in the novel to kill Sula. Black people
never annihilate evil. They don't run it out of their neighborhoods,
chop it up, or burn it up. They don't have witch hangings. They
accept it. It's almost like a fourth dimension in their lives. They try
to protect themselves from evil, of course, but they don't have that
puritannical thing which says if you see a witch, then burn it, or if
you see something, then kill it.

   Childress: I happen to disagree a bit here with you, Toni. Look at
how Black people are destroying each other in the Black communities, and hurting and harming each other.

   Morrison: I'm *not* saying that Black people don't kill each other.
I'm talking about the way in which they *perceive* evil and how they
act upon that perception. They don't destroy evil. It's as though God
has four faces for them—not just the Trinity, but four. I know
instinctly that we do not regard evil the same way as white people do.
We have never done that. White people's reaction to something that
is alien to them is to destroy it. That's why they have to say Black
people are worthless and ugly. They need all the psychological "do"
in order to do something simple like ripping some people off. That's
why they behave the way they do.

   Childress: Also their concept of being kind to the Black artist
because he's new is directly related to what you're saying here. If
what you say or write about a white man frightens him you'll find out
how fast he is to criticize you without kindness.

   BC: Are there other themes you see as being dominant in the
literature of the seventies?

   Childress: I think that all Black writers, whether they intended to
or not have been writing about not being free. Always—from the
beginning of America right up to now. Of course, you find a great
many white writers who have written about freedom in their own
terms, but I don't think in ever so great a concentrated flood and
fashion as Black writers. At least it seems to me that in any Black

book, no matter what it deals with or what the story line is, you realize that the people are not free. You know the conversation always starts off with "The trouble with us is . . ." We've heard that millions of times. The trouble with us is that we're not free. We're not free. So I think the lack of freedom is the omnipresent theme in any Black writer's work today.

Intimate Things in Place: A Conversation with Toni Morrison

Robert Stepto / 1976

From the *Massachusetts Review* 18 (1977): 473–89.

This interview was conducted in Ms. Morrison's office at Random House Publishers in New York City on 19 May 1976.

Stepto: I want to start with something we've talked about before, and that is this extraordinary sense of place in your novels. By that I mean you create communities, the community that Pecola, Claudia and the rest live in, in *The Bluest Eye*, and of course, in *Sula*, the Bottom. The places are set in time; there are addresses—we know Sula's address, right down to the house number. Years are mentioned, seasons are mentioned, details are given, and I was struck by these features in two ways. First, by the extent to which you seem to be trying to create specific geographical landscapes, and second, by how landscape seems to perform different functions in the two novels.

Morrison: I can't account for all aspects of it. I know that I never felt like an American or an Ohioan or even a Lorainite. I never felt like a citizen. But I felt very strongly—not much with the first book; more with the second; and very much with the one I'm working on now—I felt a very strong sense of place, not in terms of the country or the state, but in terms of the details, the feeling, the mood of the community, of the town. In the first book, I was clearly pulling straight out of what autobiographical information I had. I didn't create that town. It's clearer to me now in my memory of it than when I lived there—and I haven't really lived there since I was seventeen years old. Also, I think some of it is just a woman's strong sense of being in a room, a place, or in a house. Sometimes my relationship to things in a house would be a little different from, say my brother's or my father's or my sons'. I clean them and I move them and I do very intimate things "in place": I am sort of rooted in it, so that writing about being in a room looking out, or being in a world looking out, or living in a small definite place, is probably very common among most woman anyway.

The other thing was that when I wrote *Sula* I was interested in making the town, the community, the neighborhood, as strong as a character as I could, without actually making it "The Town, they," because the most extraordinary thing about any group, and particularly our group, is the fantastic variety of people and things and behavior and so on. But nevertheless there was a cohesiveness there in my mind and it was true in my life. And though I live in New York, I don't relate easily to very, very large cities, because I have never lived in a huge city except this one. My tendency is to focus on neighborhoods and communities. And the community, the black community—I don't like to use that term because it came to mean something much different in the sixties and seventies, as though we had to forge one—but it had seemed to me that it was always there, only we called it the "neighborhood." And there was this life-giving, very, very strong sustenance that people got from the neighborhood. One lives, really, not so much in your house as you do outside of it, within the "compounds," within the village, or whatever it is. And legal responsibilities, all the responsibilities that agencies now have, were the responsibilities of the neighborhood. So that people were taken care of, or locked up or whatever. If they were sick, other people took care of them; if they needed something to eat, other people took care of them; if they were old, other people took care of them; if they were mad, other people provided a small space for them, or related to their madness or tried to find out the limits of their madness.

They also meddled in your lives a lot. They felt that you belonged to them. And every woman on the street could raise everybody's child, and tell you exactly what to do and you felt that connection with those people and they felt it with you. And when they punished us or hollered at us, it was, at the time, we thought, so inhibiting and so cruel, and it's only much later that you realize that they were interested in you. Interested in you—they cared about your behavior. And then I knew my mother as a Church woman, and a Club woman—and there was something special about when she said

"Sister," and when all those other women said "Sister." They
meant that in a very, very fundamental way. There were some
interesting things going on inside people and they seemed to me the
most extraordinary people in the world. But at the same time, there
was this kind of circle around them—we lived within 23 blocks—
which they could not break.

S: From what you're telling me, it would seem that creating Medallion in *Sula* might have been a more difficult task than creating the
neighborhood in *The Bluest Eye*.

M: Oh, yes, Medallion was more difficult because it was wholly
fabricated; but it was based on something my mother had said some
time ago. When she first got married, she and my father went to
live in Pittsburgh. And I remember her telling me that in those days
all the black people lived in the hills of Pittsburgh, but now they lived
amid the smoke and dirt in the heart of that city. It's clear up in
those hills, and so I used that idea, but in a small river town in Ohio.
Ohio is right on the Kentucky border, so there's not much difference
between it and the "South." It's an interesting state from the point
of view of black people because it is right there by the Ohio River, in
the south, and at its northern tip is Canada. And there were these
fantastic abolitionists there, and also the Ku Klux Klan lived there.
And there is only really one large city. There are hundreds of small
towns and that's where most black people live. You know, in most
books, they're always in New York or some exotic place, but most of
our lives are spent in little towns, little towns all throughout this
country. And that's where, you know, we live. And that's where the
juices came from and that's where we *made it*, not made it in terms
of success but made who we are. So I loved writing about that
because it was so wide open.

Sula was hard, for me; very difficult to make up that kind of
character. Not difficult to think it up, but difficult to describe a
woman who could be used as a classic type of evil force. Other
people could use her that way. And at the same time, I didn't want to
make her freakish or repulsive or unattractive. I was interested at
that time in doing a very old, worn-out idea, which was to do
something with good and evil, but putting it in different terms. And I
wanted Nel to be a warm, conventional woman, one of those people
you know are going to pay the gas bill and take care of the children.

You don't have to ask about them. And they are magnificent, because they take these small tasks and they do them. And they do them without the fire and without the drama and without all of that. They get the world's work done somehow.

S: How did Nel get to that point, given the background you provided her with? Why does her grandmother have those "questionable roots"? How does that lead to Nel?

M: It has to do with Nel's attraction for Sula. To go back, a black woman at that time who didn't want to do the conventional thing, had only one other kind of thing to do. If she had talent she went into the theater. And if she had a little voice, she could sing, or she could go to a big town and she could pretend she was dancing or whatever. That was the only outlet if you chose not to get married and have children. That was it. Or you could walk the streets; although you might get there sort of accidentally; you might not choose to do that. So that Nel's grandmother just means that there's that kind of life from which Nel comes; that's another woman who was a hustler; that part is already in Nel and accounts for her attraction to Sula. And also those are the kinds of women there were. Here is this woman, Nel, whose mother is just busy, busy, busy reacting against her own mother, and goes to the far extreme of having this rather neat, rather organized, rather pompous life, forcing all of the creativity out of Nel. But Nel wants it anyway, which is what makes it possible for her to have a very close friend who is so different from her, in the way she looks at life. And I wanted to make all of that sort of reasonable. Because what was the attraction of Nel for Sula? Sula for Nel? Why would they become friends in the first place? You see? And so I wanted to say, as much as I could say it without being overbearing, that there was a little bit of both in each of those two women, and that if they had been one person, I suppose they would have been a rather marvelous person. But each one lacked something that the other one had.

S: It's interesting you should mention this, because my students wanted to pursue the question of Sula and Nel being perhaps two sides of the same person, or two sides of one extraordinary character. But this character is nevertheless fractured into Sula and Nel.

M: Precisely. They're right on target because that was really in my mind. It didn't come to me quite that way. I started by thinking that one can never really define good and evil. Sometimes good looks like evil; sometimes evil looks like good—you never really know what it is. It depends on what uses you put it to. Evil is as useful as good is, although good is generally more interesting; it's more complicated. I mean, living a good life is more complicated than living an evil life. I think. And also, it wasn't hard to talk about that because everyone has something in mind when they think about what a good life is. So I put that in conventional terms, for a woman: someone who takes care of children and so on and is responsible and goes to church and so on. For the opposite kind of character, which is a woman who's an adventurer, who breaks rules, she can either be a criminal—which I wasn't interested in—or lead a kind of cabaret life—which I also wasn't interested in. But what about the woman who doesn't do any of that but is nevertheless a rule-breaker, a kind of law-breaker, a lawless woman? Not a law-abiding woman. Nel knows and believes in all the laws of that community. She *is* the community. She believes in its values. Sula does not. She does not believe in any of those laws and breaks them all. Or ignores them. So that she becomes more interesting—I think, particularly to younger girls—because of that quality of abandon.

But there's a fatal flaw in all of that, you know, in both of those things. Nel does not make that "leap"—she doesn't know about herself. Even at the end, she doesn't know. She's just beginning. She just barely grabs on at the end in those last lines. So that living totally by the law and surrendering completely to it without questioning anything sometimes makes it impossible to know anything about yourself. Nel doesn't even know what questions she's asking. When they come to touch one another in the bedroom, when Sula's sick—Nel doesn't even know why she's there. Sula, on the other hand, knows all there is to know about herself because she examines herself, she is experimental with herself, she's perfectly willing to think the unthinkable thing and so on. But she has trouble making a connection with other people and just feeling that lovely sense of accomplishment of being close in a very strong way. She felt that in a way, of course, with Nel, but then obviously they lost one another in friendship. She was able to retrieve it rather nicely with a man, which is lovely, except that in so many instances, with me, the very thing that would attract a man to a woman in the first place might be the one thing she would give over once she learned Nel's lesson, which is love as possession. You own somebody and then you begin to want them there all the time, which is a community law. Marriage, faithfulness, fidelity; the beloved belongs to one person and can't be shared with other people—that's a community value which Sula learned when she fell in love with Ajax, which he wasn't interested in learning.

S: Richard Wright said in "How Bigger Was Born" that there were many Biggers that went into creating Bigger Thomas. Are there many Pecolas in Pecola? Or many Sulas in Sula?

M: Oh, yes! Well, I think what I did is what every writer does— once you have an idea, then you try to find a character who can manifest the idea for you. And then you have to spend a long time trying to get to know who those people are, who that character is. So you take what there is from whomever you know. Sula—I think this was really part of the difficulty—I didn't know anyone like her. I never knew a woman like that at any rate. But I knew women who looked like that, who looked like they *could be* like that. And then you remember women who were a little bit different in the town, you know; there's always a little bit of gossip and there's always a little bit of something. There's a woman in our town now who is an absolute riot. She can do anything she wants to do. And it occurred to me about twenty years ago how depleted that town would be if she ever left. Everybody wanted her out, and she was a crook and she was mean and she had about twenty husbands—and she was just, you know, a huge embarrassment. Nevertheless, she really and truly was one of the reasons that they called each other on the telephone. They sort of used her excitement, her flavor, her carelessness, her restlessness, and so on. And that quality is what I used in Sula.

S: What about Sula's mother and grandmother?

M: Oh, Hannah, the mother—I tell you, I think I feel more affection for her than for anybody else in that book. I just loved her. What I was trying to do was to be very provocative without using all of the traditional devices of provocation. And I think—that's why I wrote so slowly—I think I know how to do it by simply relying an awful lot on what I believe the reader already knows. I wanted Sula to be missed by the reader. That's why she dies early. There's a lot of book after she dies, you know. I wanted them to miss her presence in that book as that town missed her presence. I also wanted them to dislike her a lot, and to be fascinated, perhaps, but also to feel that thing that the town might feel—that this is something askew. And I wanted for them to realize at some point—and I don't know if anybody ever realizes it—that she never does anything as bad as her grandmother or her mother did. However, they're alike; her grandmother kills her son, plays god, names people and, you know, puts her hand on a child. You know, she's god-like, she manipulates—all in the best interest. And she is very, very possessive about other people, that is, as a king is. She decided that her son was living a life that was not worth his time. She meant it was too painful for her; you know, the way you kill a dog when he breaks his leg because he can't stand the pain. He may very well be able to stand it, but you can't, so that's why you get rid of him. The mother, of course, was slack. She had no concept of love and possession. She liked to be laid, she liked to be touched, but she didn't want any confusion of relationships and so on. She's very free and open about that. Her relationship to her daughter is almost one of uninterest. She would do things for her, but she's not particularly interested in her.

S: That conversation in the kitchen . . .

M: That's right: "I love her, but I don't like her," which is an honest statement at any rate. And she'd sleep with anybody, you know, husbands. She just does it. But interestingly enough, the point was that the women in the town who knew that—they didn't like the fact—but at the same time *that* was something they could understand. Lust, sexual lust, and so on. So that when she dies, they will come to her aid. Now Sula might take their husbands, but she was making judgments. You see what it was—it wasn't about love. It wasn't about even lust. Nobody knows what that was about. And also, Sula did the one terrible thing for black people which was to put her grandmother in an old folks' home, which was outrageous, you know. You take care of people! So *that* would be her terrible thing. But at the same time, she is more strange, more formidable than either of those other two women because they were first of all within the confines of the community and their sensibilities were informed by it. Essentially, they were pacific in the sense of what they did do. They wanted to make things come together; you know, bring it together. Hannah didn't want to disturb anything. She did her work and she took care of people and so on; and Eva was generous, wide-spirited, and made some great sacrifices.

S: I'm fascinated by all the women in the two novels: your portraits are so rich. It's not just the main characters—you get that woman from Meridian, Geraldine, in *The Bluest Eye*, and of course Mrs. McTeer, who isn't always talked about, but she certainly is the kind of figure you were describing earlier as a mother to anybody and everybody who will take you in and knows how to raise everybody. With all of these various characters that you've created, certainly you must have some response to the feeling in certain literary circles that black women should be portrayed a certain way. I'm thinking now of the kinds of criticism that have been lodged against Gayl Jones.

M: Do you mean black women as victims, that they should not be portrayed as victims?

S: Either that or even—and I'm thinking more of Sula here—as emasculating.

M: Oh yes. Well, in *The Bluest Eye,* I try to show a little girl as a total and complete victim of whatever was around her. But black women have held, have been given, you know, the cross. They don't walk near it. They're often on it. And they've borne that, I think, extremely well. I think everybody knows, deep down, that black men were emasculated by white men, period. And that black women didn't take any part in that. However, black women have had some enormous responsibilities, which in these days people call free-doms—in those days, they were called responsibilities—they lived, you know, working in other people's, white people's, houses and taking care of that and working in their own houses and so on and they have been on the labor market. And nobody paid them that much attention in terms of threats, and so on, so they had a certain amount of "freedom." But they did a very extraordinary job of just taking on that kind of responsibility and in so doing, they tell people what to do. Now I have to admit, however, that it's a new idea to me—the emasculating black women. It really is new—that is, in the last few years. I can only go by my own experience, my own family, the black men I knew—the men I knew called the shots, whether they were employed or unemployed. And even in our classic set of stereotypes—Sapphire and Kingfish?—he did anything he was big enough to do! Anything! Talk 'bout free! And she bitched—that she was going to work and so on. But there is an incredible amount of magic and feistiness in black men that nobody has been able to wipe out. But everybody has tried.

Now, Sula—I don't regard her as a typical black woman at all. And the fact that the community responds to her that way means that she's unusual. So she's not the run-of-the-mill average black woman.

S: If she weren't unusual, they'd know how to deal with her.

M: That's right. There wouldn't have been that confusion about her. They did not know how to deal with her. So she's very atypical and perhaps she would be, you know, a kind of ball-breaker, in that sense. However, the one man who talked to her, and thought she was worthy of conversation, and who let her be, was the one man she could relate to on that level that would make her want something she had never been interested in before, which was a permanent relationship. He was a man who was not intimidated by her; he was interested in her. He treated her as a whole person, not as an extension of himself, not as a vessel, not as a symbol. Their sex was not one person killing the other—that's why I pictured her on top of him, you know, like a tree. He was secure enough and free enough and bright enough—he wasn't terrorized by her because she was odd. He was interested. I think there was a line in the book—he hadn't met an interesting woman since his mother, who was sitting out in the woods "making roots." When a man is whole himself, when he's touched the borders of his own life, and he's not proving something to somebody else—white men or other men and so on—then the threats of emasculation, the threats of castration, the threats of somebody taking over disappear. Ajax is strong enough. He's a terribly unemployed dude, who has interests of his own, whose mother neglected him, but nevertheless assumed all sorts of things about him that he lived up to like he knew he was doing. So he had a different kind of upbringing. Now that, I think, is interesting; that part of it interested me a lot, so that when he would see a woman like Sula, who had been somewhere and had some rather different views about life and so on, he was not intimidated at all. Whereas a man like Jude, who was doing a rather routine, macho thing, would split—you know, he was too threatened by all of that. Just the requirements of staying in the house and having to apologize to his wife were too much for him.

S: Now you mention Jude, and that balance between Jude and Ajax is clear in the book. What about Ajax and Cholly Breedlove in *The Bluest Eye*?

M: Exactly alike, in that sense. I don't mean that their backgrounds were alike. But in a way, they sort of—through neglect of the fact that someone was not there—made up themselves. They allowed themselves to be whomever they were. Cholly, of course, lives a very tragic life, tragic in the sense that there was no reward, but he is the thing I keep calling a "free man," not free in the legal sense, but free in his head. You see, this was a free man who could do a lot of things; and I think it's a way of talking about what some people call the "bad nigger." Not in the sense of one who is so carousing, but that adjective "bad" meaning, you know, bad and good. This is a man who is stretching, you know, he's stretching, he's going all the way within his own mind and within whatever his outline might be. Now that's the tremendous possibility for masculinity among black men. And you see it a lot. Sometimes you see it when they do art things, sometimes just in personality and so on. And it's very, very deep and very, very complex and such men as that are not very busy. They may end up in sort of twentieth-century, contemporary terms being also unemployed. They may be in prison. They may be doing all sorts of things. But they are adventuresome in that regard.

And then when you draw a woman who is like that, which is unusual and uncivilized, within our context, then a man like that is interested in her. No, he doesn't want to get married, he doesn't want to do all those things, for all sorts of reasons, some of which are purely sociological. The other kind of man who is more like the Nel syndrome would be very, very preoccupied with it, and his masculinity is threatened all the time. But then you see a man who has had certain achievements—and I don't mean social achievements—but he's been able to manipulate crap games or, you know, just do things—because Cholly has done *everything*—in his life. So that by the time he met Pauline, he was able to do whatever his whims suggested and it's that kind of absence of control that I wanted—you know, obviously, that I'm interested in characters who are lawless in that regard. They make up their lives, or they find out who they are. So in that regard Cholly Breedlove is very much like Ajax.

S: Is the progression from girlhood in *The Bluest Eye* to womanhood in *Sula* an intentional progression? Might we view the two novels in these terms?

M: Yes. I think I was certainly interested in talking about black girlhood in *The Bluest Eye* and not so interested in it in *Sula*. I wanted to move it into the other part of their life. That is, what do the Claudias and Friedas, those feisty little girls, grow up to be? Precisely. No question about that.

The book that I'm writing now is about a man, and a lot of the things that I learned by writing about Cholly and Ajax and Jude are at least points of departure, leaping-off places, for the work that I'm doing now. The focus is on two men. One is very much like Ajax and Cholly in his youth, so stylish and adventuresome and, I don't know, I think he's truly masculine in the sense of going out too far where you're not supposed to go and running toward confrontations rather than away from them. And risks—taking risks. That quality. One of the men is very much like that. The other will learn to be a complete person, or at least have a notion of it, if I ever get him to the end of the book. When I wrote that section on Cholly in *The Bluest Eye*, I thought it would be very hard for me because I didn't know that as intimately as I knew Pauline. And I thought, well, let me get started on this 'cause I'm going to have a tough time trying to really feel that kind of thing. But it's the only time I've ever written anything in my life when it all came at once. I wrote it straight through. And it took me a long time, maybe eight or nine hours the first time, not stopping at all.

When I got to Pauline, whom I knew so well, I could not do it. I would not make it. I didn't know what to write or how. And I sort of copped out anyway in the book because I used two voices, hers and the author's. There were certain things she couldn't know and I had to come in. And then there were certain things the author would say that I wanted in her language—so that there were the two things, two voices, which I had regarded, at any rate, as a way in which to do something second-best. I couldn't do it straight out the way I did every other section. That was such a fascinating experience for me to perceive Cholly that way.

S: Will these two men in the new book balance as Nel and Sula do?

M: No. That is, they're friends and they're different from each other, but they're not incomplete the way Nel and Sula are. They are completely whoever they are and they don't need another man to give them that. They love each other—I mean, men love the company of other men—they're like that. And they enjoy the barber shop and the pool room and so on, and there's a lot of that because they aren't just interested in themselves. But their relationship is based on something quite different. And I think in the friendship between men there is, you know, something else operating. So the metaphors changed. I couldn't use the same kind of language at all. And it took a long time for the whole thing to fall together because men are different and they are thinking about different things. The language had to be different.

S: Will neighborhood or a sense of neighborhood be just as important in this book?

M: Yes. Well, I have one man who is a sort of middle-class black dude, whose mother was the daughter of the only black doctor. His father, who is a kind of self-taught man, owns a lot of shacks in the black part of the town and he loves things, you know, he's accumulating property and money and so on. And his son is the main character who makes friends with people in the kind of community that is described in *Sula*. You know, it's a different social class, there is a leap, but I don't think the class problems among black people are as great as the class problems among white people. I mean, there's just no real problems with that in terms of language and how men relate to one another—black men relate to one another whatever class they come from.

S: Sort of like people living on the same block, going to the same barber shop . . .

M: Yes, because whatever it is, you know, the little community is by itself. You go to the same barber shop and there you are. So this one has a little bit of money and that one doesn't but it doesn't make any difference because you're thrown into the same and you get your "stuff" from one another.

S: Will there also be a character somewhat like Soaphead Church or Shadrack in this book? Tell me something about your two crazies.

M: Well, in the first place, with Shadrack, I just needed, wanted, a form of madness that was clear and compact to bounce off of Sula's strangeness. And you know, he likes her and she goes to his house and he remembers her and so on. So there's a connection between the two of them. And I wanted the town to respond to him in one way and to her in another. They're both eccentrics, outside the law, except that Shadrack's madness is very organized. He has organized the world. He just wants all this to be done on one day. It's orderly, as madness is—isolation, total isolation and order. You know, it's trying to get order in what is perceived by the madman as a disordered world. So the town understands his own way of organizing chaos, once they find out what he's doing—you know, National Suicide Day.

With Soaphead, I wanted, needed someone to give the child her blue eyes. Now she was asking for something that was just awful—she wanted to have blue eyes and she wanted to be Shirley Temple, I mean, she wanted to do that white trip because of the society in which she lived and, very importantly, because of the black people who helped her want to be that. (The responsibilities are ours. It's our responsibility for helping her believe, helping her come to the point where she wanted that.) I had to have someone—her mother, of course, made her want it in the first place—who would give her the blue eyes. And there had to be somebody who *could*, who had the means; that kind of figure who dealt with fortune-telling, dream-telling and so on, who would also believe that she was right, that it was preferable for her to have blue eyes. And that would be a person like Soaphead. In other words, he would be wholly convinced that if black people were more like white people they would be better off. And I tried to explain that in terms of his own Western Indian background—a kind of English, colonial, Victorian thing drilled into his head which he could not escape. I needed someone to distill all of that, to say, "Yeah, you're right, you need them. Here, I'll give them to you," and really believe that he had done her a favor. Someone who would never question the request in the first place. That kind of black. It was very important in the story that the miracle happen, and she does get them, although I had to make it fairly logical in that only she can see them and that she's really flipped by that time.

S: Does your job as an editor get in the way of your writing? I ask

this partly because I remember so well having a creative writing
teacher who told me once how his being an English major in college
got in the way of his writing, so he became an anthropology
major . . .

M: In order to free himself?

S: Yes. A number of things can get in the way of writing; lots of
teachers of literature would like to write, but perhaps their teaching
gets in the way of the writing. Now, you are a writer, and an editor,
and a teacher—how do you do it?

M: Well, I suspect that full-time teaching would get in the way of
writing for me because you have to think a certain way about the
literature you're teaching, and I think that would spill over into the
way in which one has to think when writing. The critical stance—
which is what teaching is—sometimes makes me feel, if I move right
into my writing, too self-conscious. You're so aware of the theory
and the effort and so on, that you become very self-conscious and
maybe a little too tight about it. For me, it has to be very private and
very unrelated. When I write, I can't read other people that I like. I
have to read detective stories or things like that. I have to feel as if
it's being done almost in a very separate womb of my own construction. Wholly free. And because it's the only activity at all that I
engage in wholly for myself. It's the one place that I can't have any
other interference of that sort.

The editing is no problem, because that is such a different way of
thinking about things. I don't have to exercise the same skills or
talent. I don't create as an editor, I simply do more of what one does
in teaching, but in terms of someone who is creating—you see, that is
my work, so I don't feel anything strong or deeply personal about it
at all. What I want to do with an author is to get him into the position
to do the best work he can, and then to try to publish it so it will
receive the widest amount of attention, and look elegant, and be well-
received. That's quite different. It's sort of like fishing—you catch
fish, which is different from cooking them. You don't have to know
one in order to do the other, and you can do one well and not do the
other well. So that I don't find a conflict there. The problem, of
course, is time, trying to find enough time for all of those things. And
I like it all, you know, but probably the only one that I couldn't live
without is the writing. I think that if all the publishers disappeared, I

would write anyway, because that is a compulsion with me. To write, to think that way.

S: How did the teaching go this term?

M: Oh, I enjoyed it. I really did. I had a good time in both classes and in the "Black Women and Their Fiction" class, it was nice because I was able to discuss contemporary women and maybe introduce students to some women that they had never read before. And also, it was nice going into almost untrammeled territory with them. There isn't a lot of first-rate criticism about black women writers, so that in their papers I insisted that they make reference to the text that we had read in class. And I had given them outlines and general questions which we dealt with in class to get around to a decent topic for term papers. But they knew that they were very free to introduce ideas—in other words, there were not a lot of secondary sources to which they could go. I told them to feel free to draw their own conclusion. A couple of them did really first-rate work.

S: You're quite right—there isn't very much good criticism of black literature and particularly of the literature of black women. What kinds of things do you feel, as a writer, a teacher, and as an editor, need to be pursued in this regard? Should criticism take a particular direction—do certain questions need to be asked more than others.

M: Certain questions occur to me when I try to think of the body of black literature that there is in general and the body of black literature that women have produced. In the course, for example, I was very interested in how contemporary black women looked at the stereotype of black women. Did they accept that role? Did the writers believe, in the works we studied, that that was pretty much the way we were? Were there characters representative of the mammy, whore, whatever? show-girl, whatever? And emasculation and so on? How political were they? Were the writings very, very directed by new political awareness or were they distant from that, were they outside the so-called realm of politics? What were their perceptions about their role? How did they really see themselves? And even—if we could get a little bit deeper, if you could think in terms of not just characters but plot and tone and the attitude of the woman writer toward the world in which she lives—does she really feel burdened and harassed? Frequently, what I found so lacking in most black writing by men that seems to be present in a lot of black women's writing is a sense of joy, in addition to oppression and being women or black or whatever. With some exceptions, Gayl Jones is an exception to that. She never writes about joy. I think that's because she's young. But with others, there is a sense of comfort in being who one is, there's an expression of good times, not in the sense of "going out somewhere." There's a scene in *Sula* where the women are just having some fun, talking to one another. They enjoy that. That kind of woman. In Lucille Clifton's *Generations*, there's that sense of fun and joy. In Toni Cade, there's that sense of high-spiritedness. I don't mean comedy, and I don't mean jokes or anything. But part of this business of living in the world and triumphing over it has to do with a sense that there's some pleasure. And where do they get that pleasure from: How do they look at what we would call beauty in the world? What do they think it is? What pleases them? Just to see what the black woman's sensibilities are when she writes. What is she preoccupied with? What does she think are the crucial sorts of questions about existence, life, man-woman relationships? Are they seen the same way as the way in which the men have seen them?

S: Most of the major male characters in black literature are in motion. They're frequently much more like Ajax—maybe not always as grand and high-spirited as Ajax—but mobile. I think of such books as *Invisible Man* and *Autobiography of an Ex-Colored Man*, where there's this movement and quite often, there's no name, in contrast to how women are named, how they are lovingly named. An exception to this might be Leon Forrest.

M: But even there, he has that marvelous man, James Fishbond, you know, who is just a traveling man. Both of these things are very interesting to me. The name thing is a very, very strong theme in the book that I'm writing, the absence of a name given at all, the odd names and the slave names, the whole business, the feeling of anonymity, the feeling of orphanage. That's very important and became immediately clear to me in this new book. But the first thing you said about being in motion is also true, because I think that one of the major differences between black men's work—the major black characters—and black women's work is precisely that. The big scene is the traveling Ulysses scene, for black men. They are moving. Trains—you hear those men talk about trains like they were their first lover—the names of the trains, the times of the trains! And, boy, you know, they spread their seed all over the world. They are really moving! Perhaps it's because they don't have a land, they don't have dominion. You can trace that historically, and one never knows what would have been the case if we'd never been tampered with at all. But that going from town to town or place to place or looking out and over and beyond and changing and so on—that, it seems to me, is one of the monumental themes in black literature about men. That's what they do. It is the Ulysses theme, the leaving home. And then there's no one place that one settles. I mean, one travels. And I don't mean this in the sense of the Joycean character or even in the sense of just going off to find one's fortune in the classic sort of fairy tale, going off to see where the money is. But something else. Curiosity, what's around the corner, what's across the hill, what's in the valley, what's down the track. Go find out what that is, you know! And in the process of finding, they are also making them-selves. Although in sociological terms that is described as a major failing of black men—they do not stay home and take care of their children, they are not there—that has always been to me one of the most attractive features about black male life. I guess I'm not sup-pose to say that. But the fact that they would split in a minute just delights me. It's part of that whole business of breaking ground, doing the other thing. They would leave, go someplace else. There was always that possibility. They were never—I don't say they were never, obviously there were expectations to all of this—but they didn't just let it happen, just let it happen. That's part of that interesting magic I was talking about. And you know, the traveling musician, the theater group, those people who just stayed on the road, lived a different life. It's very beautiful, it's very interesting, and in that way, you know, they lived in the country, they lived here, they went all over it.

S: It's interesting to compare that motif to what you did to Sula, in that she is in motion in a sense . . .

M: Very much.

S: . . . at the same time that she is most stationary and in those enclosures, like that bedroom where she dies.

M: She is a masculine character in that sense. She will do the kind of things that normally only men do, which is why she's so strange.

She really behaves like a man. She picks up a man, drops a man, the same way a man picks up a woman, drops a woman. And that's her thing. She's masculine in that sense. She's adventuresome, she trusts herself, she's not scared, she really ain't scared. And she is curious and will leave and try anything. So that quality of masculinity—and I mean this in the pure sense—in a woman at that time is outrage, total outrage. She can't get away with that—unless she were in this sort of strange environment, this alien environment—for the normal—which would be the theater world, in which you realize, the people are living, even there, by laws. You know, somebody should do something interesting on that kind of show business woman—Billie Holiday, Bessie Smith—not just their art form, but their lives. It's incredible, that sense of adventure that those women had. And I think that's why they were there in the first place. They were outside of that little community value thing. It's more normal among men, but it's attractive, and with me, it seems to me to be one of the very interesting things to talk about when one is doing any criticism of black writing, rather than doing those books in which you do five hundred people and you say a little bit about this one, a little bit about that one. If somebody could get one or two of the really major themes that are part and parcel of this canon. And there are some traceable, identifiable themes, and that's the kind of criticism that I would love to see. There may be some things that you could do with both men and women. But certainly this seems to me one of the major themes. And then there's the black woman as parent, not as a mother or father, but as a parent, as a sort of umbrella figure, culture-bearer, in that community with not just her children but all children, her relationship in that sense, how that is handled and treated and understood by writers, what that particular role is. We talk about all these things in terms of what her huge responsibilities have been, but a really penetrating analysis might be very helpful.

S: You've just described, very well, some new directions for criticism. Can you say something about new directions in fiction?

M: What I think is happening?

S: Well, what you think is happening, what may happen in fiction by some of the writers we've been discussing, in this decade.

M: Oh, I went to some meeting recently and there was a great deal of despair, it seemed to me, about what was happening in publishing and black fiction, the suggestion being that there was not much being published but that now it's not so popular anymore and that white publishers have decided that our age is over and that we are no longer fashionable as we were in the late sixties or early seventies. I think part of that's right—that is, we're no longer fashionable in that sense—all of which I am so grateful for, absolutely relieved to find, because some brilliant writers, I think, can surface now. Once you get off of the television screen, you can go home and do your work, because your responsibilities are different. Now I don't mean that there's any lessening of political awareness or political work, but I do think that one can be more fastidious, more discriminating. And it's open, it's just freer, that's all, and there's room, there's lots of room. People tend to think that the whole literary thing is a kind of pyramid, that somebody is on top, which is total anathema to me. There is enormous space! I think of it in terms of the one other art form in which black people have always excelled and that is music, an art form that opens doors, rather than closes them, where there are more possibilities, not fewer. But to continue to write the way somebody believes is the prescribed way is death. And if I know anything about black artists, I know they don't pay any attention to any prescriptions that nobody gives them at all!

It's harder perhaps in literature, because it has to be purchased by somebody in a publishing house, so that you're always under the eye of some other person. Nevertheless, it's exciting and it's new and it's marvelous and it's as though somebody pulled out the plug and we were left again to our own devices, not somebody else's, not the television's devices, not the *New York Times'* version of what we were supposed to do, but our own devices, which are the ones which we have to be left to. White writers, you know, write about us all the time. There are major black characters in Updike, in *Ragtime*, in all of them. That's where all the life is. That's where the life is. And the future of American literature is in that direction. I don't mean that's the only group, but that certainly is one of the major groups. Obviously, lots of people are interested in it, not just for research purposes as you know, but in terms of the gem, the theme, the juice, of fiction. And we are certainly, obviously, interested; we have all sorts of philosophical attitudes about "the predicament." There's that incredible kind of movement which yields an artistic representation of something that one takes for granted in history. I think that accounts for the success of Gayl Jones's first book, where you have the weight of history working itself out in the life of one, two, three people: I mean a large idea, brought down small, and at home, which gives it a universality and a particularity which makes it extraordinary.

But there's so much that nobody ever, ever does. You know, I go sometimes and, just for sustenance, I read those slave narratives—there are sometimes three or four sentences or half a page, each one of which could be developed in an art form, marvelous. Just to figure out how to—you mean to tell me she beat the dogs and the man and pulled a stump out of the ground? Who is she, you know? Who is she? It's just incredible. And all of that will surface, it *will surface*, and my *huge* joy is thinking that I am in some way part of that when I sit here in this office and that somehow there must be those of us in white established publishers where a black author can feel that he's going to go and get some respect—he doesn't have to explain everything—somebody is going to understand what he's trying to do, in his terms, not in somebody else's, but in his. I'm not saying that only black editors can do it, but I'm certainly saying that it's important that we are here to participate, to contribute to "the shelf"—as Forrest likes to call it.

S: I have one last question. What's the name of the new novel?

M: At the moment, it's called *Milkman Dead*. [The novel was published as *Song of Solomon* in the fall of 1977.]

The Seams Can't Show: An Interview with Toni Morrison

Jane Bakerman / 1977

From *Black American Literature Forum* 12.2 (Summer 1978):
56–60. Copyright © 1978 Indiana State University.

The funding for this project was provided by a grant from
the Indiana State University Research Committee. The interview took place in May 1977, in Morrison's Random House
office.

Toni Morrison is hooked on writing. Though she didn't intend to
become an author, she turned to fiction during a period of stress,
driven, she thinks, by loneliness:

> I never planned to be a writer. I was in a place where there was nobody
> I could talk to and have real conversations with. And I think I was also
> very unhappy. So I wrote then, for that reason. And then, after I had
> published, it was sort of a compulsive thing because it was a way of
> knowing, a way of thinking that I found really necessary.

Since the readers of *The Bluest Eye* and *Sula* are themselves
hooked on Morrison's fiction, the fact that she can't imagine not
writing is both a comfort and a source of satisfaction. The new novel,
Song of Solomon, appeared last fall, published by Knopf, the same
firm which brought out *Sula*, and a fourth novel is just beginning
to take shape. It will be called *Tar Baby*, and is just in its initial
stages now, too new to be discussed. Morrison says that she can be
coherent only about the title at this point, "because it's in the note-
taking stage. The story is fairly clear, but there are whole worlds of it
that I don't have yet, so that anything I said about it might be
altered."

As a rule, Toni Morrison never knows what the next book is going
to be while she is immersed in the current project, but the idea
always comes, even if it's

after a long period of *total* depression. After *Sula*, it was very depressing; I missed all the characters. And then it meant that I didn't have anything to think about in *that* way while I was going about the world. When one is working on a book, whatever one does, whether you're feeling good or you don't feel so good, your writing is something going on inside. So that's what I was really missing. I would write if there were no publishers at all! It's the only thing I do for myself alone.

But following the composition of *Song of Solomon*, the period of depression, if it existed at all, was very brief, and the thinking process is centered on *Tar Baby*.

Generally, it takes Morrison about two to two and a half years to produce a novel, and there are several reasons for that time span. One is that she aims for a genuinely polished, beautiful whole. Well aware of the work and even the struggle which go into the preparation of a novel, she insists that that part of the process ought not to be apparent to the reader: "The point is so that it doesn't look like it's sweating like that *effort*, you see? It must appear effortless! No matter what the style, it must have that. I mean the seams can't show." Another reason for the substantial incubation times for the novels is the simple fact that Toni Morrison is a very busy person, busy being a mother, editor, and teacher, as well as an author. Here, too, one has the feeling that in her hands life is balanced and handled so as to appear seamless. To balance her professional obligations, she's learned to organize and to simplify her life as far as possible.

What happens, I think, when you do several things is that you cut a lot of things out. So I don't entertain people very much and I'm *not* entertained very much. So, if you don't go to a dinner party, you have three hours to do something else in. Also, I don't live in the city; I live in the country, and I get up early—I always have—it's not any effort for me to do that, and take care of the house business with the children—Slade, 12, and Dino, 16—take them to school and so on.

This job, as Senior Editor at Random House, is very demanding, but doesn't so much require being *in* the office. Most of the real work you do of editing is done at home. Then, I teach at Yale one day a week, during one semester; that takes up all of Friday.

But I don't write every day. I only think about it every day. But I think one thing that happens is that you learn to use time for more than one thing. If you're cutting the lawn, you really can't focus all of your mind on that, so you really are in the business of thinking through some *different* kinds of things. When I'm writing a book, there's almost no time when it's

not on my mind—when I'm driving, doing dishes, or what have you. So by
the time I get to the manuscript page, I have had some very clear thoughts
about what I want to do!

Although most writers comment that they need long periods of
sustained time to be alone to work, Morrison's obligations don't
allow her that pattern. In fact, she now does her writing with the
children there, in the room. While her sons are, of course, proud of
their mother's accomplishments,

> if I say that I have to write, that's annoying to them; it takes me away from
> what I'm supposed to be doing, which is mothering them! I used to go into
> the back room to write, and they would come in there frequently, asking
> for things or fighting each other. And then it occurred to me that they
> *didn't* want me to separate myself from them, so now I write in the big
> room where we all generally stay.
>   They didn't *want* me and they didn't have anything to say to me
> particularly; they just wanted the presence. . . .

And so another seam disappeared.
Other seams which must be obliterated develop because of Morrison's writing method. For one thing, she doesn't necessarily start
at the beginning of the book:

> No, I hit certain scenes that are clear to me, that I have a feeling, the
> language, the metaphor, for. I do those, and they may appear at any point
> in the book. I've never written the beginning of any book first; I didn't
> know the beginning. I just *start*!
>   I think the beginnings can stop you, if you don't have them right, and
> some people never go on, so I just start. And then, when I'm finished,
> sometimes I know what the beginning should have been, *is* . . . then I write
> it. I did that on *Sula*; I started on Shadrack.

On the other hand, she *always* knows the endings before she starts,
even

> the words, the sentences. As a matter of fact, on *Sula*, I knew myself from
> the beginning that the last words would be, "Oh . . . girl, girl,
> girlgirlgirl. . . ." So I wrote it, but then I wrote some more, and I wrote
> some more!
>   When my editor saw it, he said, "Tell me, where does the book end?"
> And I pointed to that sentence, which is where it had ended in my mind—
> and then I had added one more, which was really a close.

> But I knew from the start the language of the ending and where it would be.

The earliest written stage of a Morrison novel consists of extensive comments aimed at giving *her* a true sense of the work. This stage is *Tar Baby*'s current status:

> I don't have an outline. Sometimes I sit down and write out what *could* be called a précis, except that it goes on and on and on. It's like a plot, but it isn't; it's just things I think about the people and what happens. Notes. They're notes, I suppose, but sometimes they have continuity. Parts of that stuff, I'm able to use verbatim, and some of it, I'm not. But it does give me a sense of the whole.
>
> The reason I do that is because I have so many other things to do: I have to get it *down* someplace so that I can refresh my memory about certain things, not about the overall work I'm doing, but about the details which could slide by me and slip away.

At one point in the construction of *Song of Solomon*, for instance, Morrison was looking for a way of invoking the feeling of a very, very small rural town. She turned to her notes.

> And I came across a sentence in that pile of stuff that I had written some time ago, that I had forgotten. I had written about how the women in the town walked down the streets with nothing in their hands . . . no pocketbooks, no money, no keys. That was just what I wanted to say because the place where one can do that, just get up and walk out the door and go, some*where*, on some business and not have to remember to take the key or money or whatever, would be a place in which you either felt extremely comfortable or be so far back in the backwoods . . . you know, be a small, little community. So that reminded me, and I used it so the reader would know what kind of place that must be.

During the writing of *Sula*, another kind of preparatory note came in handy. In addition to the précis, Morrison often jots down, sometimes on tiny scraps of paper, ideas or phrases which will "open the door to a scene," will convey a tone or a mood. In this instance it was "It was too cool for ice cream," a phrase that for her meant "just a certain kind of day." From that small trigger, the whole scene arose.

Doing the books by scenes, in this way, does, of course, demand very careful revision in order to achieve the polished, seemingly

effortless whole Morrison is after. Fortunately, that step affords her
enormous satisfaction.

> I love that part; that's the best part, revision. I do it even after the books
> are bound! Thinking about it before you write it is delicious. Writing it all
> out for the first time is painful because so much of the writing isn't very
> good. I didn't know in the beginning that I could go back and make it
> better; so I minded very much writing badly. But now I don't mind at all
> because there's that wonderful time in the future when I *will* make it
> better, when I can see better what I should have said and how to change it.
> *I love that part!*

Sometimes, doing that polishing is arduous because it cannot and
must not be forced. Over and over, Morrison stresses that the time
spaces around composing and polishing periods are really essential.
As a reader, she is certain that she knows instinctively when a writer
has written too fast (even if he's very, very good at his craft) because
the passage just doesn't feel natural. She says she's done that herself,
but "I've learned not to fight it. The right thing will happen if you're
not frightened and you relax." Now, it might take months for the
right thing to happen, but it does happen, often as a result of longer,
even more careful thinking about the characters because they will
often lead to the resolution of the problem. There are certain things
they will or will not do, will or will not feel, and, of course, they
must be allowed to behave as they genuinely would.

> I remember writing that scene where Nel discovers Sula and her [Nel's]
> husband making love. And she goes off into the bathroom and thinks.
> When I wrote it, I thought it was absolutely beautiful, purely distilled pain.
> And my editor said that it was—but it wasn't hers; it was mine. And he
> was right. I had written that scene the way *I* would have said it, had I felt
> this thing. And I had to write it again the way *she* would see it or feel it or
> think about it, what *her* images were.

This exploration of various characters is one quality which makes the
novel form so attractive to Morrison; one has to put aside her own
assumptions and explore those of a whole range of personalities,
making the novel "the most demanding and the most challenging"
genre.

Morrison has a *lot* of faith in the future of the novel, despite its
frequently reported demise.

Novels aren't dying! People *crave* narration. Magazines only sell because
they have stories in them, not because somebody wants to read those ads!
Aside from the little game shows, television is all narrative. People want to
hear a story. They love it! That's the way they learn things. That's the way
human beings organize their human knowledge—fairy tales, myths. All
narration. And that's why the novel is so important!

So Morrison's aim is to provide narratives which will help readers to
organize their knowledge, and to do it in a beautiful way. She's very
conscious of style, and she's open to experimentation. At the outset,
"I wanted to write in a very economical way because I wanted to
provoke, evoke, and I rely very heavily on the reader to know a *lot*
about what he *does* know. I just wanted to pull that *out*, so the
writing would be extremely suggestive." But *Song of Solomon*, she
judges, is different:

I made a serious attempt to write it all out and not to write in a hermetic,
closed way . . . simply because I hadn't done it before and also because
this book, I think, required it. It was a joyous but very difficult thing
for me to do.
   But I was so elated, and I felt as though I were taking huge risks in doing
it because my way is usually to say less rather than more in writing. To try
to say a lot in a line.

To say a lot in a line, of course, requires close attention to the
symbol structure of each book; for Toni Morrison, those symbols are
often the route into a character or a scene.

You have to find the key, the clue. In language all you have are those 26
letters, some punctuation and some paper. So you have to do everything
with just that.
   A metaphor is a way of seeing something, either familiar or unfamiliar,
in a way that you can grasp it. If I get the right one, then I'm all right. But
I can't just leap in with words, I have to get a hook. That's the way I think;
I need it, the phrase or the picture or the word or some gesture. I need
that thing over Sula's eye [the birthmark, "shaped something like a
stemmed rose," on Sula's eyelid].

She looks, then, for features that "become integral parts of how
people describe people," and these devices come to stand for characterization, attitudes, roles in society. For the readers and for the
characters who surround Sula, for instance, the birthmark can stand

for beauty, for danger, for uniqueness; the symbol becomes the
evocation of the character.

Sometimes, it's easy to find the intellectual rationale which makes
a symbol work. Again, a good example comes from *Sula*.

> When Sula comes back, I knew that there would be a natural distortion,
> something out of kilter in nature. I wanted something undramatic, since
> dramatic and explosive things are happening in the plot. And I wanted
> something that was both strange and common. A plague of robins is very
> strange, but aberrations like that in nature are not.
>
> I wanted two things to happen: first, to get the awful feeling of those
> birds everywhere at the moment of her arrival. And it *is* awful, her kicking
> them aside as she walks in. Second, it's almost like the violin music in the
> score of a film; you know something is about to happen.
>
> And I also use repetition; I might mention it later in the book, or I might
> have mentioned it early in the story, so that the reader anticipates the
> plague of robins or some other symbol.

At other times, however, the process is not intellectual but rather
almost wholly emotional or intuitive; it doesn't lend itself readily
to explanation.

> A lot of what you write is right for you as a writer, but you can't say
> why. You just know that that's the way it must be. There's *some* intelli-
> gence behind it, but not a whole lot. I guess that's why people talk about
> muses! You can't always explain it. I've had things like that happen. . . .

The example Morrison cites here has to do again with *Sula*. She was
working on a scene in which Eva's husband, who had abandoned
her, returned briefly. Originally, as BoyBoy left the house, Eva stood
waiting to see what would happen, how she would feel when the
numbness wore off. "He jumped into a T-Model Ford that was pea-
green, and he hit the horn, and it said 'oogah, oogah!!!' . . . the way
those old cars did. And as soon as she heard that sound, then she
knew what to think; she *hated* him." To Morrison, the scene seemed
to work, and it did—except for the fact that, as her editor pointed
out, the time was too early for Model-T's! So the scene had to be
rewritten.

As it now stands, BoyBoy leaves the house to meet a woman in a
pea-green dress who laughs "a high-pitched big-city laugh that
reminded Eva of Chicago." The important point here is that for

Morrison, *and* for her character, Eva's emotions could be released only by the combination of the pea-green color and the loud, braying, "big-city" sound of the car or the woman's laugh.

> In my mind, whatever he was going to, was something that was pale green and there was a sound that came from it that would connect, you see. And that way it would release whatever the stuff was that Eva had not taken the trouble to see. . . . Now, that's the way *I* saw it. It's not important, except to me; it doesn't *mean* anything, except that's the way I visualized it.

In either case—whether the scene's symbol is intellectually or emotionally stimulated—Morrison's goal is spare, evocative prose. This pattern is consistent even in very sensual passages. Too much detail is, she believes, damaging.

> It's *boring*. I can't really get into it. But I do know that whatever the reader has in his experience or his imagination, if you give him enough of the outline, enough suggestion, . . . if you give him the language, he will understand.
> Like when Sula is making love to Ajax . . . she may be talking about something entirely different, but they become sensual words because the reader is supplying it. As *I* am. I mean I'm putting in my own feelings and understanding. In other words, it's like a painter uses white space, a musician uses silence. So a writer has to use the words he does *not* use in order to get a certain kind of power.

And she underscores the point with another image: "I think the problem (as an editor and as a writer) is to say the thing properly so that you really remove cataracts and you let people know where their power is!"

Naturally, one of the chief factors in establishing any story and a particularly important factor in creating spare prose is the point of view employed. Morrison uses both the first and the third persons, but sometimes a combination is necessary to arrive at the proper effect.

> I *like* the first person, when I'm assuming the character, but it's harder; it's too hard. When I wrote the section in *The Bluest Eye* about Pecola's mother, I thought I would have no trouble. First I wrote it out as an "I" story, but it didn't work because she, herself, didn't know a lot about things. Then I wrote it out as a "she" story, and *that* didn't work out very

well because I couldn't get her thing into it. It was me, the author, sort of
omnipotent, talking.

I was never able to resolve that, so I used both. The author said a little
bit and then she said a little bit. But I wish I had been able to do the "I"
thing with her. I really wanted to.

But it's hard because you are faced with the limitations of the character.
And if they don't know it, they're not going to tell you! And they can't
say it.

Although Morrison is very aware of her readers because of their
warm response to her work, she does not keep any group of readers
or any sort of "ideal" reader in mind as she writes. In part, that's
not necessary because she rightly trusts her own good judgment as a
reader, a skill she employs constantly in both her editorial work and
in her fiction.

I'm sure I'm *not* the ideal reader in any way, but it's just a very
important part of my life. And when you read something that you like, it's
just so tremendous a thing.

I use myself as the Black audience, and I am a discriminating reader
about things I like. I just try to continue to do that to my work after I've
written it, read it discriminatingly.

When I'm writing, it all seems wonderful, but later on it doesn't, and I
change it. I *rely* on that judgment.

The trust in herself as both specifically a Black reader and a
general reader and her insistence on not explaining too much merge
in her comments about her responsibilities as a Black writer.

Yes, I do. I feel a responsibility to address—well, I say myself!

At first, I didn't feel anything; I just thought that I wanted to write the
kind of a book that I wanted to read. Later on, it changed. There was also
something else—I felt that nobody talked about or wrote about those
Black people the way I knew those people to be. And I was aware of that
fact, that it *was* rare. Aware that there was an enormous amount of
apology going on, even in the best writing.

But more important than that, there was so much explanation . . . the
Black writers always explained something to somebody else. And I didn't
want to explain anything to anybody else! I mean, if I could understand it,
then I assumed two things: (a) that other Black people could understand
it and (b) that white people, if it was any good, would understand it also.

If I could understand Emily Dickinson—you know, she wasn't writing
for a *Black* audience or a *white* audience; she was writing whatever she

wrote! I think if you do that, if you hone in on what you write, it will *be* universal . . . not the other way around!

If you start out writing for some people that you're going to have in mind, it loses something, gets sort of watered down and didactic.

Midwesterners hail Morrison as an important, new Midwestern writer, and she acknowledges that fact. In *Song of Solomon*, for instance, "I think I call it Michigan; they sort of travel around a little bit. But all of mine start here in the Midwest!" Lorain, of course, is a real town, but Medallion isn't, "I just thought it up," and

> I used something that my mother had said to me when I was young, about her living in Pittsburgh when she was first married—how all the Black people lived in the hills and all the white people lived in the valley because the land was rich. Later on, when they had the blast furnaces, all the smoke came down there, and so they sort of flipped it. I just remembered that and so I used it, a similar situation without having Pittsburgh or Bessemer furnaces.

While the author says that all her experiences in life are grist for her fictional mill, she does *not* write autobiographically. Her own experiences are "useful to me as fodder, but not to write about," at least up to this point in her life; "I will use what I have seen and what I have known, but it's never about my life."

She points out that instead she uses what she defines as the true "process of invention for a writer."

> I can easily project into other people's circumstances and imagine how I might feel *if*. . . . I don't have to have done those things. So that if I'm writing of what I disapprove of, I can suspend that feeling and love those characters a lot. You know, sort of get inside the character because I sort of wonder what it would be like to *be* this person. . . .

The process isn't always comfortable, however, because it means that she must always be willing to "think the unthinkable."

> Sometimes, it's a little frightening. I wouldn't like to know anybody like some of those people. I would be horrified. But it's safe in a book! Because I can do it there and it's real and not real, you know.
>
> When Sula dies, I remember thinking or feeling that well, it's not a pleasant thing, but I'm willing to contemplate death. To contemplate what it must be like really to be sick and really dying, and to be interested in it

while you're dying . . . which I would never do. It sounds horrible, but I'm
willing to do it *then*, for the book; I'm not willing to do it otherwise. . . .
  That's what I mean when I say that one takes huge risks. Because you
do start to think all the way through character and event and situation,
often those not pleasant to think about, normally. To think, as in *The
Bluest Eye*, about a little girl who is raped and left on the floor. . . . I've
never been raped, and I don't know what it feels like, but suppose—That's
where the courage or something in the thinking process comes in.

This projection into the character comes only after the original idea
or theme presents itself, "and then I have to find somebody who can
work it out for me." At first glance, the themes seem varied, and
certainly their treatments are, but Morrison responds in this way to a
question about her basic themes:

Beauty, love . . . actually, I think, all the time that I write, I'm writing
about love or its absence. Although I don't start out that way.
  I thought in *The Bluest Eye*, that I was writing about beauty, miracles,
and self-images, about the way in which people can hurt each other *about*
whether or not one is beautiful.
  In *Sula*, I thought I was writing about good and evil and the purposes to
which they are frequently put, the way in which the community can use
them.
  In this last book, *The Song of Solomon*, about dominion (that book is
about men, the leading characters are men). And I thought I was writing
about the way in which men do things or see things and relate to one
another.
  But I think that I still write about the same thing, which is how people
relate to one another and miss it or hang on to it . . . or are tenacious about
love.
  About love and how to survive—not to make a living—but how to
survive *whole* in a world where we are all of us, in some measure, *victims*
of *something*. Each one of us is in some way at some moment a victim and
in no position to do a thing about it. Some child is always left unpicked up
at some moment. In a world like that, how does one remain whole—is it
just impossible to do that?

Because her "effort is always to push every emotion all the way to
its final consequence because it interests me more that way," Morrison often has to explore violence, and she believes that possibly all
of us, at least in part, are violent creatures.

We have a lot of rage, a lot of violence; it comes too easily to us. The amazing thing to me is that there is so much love also. And two things operate.

One is that with the best intentions in the world, we can do enormous harm, enormous harm. Lovers and mothers and fathers and sisters, they can hurt each other a *lot*.

Also, it always amazes me that sometimes, when we have a choice, we take the *best* one! And we do the nicer thing.

All about love . . . people do all sorts of things, under its name, under its guise. The violence is a distortion of what, perhaps, we want to do.

Good examples of that violence as distortion are found in her fiction. Eva, for instance, in *Sula*, could "jump out of the window for one daughter, burn up another child, all about love!" In *The Bluest Eye*, Cholly, Pecola's father, is a broken man, chained by poverty and circumstance, so "he might love her in the worst of all possible ways because he can't do this and he can't do that. He can't do it normally, healthily and so on. So it might end up this way [in the rape]. I want, here, to talk about how painful it is and what the painful consequences are of distortion, of love that isn't fructified, is held in, not expressed."

One of the great attractions of *Sula*, perhaps particularly for female readers, is its examination of a friendship between two women. On the surface, one is a good woman, Nel, and the other a bad woman, Sula. Certainly, those neat categories are the handy tags their society puts upon them. Actually, according to Morrison, Sula and Nel are the two sides to one personality, "if they were one woman, they would be complete," and the loss of their friendship, which is actually the balance wheel for each woman, is central to the book. Often, in her fiction, Morrison explores such losses because that's "my way of saying to the reader, *don't let it happen!*" Only at the very end of that novel, does Nel come fully to understand her loss; Morrison has understood it all along.

Love is always passing us by, always passing us by . . . and always the ego interferes: some pride, some sort of arrogance . . . and it just slips through our fingers. And there's some reason why we don't hang in with a husband or sweetheart or what have you. Something comes up, and we frequently just cannot rise above it. And I think that is simply more true than not.

Friends, husbands, sweethearts—but the problem doesn't stop there.

> Parent-child relationships are the most obvious ones. Parents who
> simply adore their children and really and truly do want the best for them
> may, in fact, destroy them. They say to them, as Eva did, "Your life is not
> worth living." They may not kill them, as she does, but they say, "If you
> do not behave the way *I want you to behave*, then leave or get out. You
> must live *this* way." Too frequently love has to do with owning that other
> person.

Just as Morrison anticipates that her readers will bring their experiences to bear on her fiction, so she hopes that the experiences they live with her characters will help them "not to let it happen" in their lives. The novels, however, are never didactic; they do not preach, they teach. As she has hoped to do, she does "remove the cataracts" to show us, the people, the power we have—for evil and for good. The books work. The reason they do lies in Toni Morrison's willingness to explore the limits of emotion and then to think long and deeply about her work, to hone and polish it to a gleaming finish. To perfect it so the seams don't show.

Talk with Toni Morrison

Mel Watkins / 1977

From the *New York Times Book Review* 7(11 September 1977):48–50. Copyright © 1977 by The New York Times Company. Reprinted by permission.

In her office at Random House, where she is a senior editor, Toni Morrison sat behind a desk stacked high with correspondence and typed looseleaf manuscripts. Around her the walls were lined with copies of books she had edited—most prominently, an over-sized facsimile of Muhammad Ali's *The Greatest*. And, of course, there were copies of her own novels: *The Bluest Eye* (1970), *Sula* (1974) and her latest, *Song of Solomon*.

At 46, Miss Morrison has become one of the most successful black writers in America. Each of her first two books was a critical success, and *Song* promises to outstrip both of them. First serial rights have been sold to *Redbook*, and it is the first novel written by a black since Richard Wright's *Native Son* (1940) to be chosen as a main selection of the Book-of-the-Month Club. It is a notable achievement, particularly when one considers that she has been only a part-time writer. In addition to her job at Random House, Miss Morrison, a divorcée, is the mother of two teen-age boys, teaches courses at Yale in the technique of fiction and the writings of black women, and spends considerable time on the lecture circuit. (On the evening that we talked she was preparing for a 10-day stint at Breadloaf as a lecturer.)

"It does seem hectic," she said of her busy schedule. "But the important thing is that I don't do anything else. I avoid the social life normally associated with publishing. I don't go to the cocktail parties, I don't give or go to dinner parties. I need that time in the evening because I can do a tremendous amount of work then. And I can concentrate. When I sit down to write I never brood. I have so many other things to do, with my children and teaching, that I can't afford it. I brood, think of ideas, in the automobile when I'm driving to work or in the subway or when I'm mowing the lawn. By the time I get to the paper something's there—I can produce.

"Even so, I wish I were more organized. I might write each day for three months, then not write at all for the next three months. I always thought I should have a routine of some kind, but I've discovered I can never force it. If I don't feel the stride I can't do it. But once I get the hook, the right metaphor for a scene, I'm all right. In *Song* I worried over how I could say that Milkman, the hero, was in this small town that was different from any place he'd ever been— that it was really the country, the backwoods. Lots of things came to me, but once I was able to visualize that the women there walked down the streets with nothing in their hands I knew I had it. First I had to get it set—that phrase did it for me. I knew what was going to happen but I couldn't get the language and the feeling, the fabric, until then. Not until I knew what would make the reader and me and Milkman know this was the small, rural town I'd imagined—then I could do the whole chapter.

"Still, I feel I've been spreading myself too thin. I've always thought about writing full time, but there was so much insecurity about not having a job. I wanted to make a big score first—now I've begun to make arrangements to work a little differently at Random House. Starting in October I'll spend more time at home. I'll still edit four or five books a year, but I'll have more time for writing."

Writing then has become Miss Morrison's primary pursuit, which is ironic because as she tells it she started almost by accident. "I never wanted to be a writer," she said, "but I was always an avid reader of fiction. I really began writing myself when I drifted into a writer's group while teaching at Howard University in 1962. There were about 10 of us who got together once a month, and the only rule was that you couldn't come unless you brought something to read. The others were mostly poets, but Claude Brown was part of it for a time. Anyway, I brought all that old junk I'd written in high school. Then one day I didn't have anything to bring, so I wrote a little story about a black girl who wanted blue eyes. It was written hurriedly and probably not very well, but I read it and some liked it—I was 30 years old then so I wasn't a novice. Still, I thought it was finished; I'd written it, had an audience, so I put it aside.

"In 1964, I left Howard and went to Europe for the summer. When I returned I was divorced and in a state of unhappiness. I got a job in Syracuse and was very lonely there. So I started to work on that story—it was a way of communicating and, with few friends, I had to talk to someone. About three-fourths of the way through I sent it to a young editor at Macmillan and it got a positive response. Later he moved to Holt and called to ask me about the story. It was eventually published there.

"After I had written that book, I began to order my experience in that form. I thought of myself as a writer, even when I took the job of editor here. I wasn't able to stop. It was for me the most extraordinary way of thinking and feeling—it became the one thing I was doing that I had absolutely no intention of living without. I just wanted to do it better and better. . . . It's still difficult, but I never approach it with dread or fear; I look forward to it. It stretches you, makes you think the unthinkable, project yourself into people you even dislike, people I couldn't stay in a room with for over 20 minutes. It makes you stay in touch with yourself; I guess it's like going under water for me, the danger, yet I'm certain I'm going to come up.

"And sometimes, when the language is right, there's even more; I begin to react to the characters who say certain things. In *Song* when Milkman's mother says to his father, 'What harm have I done you on my knees?', then I loved her. I felt all kinds of chilling things. When the language fits and it's graceful and powerful and like what I've always remembered black people's language to be, I'm ecstatic. It's always seemed to me that black people's grace has been with what they do with language. In Lorain, Ohio, when I was a child, I went to school with and heard the stories of Mexicans, Italians and Greeks, and I listened. I remember their language, and a lot of it is marvelous. But when I think of things my mother or father or aunts used to say, it seems the most absolutely striking thing in the world. That's what I try to get into my fiction."

In fact, Miss Morrison's first two novels received their greatest praise for her lyrical, precise use of language. Thematically both of those books focused on the insulated, parochial world of black women. *Song of Solomon*, however, marks a dramatic departure from that narrower theme.

"This book was different," she said, "men are more prominent. They interested me in a way I hadn't thought about before, almost as a species. I used what I knew, what I'd heard. But I had to think of

becoming a whole person in masculine terms, so there were craft
problems. I couldn't use the metaphors I'd used describing women. I
needed something that suggested dominion—a different kind of drive.
I think *Song* is more expansive because of that; I had to loosen up. I
could not create the same kind of enclosed world that I had in
previous books. Before it was as if I went into a room and shut the
door in my books. I tried to pull the reader into that room. But I
couldn't do that with Milkman. It's a feminine concept—things
happening in a room, a house. That's where we live, in houses. Men
don't live in those houses, they really don't. My ex-husband is an
architect and he didn't live there; every house is a hotel to him. So
the forces were different in this book, I had to look outward.

"I also wanted to use black folklore, the magic and superstitious
part of it. Black people believe in magic. Once a woman asked
me, 'Do you believe in ghosts?' I said, 'Yes. Do you believe in
germs?' It's part of our heritage.

"That's why flying is the central metaphor in *Song*—the literal
taking off and flying into the air, which is everybody's dream. My
children used to talk about it all the time—they were amazed when
they found they couldn't fly. They took it for granted that all they
had to do was jump up and flap their arms. I used it not only in the
African sense of whirling dervishes and getting out of one's skin, but
also in the majestic sense of a man who goes too far, whose adventures take him far away . . . black men travel, they split, they get on
trains, they walk, they move. I used to hear those old men talk about
traveling—which is not getting from here to there, it's the process—
they even named themselves after trains. It's a part of black life, a
positive, majestic thing, but there is a price to pay—the price is the
children. The fathers may soar, they may triumph, they may leave,
but the children know who they are; they remember, half in glory
and half in accusation. That is one of the points of *Song*: all the men
have left someone, and it is the children who remember it, sing about
it, mythologize it, make it a part of their family history."

The mythical aspects of *Song of Solomon* seem in some ways
similar to those of Gabriel García Márquez's magical and surreal
family chronicle *One Hundred Years of Solitude* but, although she
admits that Márquez, Miguel Asturias and other Latin Americans are
among those authors that she envies, Miss Morrison doesn't feel

that their work consciously influenced her. "I may be influenced by what I read," she said, "but I'm just not aware of it. When I think of influences I think of painters. In *Song*, for instance, I was working on a scene where Milkman is in a small Southern town—he is anxious, feeling lost, out of place—and I literally picked a painting by Edvard Munch that I had seen in Oslo. 'Spring Evening on Karl Johan Street' I think it was, which I felt conveyed the atmosphere I wanted. In paintings I can see scenes that connect with words for me, and I think it helps me get the visual, visceral response I want."

Other writers she admires are John Gardner, James Dickey— whose novel *Deliverance* impressed her because of its implicit moral commitment—Nadine Gordimer, Eudora Welty and Lillian Hellman. Explaining the latter three choices she said: "Perhaps it's because they are all women who have lived in segregated areas of this country or in an area where there is apartheid. They are fearless. Nadine Gordimer and Eudora Welty write about black people in a way that few white men have ever been able to write. It's not patronizing, not romanticizing—it's the way they should be written about."

As to her next book, she is already at work on a novel based on the tale of the Tar Baby. "I was always terrified by that story," she said, "and I never knew why. But it's an example of black folklore as history. It's incredible, but it's right there on the surface—both as prophecy and as a reflection of the past. It's a love story, really: the tar baby is a black woman; the rabbit is a black man, the powerless, clever creature who has to outwit his master. He is determined to live in that briar patch, even though he has the option to stay with her and live comfortably, securely, without magic, without touching the borders of his life.

"Do you think she would go into that briar patch with him?" she asked, rhetorically. "Well, that's what it's all about. If there is any consistent theme in my fiction, I guess that's it—how and why we learn to live this life intensely and well."

The Song of Toni Morrison

Colette Dowling / 1979

From the *New York Times Magazine* 6 (20 May 1979):40 +.
Reprinted by permission of Colette Dowling.

It is an evening in early spring. A group called the Friends of Sarah
Lawrence Library has sponsored the evening's speaker, which
means it has met her rather sizable fee, sent a limousine into Manhattan to fetch her, and wined and dined her in the Tudor mansion of
the college president.

Now, in the intimate auditorium of Sarah Lawrence College in
Bronxville, N.Y., smiling graciously, the picture of warmth and ease,
Toni Morrison walks to the podium. She has changed notably since
she gave her first public reading five years earlier in the back room of
a Harlem book store. Success has both softened her appearance and
charged her with presence. Her eyebrows, no longer plucked and
drawn like stab wounds, arch gently. She is dressed in black, with
pale, ivory-colored beads and gold hoop earrings, and she is very
much in command of the situation. Toni Morrison adjusts the height
of the microphone, deftly passing her hand over its head the instant
feedback leaks out. She leans forward, adopting that disarmingly
intimate tone with which she will sometimes deliver a line she knows
to be socko. "What is curious to me," she says, "is that bestial
treatment of human beings never produces a race of beasts." She
lingers slightly on the "bestial."

Not a new idea, but stated so bluntly to this mostly white academic
audience, it certainly snares attention. She talks for a while, lectures
in a casual, self-assured way, then drops her voice, almost whispers,
takes up the honeyed cadences that make her readings among the
most effective of any writer's living today. Then she picks up her
best-selling *Song of Solomon* and begins to read about a farm, "a
little bit a place," called Lincoln's Heaven: "It was . . . maybe 150
acres. We tilled 50. About 80 of it was woods. Must have been a
fortune in oak and pine; maybe that's what they wanted—the lumber,
the oak and the pine. We had a pond that was four acres. And a

stream, full of fish. . . . And all around the mountains was deer and wild turkey. You ain't tasted nothing till you tasted turkey the way Papa cooked it.''

That farm was a long lost part of Toni Morrison's history.

Nowadays, Toni Morrison is reading and lecturing everywhere—at colleges, publishers' meetings, the Library of Congress and on television, which is all-important in beguiling a large reading audience. She has also had a show devoted to her life on the PBS series, "Writers in America.'' Her third and most recent novel, *Song of Solomon*, was condensed in *Redbook*. Book-of-the-Month Club picked it up, making her the first "main selection" black author since Richard Wright (*Native Son*) in 1940. The same month in which it was published by Knopf, it sold to the paperback house, New American Library for a reputable $115,000. It rapidly became a paperback best seller and 570,000 copies are now in print. In addition, translation rights have been sold in 11 countries.

Her success can be measured in more than numbers. The National Book Critics' Circle gave *Song of Solomon* their fiction award, as did the American Academy and Institute of Arts and Letters. And John Leonard didn't exactly hurt the book's chances when, in *The New York Times*, he put it in the same class with Vladimir Nabokov's *Lolita*, Gunter Grass's *The Tin Drum* and Gabriel Garcia Marquez's *One Hundred Years of Solitude*.

A few months ago, Chatto and Windus, Toni Morrison's British publisher, brought her to England, where she spoke at Oxford and the University of London, and gave a reading on the BBC. Back home now, she continues her hectic schedule. She is a senior editor at Random House (where she has been for 13 years). She is at work on her fourth novel. Within the next several weeks, she will give no fewer than four commencement addresses. Toni Morrison has traveled a long way from Lincoln's Heaven.

Long before she went to Howard, majored in English, and decided to change her name, before she went on to do graduate work at Cornell, to teach English in various colleges, marry, have children, get divorced, and become a New York book editor—before all those things, Toni Morrison was Chloe Anthony Wofford, born in the windy, steel-working town of Lorain, Ohio.

Chloe's father, a shipyard worker, was George Wofford. Her

mother is Rahmah (a name picked out "blind" from a page in the Bible). There were four children. If one takes *The Bluest Eye* to be at all autobiographical, Chloe was a smart, feisty little girl who took issue with most things around her. She eschewed the plastic celebrities of white culture—hating, for example, the ground sweet Shirley Temple walked on.

Chloe got her true education from watching the town's outcasts and characters—women like Reba, in *Song of Solomon* who "lived from one orgasm in another," women who worked roots and did healing, strange, obsessional preachers, wonderful children, toying whores. Chloe, whose mother sang in the choir and whose proud father used to write his name in the steel sides of ships whenever he welded a perfect seam, was able to enjoy the luxury of going outside herself to examine these people's lives because she was secure. There were times when the family was on relief. There were times when her father would become terribly, terribly angry (once George Wofford threw a white man down the stairs). Still, Chloe Wofford got the juices she needed for growing up—and out.

Each night, the family would tell ghost stories. "My father's were the best," Toni says now, "the scariest. We were always begging him to repeat the stores that terrified us the most."

Chloe was a reader of books, and the teachers at Lorain High School plied her with them, taught her, among other things, four years of Latin, and watched her be inducted into the National Honor Society. Then, because her father, by holding down three jobs simultaneously for the better part of 17 years, was able to help out, they watched her leave Lorain and go East.

Because the people at Howard seemed to have difficulty in pronouncing her name properly, she changed it to Toni. She did find herself growing bored with the people at Howard. What saved those four years were the Howard University Players, the repertory company that took plays on the road and showed her, for the first time, what life was like for black people in the South in the late 40's and early 50's. This was a crucial experience in Toni's life, bringing into focus certain ancestral information—particularly the iniquitous loss of family land to whites—the pain and the glory of which would, 15 years later, drive her to writing.

I was eager to meet Toni Morrison and waited for her at a table in a

small restaurant in the East 50's. She is, at 48, a big, handsome,
woman with beginning to gray hair. She is often breathless, often
running, often (I was to learn) late—a woman who fights continually
against overextending herself and seems always on the verge of
losing.

She had been out on the road giving interviews, doing television
shows and now she wanted to be holed up again working on her new
novel. Her defensiveness was palpable. I would soon learn that she is
a woman of many moods. Not just ordinary moods abrupt, seismic
shifts, as if the energy within were caught between opposite poles—
the need to express and the need to defend.

She will often put on an act in conversation, she might suddenly
"get down" and be very chicken-and-ribs, sucking her teeth, poking
a finger into her scalp and scratching—a strange, primitive gesture
that makes her hairdo rock back and forth on her scalp like a wig.
It's not difficult to get the impression that she's putting you on,
at times, taking pleasure in watching you try to figure her out.

"I probably spend about 60 percent of my time hiding," she would
tell me, some months after we had our first lunch together. "I teach
my children that there is a part of yourself that you keep from white
people—always."

Toni Morrison slipped into writing spontaneously. After getting her
master's degree in English at Cornell University and teaching briefly
at Texas Southern University, she returned to Howard to teach. In
1962, she joined a writers' group there and started a short story
"about a little black girl who wanted blue eyes."

A few years were to pass before she resumed work on what
eventually would become a novel about the tragedy that befalls
children too fragile to survive in a hostile world. In the meantime,
while teaching at Howard, she married Harold Morrison, a young
architect from Jamaica. They lived in Washington, had two sons, but
they were at odds.

"Women in Jamaica are very subservient in their marriages," she
says, explaining some of the difficulties in their relationship. "They
never challenge their husbands. I was a constant nuisance to mine.
He didn't need me making judgments about him, which I did. A lot."

In the summer of 1964, Toni and her husband went to Europe with
their two small boys, Slade and Ford. She returned to this country

without her husband. With no immediate job prospects and a toddler and an infant to care for, she went to her parents' home in Lorain.

A year and a half later, she saw an ad in *The New York Review of Books* for an editing job with a Syracuse textbook company, a subsidiary of Random House. She says, "The civil-rights movement was putting pressure on schools to revise the way blacks were being presented in the curriculum. I thought I might be able to make some changes."

She also took the job because they assured her she would soon be able to go to the textbook division of Random House in New York.

Against the mostly bland background of her 18 months in Syracuse, three things stand out in Toni Morrison's memories. One was hiring a white "maid" to take care of her children. Another was initiating (and eventually dropping) a $200,000 suit against a neighbor woman who, in the course of an argument about noise the Morrison children were making in the apartment, called her a tramp in their presence. "In those days I didn't even know any men," says Toni, still bristling at the memory. "That poor woman didn't know what hit her."

The third thing, that happened in Syracuse was that she began, seriously, to write: "I had two small children in a strange place and I was very lonely. Writing was something for me to do in the evenings, after the children were asleep."

What she worked on, that first snowy winter, was the story she'd begun at Howard about the little black girl. It evolved into *The Bluest Eye* and was soon picked up by a young editor at Holt, Rinehart & Winston.

In 1968, Toni Morrison left Syracuse and moved to New York. It wasn't long before Random House switched her to trade books and she was working almost exclusively on books by black writers— Muhammad Ali, Angela Davis, Toni Cade Bambara and Gayl Jones.

"We don't believe that only black editors can do a black book," says Jason Epstein, editorial director of Random House, "but it's something Toni likes to do, and it can be useful. Not long ago, we bought a novel by a black writer and Toni didn't get to see it before we bought it because she was out of town or something. When she did get around to reading it she hated the thing. She thought it

wasn't a true picture of the ways blacks live today. Judging by
the way the book has sold, I would say Toni was probably right."

Although holding down an editor's job, Toni Morrison has made
writing her main work since *The Bluest Eye* was published in 1970.
As she told Mel Watkins of *The Times*, "Writing was for me the most
extraordinary way of thinking and feeling. It became the one thing I
was doing that I had absolutely no intention of living without."

In 1974, *Sula* was published. A stronger, more fully developed
story about the relationship of two women who'd been friends since
they were 12. It received dream reviews and was nominated for a
National Book Award.

More important, *Sula* alerted the literary world to a developing
talent. *The Bluest Eye* was told through the eyes of a child. *Sula*
moved beyond childhood into a more complex vision of life. Here the
viewpoints are, alternately, those of two women. Nel, straight,
inhibited and conventional. Sula, a complete anarchist. In *Song of
Solomon* the view of the world broadens still further, geographically
and chronologically. The main character is a young man named
Macon Dead Jr., in search of himself, his roots and his future. His
odyssey reveals that not all people are like his own, that rules change
radically from one region to the next and that one must have more
than rules to live by if one is going to leave the primal coop and fly.

With *Song of Solomon* it was clear that Toni Morrison was herself
growing, transcending her past as she engaged it. The book she is
now working on called *Tar Baby* is a kind of love story.

"The tar baby," she says, "is a black woman. The rabbit is a
black man. He is determined to live in that briar patch, even though
he has the option to stay with her and live comfortably, securely,
without magic without touching the borders of his life."

"I'm used to writing on buses, while other people are staring out
the window, or while I'm standing by the sink washing dishes," Toni
Morrison says, although now, having reduced her office days to one a
week, she has long, undisturbed stretches for writing for the first
time in her life. "I keep most of my evenings for myself because I
can get a tremendous amount of work done at night."

For five years, Toni Morrison lived in Queens. In 1970, she bought
a house 45 minutes out of Manhattan, in Rockland County, and
commuted to New York every day. Until this year, when they

switched to public schools in Spring Valley, her sons Slade and Ford
went to school in Manhattan—first the United Nations International
School and then Walden School. She would drive them in with her,
drop them off at 8 in the morning, and go straight to her office. At
3:30 when the boys got out of school she left work for the day picked
them up and drove back to Spring Valley.

"You don't ask, you just do," she said, when I wondered whether
it had been difficult getting Random House to agree to her hours.
"I've always operated that way when Yale offered me a part-time
teaching job three years ago. I didn't ask anyone's permission to be
out of the office on Fridays. I simply took the job. One day my boss
announced that there'd be a production meeting or something on the
following Friday, 'I won't be able to be there,' I told him, 'I teach at
Yale on Fridays.' "

There is a history, in Toni Morrison's family, of women willing to
take action—"women," she says, "who would run *toward* the
situation rather than putting someone up in front of them, or retreat-
ing."

Growing up, Toni knew only her maternal grandparents, impover-
ished sharecroppers from Alabama. Her father's parents, from
Georgia, had died by the time her father and mother had met.

Toni Morrison's great-grandmother was an Indian who'd been
given 88 acres of land by the Government during Reconstruction. It
was the inspiration for Lincoln's Heaven, that "little bit a place" she
wrote about in *Song of Solomon*."

"The land got legally entangled," she tells me, "because of some
debts my grandfather, who inherited it, owed—or, rather, didn't
know he owed. It was like the old man in *Song of Solomon*. Those
people didn't really understand what was happening. All they knew is
that at one point they didn't own the land anymore and had to work
for the person who did."

In 1912, the family began the odyssey that was to end, a few years
later, in the dismal industrial town of Lorain.

"I have always thought of Toni as a touchy person," one literary
agent told me. "She's, well . . . prickly."

I was to learn how prickly she can be. Last spring, we were to
meet at the information booth in Grand Central Station 15 minutes
before taking the train to Yale, where she was teaching. She ap-

peared about a minute before the train left. Once we'd pushed
through the crowded train and found seats, I said, "I waited for you
at the information booth."

A dark look flashed from her "To tell the truth, I wasn't thinking
about you at all this morning."

It seemed the better part of wisdom to back off. I took out my
Times, she took out hers. Sitting opposite each other, our knees
almost touching, we remained silent behind our newspapers all the
way in to New Haven.

The town, when we arrived there, was gray and muddy. Before
going to her classroom, we went to a nearby coffee shop. After
coffee, smoking, her early morning pique seemed to have passed. "I
suppose you've heard whom the N.B.A. (National Book Award)
nominated for fiction," she said pleasantly.

"Have they announced it?" I asked. Many people in publishing
had considered Toni Morrison a shoo-in.

"They haven't announced officially, but we got the word at Random House yesterday," she said.

"So who got fiction?" I asked.

"Well," she paused, dramatically, "It wasn't John Cheever, for
Falconer, and it wasn't Joan Didion, for *A Book of Common Prayer*,
and it wasn't Toni Morrison either."

Perhaps this bad news had accounted for her bad mood earlier.
After breakfast, while teaching her course, "Black Women and
Contemporary Literature," she was still somewhat detached. It was
not until she joined her intimate six student writing seminar that Toni
Morrison seemed relaxed and fully engaged.

A writer before everything else, Toni Morrison says, "I don't have
much time to nurture my friends. Sometimes I'll even forget to go if
I've been invited to someone's house for dinner. At this point in
my life, anyone who's going to be a friend of mine is simply going to
have to be able to understand that."

Her involvement with her work sometimes precludes the children.
"If I'm really working, they'll get left out, too. I remember, the
summer I was finishing *Song of Solomon*, I said to my younger son,
who was 10. 'Slade, I'm afraid this isn't going to be a very good
summer for you because I'm working.' I asked him to please, please
bear with me. I told him that once it was finished, we would spend

time together. Sometimes he still says to me. 'Ma, that was a *terrible* summer!' and I say, 'But you were so *good*. Slade. Without you I could never have done it.' "

After 13 years of living alone with her children, could marriage fit into her life again. "What I like," she replies, thoughtfully, "is the minutiae, the day-to-day stuff, the 'Where are my socks?' I like *doing* things for a man." She sighs. "The trouble is, I don't have time for that kind of relationship anymore. The one time I did consider getting married, some years ago, the man expected me to go with him so he could take a job somewhere on the other side of the country. I thought he was crazy! All of a sudden it occurred to me, after not having been married for a while, that *that's* what that means: to be married, you have to go where they say."

In her writing Toni Morrison gives us exotic stuff—voodoo dolls, greenish-gray love potions, a sack of Daddy's bones hanging from the ceiling. There are natural healing practices, powders for encouraging conception, excesses of love and hate that bend the mind and fell the body. Women pull their dresses over their heads and "howl like dogs for lost love"; men who are similarly afflicted sit in doorways with pennies in their mouths. A vigilante gang, the Seven Days executes an "appropriate" white murder for every murder of a Negro it hears about or sees reported in the newspaper. More ordinary folk function according to dreams and numbers. "I write about them not because they are common characters, but because they are uncommon." Toni Morrison says, "I don't want to know what happens with somebody who does the routine."

Like a master storyteller, Toni Morrison whistles and sings a bit first. At times, her writing seems a bit too much of a virtuoso performance. Yet, like a high-wire artist, she thrills and frightens with her grace and speed—most of all, perhaps, with the confidence with which she employs her techniques. She compresses time, makes quick jump cuts in point of view and uses imagery stunningly. Telling of a child's funeral, she will say that the hands of the women in the church "unfolded like pairs of raven's wings and flew high over their hats in the air." The picture of those bony, articulate hands leads you away from sentimental involvement with the dead child and toward the survivors' awful new comprehension of mortality.

Another of Toni Morrison's techniques is the condensed heaping of one horrifying episode upon another. For just one example, in the course of six pages, Sula's stump-legged grandmother, Eva Peace, is described caring for her sick infant, then relating how and why she burned the same child to death when he became a man, then heaving herself out the window to help a daughter who has caught fire while canning vegetables in the yard.

There is an atmosphere of exoticism, honed at times to the intensity of magic, that gives much of Toni Morrison's work a surreal quality: It also contributes to occasional controversy over what the writer is about. In *The New York Review of Books*, Diane Johnson (reviewing Toni Morrison's novels along with those of another black writer, Gayl Jones) found the behavior of her characters aberrant: ". . . they entirely concern black people who violate, victimize, and kill each other. . . . No relationships endure, and all are founded on exploitation." Diane Johnson found the novels so disturbing that she finally asked, "Are blacks really like this?" She went on to say that the black novels she was reviewing did not have "the complicating features of meaning or moral commitment."

Other interpreters, however, believe Toni Morrison is writing about people with an awesome capacity for loyalty and love, not just those whom life has maimed. And they go on to point out that it is Toni Morrison's very sense of moral commitment that lends her work its horrific overtones.

As a culture, we are not yet entirely at ease with black writers' work. Diane Johnson observed that content—particularly the stuff that's most brutal or bizarre—has been consistently avoided in reviewers' discussions of Toni Morrison's writing (They usually stick to taking note of the "vigor" of her language her "lyricism," her "vitality").

The critics, white and black, seem to be tiptoeing through a minefield. You can imagine them asking themselves. Where does her material come from? From her own life? Is she taking an ironic stance vis a vis some of what she writes about?

Diane Johnson alone raised the possibility that Toni Morrison's largely white audience thrills voyeuristically to the black magic she involves that we press our noses to the window to see the black mama suckling her school age son, the black papa committing incest.

"Perhaps what is exciting about the violence and depravity in . . . Morrison," she concludes, "is that they confirm white fears . . ."

Whether or not white faces are "confirmed" by what black writers choose to write about seems irrelevant—the white reader's problem, if anyone's. It's not difficult to get Toni Morrison to tell you that what concerns her, in her writing, is what she has called "the elaborately socialized world of black people." Like anyone who grows up intelligent and gifted, leaves home, and takes off in another direction, she remains fascinated by the world she left behind, its "characters," its rules, its particular flavor and absurdities. "I wanted to find out who those people are," she says, "and why they live the way they do. I wanted to see the stuff out of which they're made."

Toni Morrison says she had little choice about leaving the community she grew up in. "If black people are going to succeed in this culture, they must always leave. There's a terrible price to pay. I could only edit in the place where the editing is being done. I had to make sacrifices. Once you leave home, the things that feed you are not available to you anymore, the *life* is not available to you anymore. And the American life, the *white* life that's certainly not available to you. So you really have cut yourself off. Still, I can remember that world I can savor it. I can write about it."

Toni Morrison told a story, brought to her by her mother, who recently came East to visit, of something that happened in Lorain last summer. From her telling of it, I got a sense of how she will take something small and vivid from the life back there and spin it out until it encompasses the larger idea, generations, a pocket of human history.

"An old man, the husband of a friend of my mother's just walked off one day," she said "You know, the way older people do. Finally, after many months, his dead body was found in a field. Apparently, he'd had a heart attack, caught his foot in the root of a tree, and fallen. My own grandfather used to walk away and we had to go out and find him. 'Go find Papa,' they'd say to my sister and me. It was often true of little towns with three or four generations of people that the children would be sent out to find the older ones, who were wandering. But there aren't any people to do that anymore, no children, no neighbors. Agencies do it. Well, the town I grew up in used to respond to an event like that almost like a chorus. Those people have a quality, a way of dealing with life that I value, and I write about it.''

Toni Morrison is both held by that world—cradled in it—and at the same time alien to it. When she goes back now, she suffers the ambiguity of both belonging and not belonging. She chose not to go back when *Song of Solomon* was published ''I didn't want those people to look at me funny. I didn't want to experience myself as separate from them. I couldn't bear the fact that old ladies who used to tell me, 'Chloe, cross your legs' would look at me in any other way than that they had the right to tell me that still.''

It is the particular irony of her life—perhaps of every novelist's— that because she sees those people, because she calls them ''them,'' because she names them (as she would say), she succeeds in separating herself from them more finally than ever she did by moving away. But using them to build her own truth, however distancing, is what she is compelled to do. ''Everything I write starts there,'' she says. ''Whether I end up there is another question, but that's the place where I start. Always. And, of course, it isn't the place that I imagine it to be, no place is. But that doesn't matter, it's my beginning, my thing, and I have distorted it, piled things on, I have done whatever it is that writers do to places, and made it my own. So it is mine now. And more and more I see it that way, and hear it that way, and feel about it that way.''

In writing about the world ''back there,'' in the very act of comprehending it, shaping it, impressing her ideas upon it, she moves out beyond its objective reality, and thus loses it. What she gets, instead, is the nowhere world of her own making, intense, vividly encountered, the solitary reflection of her own unique sensibility the only home a writer ever has.

Complexity: Toni Morrison's Women

Betty Jean Parker / 1979

From *Sturdy Black Bridges*. Ed. Roseann Bell et al. Garden City: Doubleday, 1979: 251–57.

". . . Anything I have ever learned of any consequence, I have learned from Black people. I have never been bored by *any* Black person, ever. . . ."

I noticed that the sun had forced it way over the East River through the smog and was trying desperately to energize the early morning persons rushing about on New York's fashionable East Side. A beam of light slipped through a drapery panel, in the room where I sat, and shone directly on a photograph of Muhammad Ali. Although I was partially blinded by the insistent sun, I kept staring at the eyes in the photograph which dominated the other objects on the wall. The voice that spoke to me diverted my attention from the photograph.

". . . you see, my juices come from a certain place. I am like a painter who is preoccupied with painting violins, and may never do moods or paint a tree. . . ."

Toni Morrison was testifying. Her soul was breathing. As senior editor at a major publishing house, she has for some time been deliberately encouraging and cultivating a certain kind of Black work. And, even as a personal preoccupation, she has concentrated on a specific folk element in her own fiction. Without a doubt, her office reflects her trade. Books. Some folks decorate their offices with exotic plants, ashtrays, and an ornamental book here and there. In Toni Morrison's office, books are everywhere. It reminds one, at a quick glance, of an overstuffed dinner table. Copies of *The Black Book*, a documented history of Black culture, edited by her in 1971, occupied most of the coffee table. Several copies of Henry Dumas' *Ark of Bones* and *Play Ebony Play Ivory* along with John McClusky's *Look What They Done to My Song* were neatly lined on a center bookshelf. These represented some of the fruits of her labor. Resting on the left corner of her desk was a copy of *Corregidora*, a novel by

Gayl Jones and one of Mrs. Morrison's earliest projects. Directly
behind her desk was a colossal painting of Africa dipped in red
between a faint black outline. The distance between Lorain, Ohio,
and Random House publishing company could only be a stone's
throw away for a woman who knew how to get where she had to go.
During this interview she seemed radiant and at peace with herself as
she talked to me about the parallels between living and loving in and
out of fiction.

The testimony that she was giving about her strengths and virtues
explained the presence of simple settings and full Black characterization as well as the absence of white characters in her fiction. I asked
her to explain the motive behind writing *The Bluest Eye.*

"I wrote about a victim who is a child, and adults don't write
about children. The novel is about a passive kind of person and the
people around her who create the kind of situation that she is in. I
did not think that it would be widely distributed because it was about
things that probably nobody was interested in except me. I was
interested in reading a kind of book that I had never read before. I
didn't know if such a book existed, but I had just never read it in
1964 when I started writing *The Bluest Eye.*"

An element of mysticism envelops Toni Morrison's fiction. It
comes through both of her major fiction pieces like plaited hair with
different color ribbons woven in. Each color knows exactly when
to surface. One first notices this mystic thread in *The Bluest Eye.* For
example, a strong kinship exists between Pecola's stunted growth
and the growth of the marigolds. It is sewn throughout her second
novel, *Sula,* which is steered by blackbirds and birthmarks and fire
and water. I asked her outright if she was superstitious. First, she
laughed in much the same way that I would expect the seven voodoo
sisters in Algiers, Louisiana, to laugh at such an untactful question.
Secondly, she picked up her pipe and began to refill it. She never
smoked it during the interview. She just kept stuffing it. I was
mesmerized by her serious response.

"I am very superstitious. And that is a word that is in disrepute,
but whatever it is that I am has something to do with my relationship
to things other than human beings. In *Sula* the people are like the
people I have always known who may or may not be superstitious but
they look at the world differently. Their cosmology is a little bit

different. Their relationship to evil is what preoccupied me most throughout the book. How they see it. What they do with it. Black people in general don't annihilate evil. We are not well known for erecting stoning centers or destroying people when they have disagreements. We believe that evil has a natural place in the universe. We try to avoid it or defend ourselves against it but we are not surprised at its existence or horrified or outraged. We may, in fact, live right next door to it, not only in the form of something metaphysical, but also in terms of people.''

Now her voice had staccato movements. I asked her to reflect on the women in *Sula*. They are such a disturbing bunch. And they seem motivated by a force other than Toni Morrison. Sula seems to be a mixture of Hannah, Eva, and Nel. Or are these three women fragments of Sula? I questioned. She nodded her head in understanding my concern.

''In *Sula* I tried to posit a situation where there was a so-called good and a so-called evil people. Nel and Sula are symbolic of this condition. And of course, you can't always tell which is which. Nel is the kind of person I like because I like people who 'do it.' No matter what happens, they do what they have to do. She will take care of the children and do the work but will never have the fire and the glory or the glamour. But the bread will be there. Nobody ever thinks about these people. So they just sit on buses and carry the weight of the world forever. Nel has limitations and she doesn't have the imagination that Sula has.

''On the other hand, I also like people like Sula. They are exciting, and they are willing to trust their instincts completely which is what Sula does. She has absolutely no plans for any series of moments. Yet she and Nel are very much alike. They complement each other. They support each other. I suppose the two of them together could have made a wonderful single human being. But, you see, they are like a Janus' head.''

Mrs. Morrison's telephone rang and I took the opportunity to reverse the tape in my recorder. I refocused my mind on Sula and Nel. Sula was much more complex than Nel. Her relationship with Ajax simply compounded her internal disorder. The way she acted during the course of their relationship seemed somewhat out of tune with her general behavior. After the brief telephone conversation, Mrs. Morrison talked more about Sula.

"When creating Sula, I had in mind a woman of force. In a way she is distilled. She doesn't stop existing even after she dies. In fact, what she left behind is more powerful after she is dead than when she was alive. But back to Ajax. Sula behaves like Nel while she is going with Ajax. She does a little number with the dishes and cleans up her house and puts a ribbon in her hair. Her attempt to be domestic is the thing that makes him leave because he liked her for what she was."

This analysis of Sula and Ajax was especially impressive. Despite the fact that Sula "didn't care bout nobody," she did break down and put a ribbon in her hair for Ajax. However, this need on the part of Sula to be "different" with Ajax than with other men is possibly the great flaw in the web that she has woven for herself. And, on a more general plane, all the women in the book have healthy attitudes toward the men with whom they come in contact. Mrs. Morrison played around with her pipe and continued to comment on the women.

"Sula's mother, Hannah, is sexually selfish. But she is not a selfish person. There is also nothing sinister about her, although she is lazy. She doesn't want an affair, a relationship, or a meaningful anything. She is not about the possession of other people. She has a streak of kindness about her. Sula didn't have that. Hannah is uncomplicated and really and truly knows nothing about jealousy or hostility. And when you take that kind of innocence and put it in an adult, it has reverberations. The people in the town all gossip about her but they miss her when she is gone. And they take care of her when she burns and weep for her when she dies."

The women in the community who cared for Hannah and cried for her were certainly aware of her relationship with their men. Often she made love to their men in her pantry in the afternoon and later helped the wives cook dinner and gossiped with them. Why, then, did they mourn her so? Without so much as a pause, Mrs. Morrison explained.

"Hannah makes a statement of lust about their husbands. Even though they may not want their men to be sleeping with her, it was a compliment to know that somebody else wanted them. It was this quality that made her a perfectly charming person. Of course, she couldn't keep a friend for long because they, being like most of us, have conflicts about love and marriage and who owns and who goes with and all of that. She does not flaunt or boast or go around trying to look cute. She does nothing.''

A puzzling woman, in another sense, is Eva. Whether or not she actually had her leg cut off by the train to collect insurance money may or may not be accurate or important. Nonetheless, she handled the men in her life with a special flavor. The checkers games she played with them in her quarters were spirited and non-competitional. But when her son, Plum, the one man whom she actually gave life, tried to re-enter her womb, she set his body aflame. Was this, I questioned, an act of mother's love?

"Eva is a triumphant figure, one-legged or not. She is playing God. She maims people. But she says all of the important things. She tells Nel, for example, that there is no difference between her and Sula. She tells her, 'I just saw it. I didn't watch it.' Now, 'watch' is something different from 'saw.' You have to be participating in something that you are watching. If you just saw it, you just happened to be there. But she is there at the end and she knows that they are putting something in her orange juice. So she just eats oranges. She is old and senile and Sula has put her in the old folks' home! This is the act that is so unbelievable about Sula. You know like I know that *we* don't put old people in old folks' homes. We take care of them like they took care of us. Anyway, the older you get the more prestige you have. There is nothing prestigious about being young. When old women walk into a room, people stand up and act like they have some sense.''

With all the current uproar about and among Black women, the concerns about choices and the preoccupation with roles, I asked Toni Morrison if her women were prototypic of present Black women. Or, I quizzed, were they antithetical to the current confusion?

"There is something inside us that makes us different from other people. It is not like men and it is not like white women. We talked earlier about the relationship between my women and the men in their lives. When they sing the blues it is one of those 'somebody is gone' kind of thing but there is never any bitterness. Personally, I have always felt this way and I have recognized it in other women.

They are sorry that the man is gone at the moment and may sit around on porches and cry but there is no bitterness and there is no whining, either. You see, I don't have to make choices about whether to be a mother or whether to work. I do them both because they both exist and I don't feel put out about it. I don't dwell on the idea that I am a full human being. I know that. But, speaking of choices, a woman can either choose to have a child or not to have a child, for example. Well, it also has to be the other way around. If she chooses to have it, the man can choose to ignore it. And that is a double-edged sword. If she doesn't have to be the mother and manufacture it, then obviously he doesn't have to be the father. And this is a liberty that Black men have always taken. They have always made that choice. Now, they have been cursed out for years for doing it, but nevertheless, they have always done it and there is no way to stop them. And I think that is called abandonment of the family or something. On the other hand, Ulysses abandoned his child for twenty years and he didn't go anywhere since he was just hanging out over there with the Sicilians. But he is considered a hero! His wife stayed home and did little wifely things. He knew that there was a child there and never once said that he had to go home to his son. He said he had to go home to his property. But, you see, he is a classic!''

The morning was growing into noon. By now the ray of sunlight that had stolen its way into the room had doubled in size. I thought of Zora Neale Hurston, Nella Larsen, Ann Petry. In their way and their time they had plowed the furrows of Black life through the medium of literature. Yet, even now they are only shadows in the literary world. I asked Toni Morrison why she felt that Black women writers had never been taken seriously.

"Because no women writers were taken seriously for a long time, unless they were cultivated by someone. In earlier years, Black women were not compelled to write. If they wanted to do something creative, they would generally not write. You see, if Sula had any sense she'd go somewhere and sing or get into show business. Writing is a formidable thing to break into for anybody. For most Black women in the past there was no time to write. I have never yet figured out how they found time to do all the things they did. Those who went to school and presumably had leisure had few choices.

They became teachers and things of that sort. Things are not that much different now."

Mrs. Morrison noticed that I was again looking at the eyes in the photograph that hung on the wall. She leaned back in her chair, her head almost touching the map that framed her. This time she lit a cigarette and pushed the pipe out of the ashtray.

"That picture would have been good on the cover of Ali's autobiography. It is different from anything I have seen of him. I have just finished editing his autobiography. And it is beautiful. It is also massive. It was almost like editing the Bible and every comma became a thesis. Now that it is complete, I can get back to my own work."

I asked her if she was working on another novel.

"I think I am almost finished with my third novel [*Song of Solomon*]. I must get it to my editor. There is so little time to do what we have to do. But it should be available soon."

I gathered my things and rose to leave. Toni Morrison is a legend in her time. She has certainly moved one step beyond her literary mothers. They made that possible for her just as she will continue to pave the way for others. Margaret Walker said once that literature is like a chain. Toni Morrison is easing her link into that chain in much the same way that the sun eased its way into her office.

The One Out of Sequence

Anne Koenen / 1980

From *History and Tradition in Afro-American Culture.* Ed.
Gunther Lenz. Frankfurt: Campus, 1984: 207–21.

K: As a white woman from Germany, interested in Black women's
literature, I want to ask you if you feel more comfortable with
reviews of your books when they are written by Black feminist
critics, or if you can name some aspects which I should consider in
writing about Black women's literature?

M: I'm always a little disturbed by the sociological evaluations
white people make of Black literature. Unless they are used as
servants of aesthetics. I don't think it is possible to discuss a literature without taking into consideration what is sociologically or
historically accurate, but most of the criticism in this country stops
here. It's demoralizing for me to be required to explain Black life
once again for the benefit of white people. Or to feel that I have to
write about people who are "typically Black." But Sula's an unusual
woman. That's why the town doesn't know what to do with her. She
doesn't represent all Black women at all. I think perhaps she is a
much more contemporary woman than her time allowed her to be.
For that's what makes her unusual. She's the one out of sequence, so
to speak, and she would not have the same difficulties, I think, these
days, but any woman who chose to live a rather experimental life
would have trouble even now, and certainly then.

K: Could you explain to me why Sula is considered evil? I didn't
think she was evil at all, perhaps because I could identify with her
and felt rather close to her.

M: I thought she had a serious flaw, which led her into a dangerous zone which is, and it really is dangerous, not being able to make
a connection with other people. Now it's true that she made some
tentative efforts, she tried, but that absence of . . . You see, it's
important to my idea of her that she not do anything as wicked—
socially wicked—as her mother and grandmother; they did things
that were not quite acceptable, but all of their errors or wickedness

67

came out of compassion or some human feeling. Sula's behavior looks inhuman, because she has cut herself off from responsibility to anyone other than herself, she is afraid of that area of commitment. She hasn't the tenacity and that sort of salt of the earth quality that Nel has. Even when Nel was in despair she takes good care of the children. She will do the things that must be done, simply because they are there. Now, mind you, Sula was living in a period during which human beings had to take care of each other and she's living in a town in which it's absolutely necessary. That's why the townspeople don't understand her. You see, there were no agencies then. Neighbors, individuals, plain human beings used to do that—take care of the helpless or needy. She, Sula, put her grandmother away. That is considered awful because among Black people that never happened. You must take care of each other. That's more unforgivable than anything else she does, because it suggests a lack of her sense of community. Critics devoted to the Western heroic tradition—the individual alone and triumphant—see Sula as a survivor. In the Black community she is lost.

K: I especially like your description of communities. They give me a very good idea what it is like living in such a neighborhood, and it reminds me a little bit of the neighborhood I lived in as a child, where people used to sit in front of their houses in the evenings.

M: It's that close? It's not like that now, you know. Oh, there are some communities still like that, but one's impression from looking at Black literature is a little different. I thought that the criticism and the reviews—well, I haven't read a lot of it, so I can't really speak about it, I don't get around to reading the journals that I used to read when I was teaching—but anyway, when I hear people talk about all sorts of things, they don't talk about friendships of women, or they talk about deficiencies in the communities, what was wrong with this. It all looks pathological to them, but I found it very nourishing. And I thought her, Sula, pathological in that sense, in relationships with the community, not pathological as an individual. So I don't find her evil as a single evil person, but she was used as though she were, which is helpful for the townspeople. They were very creative in that sense.

K: I remember, First Corinthians in *Song of Solomon* saying that she didn't know any grown-up women. I wonder whether this is your opinion, too, about the women characters in your books, and I want to know what woman has the potential of being an "ideal woman"?

M: First Corinthians is kept like a child, trained to be a child, as many women are, because her father and mother believed, at least to some degree, that the American Dream was worthwhile. And part of that dream is to remain infantized and to regard innocence as a virtue that's supposed to last forever. Those girls are just reared that way. The woman that is most exciting, I suppose, is Pilate, only because she has a kind of ferocity, that's very pointed, astute, and she's also very generous and wide-spirited; she has fairness, and braveness, you know, in a way I'd like to be. The woman that I feel most affection for is Hannah. I thought very tenderly about her.

K: Could you explain why?

M: I can't. She's just a person I like. Hers is a sort of life stripped down to its essentials, and that was enough for her. She was not bitter, and she was not whining. She was reliable, and she was also a little off-centre. But she wasn't so off-centre that she frightened, just a little. I think she's the only person who never deliberately caused anybody any pain, although she does say something awful to Sula, but she never wanted to hurt anybody, she didn't have the ego or the vanity to want to impose herself on anybody. And I like that. It's genuinely maternal. She reminds me more of Lyra and all those water-creature women who are competent and a little joyful. They're not dependent on men, but they don't hate them either.

K: Could you comment on your descriptions of motherhood? I thought that you are moving away from romantic concepts of motherhood. For example, when Hannah tells a friend that she loves Sula— and this sounds like a statement about a biological necessity—but that she doesn't like her.

M: I think that distinction is an important one that Hannah makes. It happens sometimes, but sometimes you don't say it. It doesn't matter if she keeps on doing what she does for the children. It was the one sentence that would turn the whole thing around. The whole business of nurturing is always very interesting. . . .

Hannah asks her mother, "Why did you never play with us?" But, you know, it's problematic playing with children when you don't know how to stay alive. The children are always hostile about it, but then they carry the same thing on. That kind of sentimental love for children is not possible, except in a certain kind of loving society, where you can relish it. Children are easy marks in aggressively oppressive societies.

K: You seem to be generally suspicious of romantic feelings, especially romantic love, like when you say in *The Bluest Eye* that the idea of romantic love is one of the most dangerous ideas which exist.

M: That was very important to me at that time. I don't make a lot of general statements, because they always seem to jump out so hard at you. Also, who wants it, romantic love? The women who would want it are precisely the kind of women I would never like to be. In other words, it's a complicity between master and servant—first of all, is the assumption that it is possible for men to *give* it to you, and second that you would want to accept something from another human being totally, that you didn't want to get the world for yourself. That you wanted it handed to you. Who wants to be taught that stuff? That's part of a lot of women's writing. I keep hearing that note. Everybody's so disgruntled because some man hasn't come along and solved their problems. It bothers me a little bit, because, even though some women sound very militant, underneath—well—if some man came along and said, "Here, here, here," I have the feeling that they'd quit everything.

K: That reminds me a little bit of First Corinthians and Porter, where he keeps saying, "This is for you instead of that." I must say that this scene troubled me a little bit. Is it just a description or what did you want to imply?

M: But he's giving her love instead of things, tenderness and care and respect. He can't give her a trip, he can't give her all those romantic things.

K: But the point for me is that love is still the most important thing in her life.

M: Indeed.

K: Would you agree with that notion of love on a more general level?

M: Oh no. I think it's important, but without it—what? It's not a deathblow. I mean it's not vital. But I am not my characters, I just try to make sense from their point of view. With a character, I do what an actress does: I get inside, I try to see what it looks like and

how they feel and let them do what I think they'd do. At the moment
I'm writing, I love all of that, I love them, but I'm not putting my
persona in there. I like the scene because of what he was saying, I
like the seduction of her which says, "I can't court you." And I
liked her simplicity, and I liked the fact that she liked it. But I like
lust, you know (that's why I like Hannah).

I like Corinthians saying, "I feel simple." It's not all that stuff in
her house, all that marriage to the right person—she's feeling closer
to that part of herself that is just simple. And I like that, I think,
personally. But it's true that she didn't have anything else, she didn't
have any "raison d'etre." Without him, I mean she was really "out
to lunch." She didn't have anything at all, so this was a distinct
improvement in her life. But you understand that my notion of love—
romantic love—probably is very closely related to blues. There's
always somebody leaving somebody, and there's never any vengeance, any bitterness. There's just an observation of it, and it's
almost as though the singer says, "I am so miserable because you
don't love me," but it's not unthinkable. You know, "I don't want to
see the evening sun go down, all is gonna be awful and all terrible,"
but there's no whining and no "Look, what I've given up for you."
You don't have the sense that something stops. It's not romantic in
that sense, and that's my educated view. It's quite contrary to
Western civilization, it's quite contrary to the overwhelming notion
of love that's the business of the majority culture. This one is different, not only that I grew up with both cultures, but the one that came
to my aid in times of crisis was always one that was not the majority
culture, when you are thrust back into small places. What I could
find useful was almost never things I learnt in school. What one
learns in school is a different kind of education that would make it
possible for you to work and talk to certain kinds of people, but it
was frequently quite the opposite of, certainly unlike, the education
one received in the community. Those are the things that interest me.

In *Sula*, I'm interested in what it means to be an outlaw, who an
outlaw is, by our definition, not by somebody else's. And it keeps me
fiddling around in my books with the past, because I have to clear
that up before I can go forward into anything more contemporary. I
don't do any research, but I try very hard to make it organic. I would
like them to behave differently a lot of times, but they don't go with

it. And I feel it very strongly. And it's credible to me, it seems authentic to me, and real to me. I had Black people say to me they don't know who Pilate is, I mean they don't even recognize that person at all; even though she is fantastic, I thought everybody knew a person like that. But some people tell me they don't. So you just write what you think is your truth. Everybody isn't everybody.

K: I'm also interested in the images the Black liberation movements had of Black women, and their influences on Black women's literature. I think the movements' images are rather flat and one-dimensional, and want to contrast them with Black women's images of themselves. Have you been influenced in any way by those images?

M: In my work, no. I don't think any of that had anything to do with the work. I was not impressed with much of the rhetoric of Black men about Black women in the Sixties, I didn't believe it. I don't think they meant it. I was distraught by the gullible young Black women who got caught up in it. But I never made any observation about any of them in print or otherwise, because it was too frail a movement to swish down certain kinds of criticism on it. It seems to me historically true that Black women have a special place in this culture which is not always perceived as an enviable one. One of the characteristics of Black women's experience was that they did not have to choose between a career and a home. They did both. Also, in times of duress, and I have to be careful here because what I have to say may sound like "Racism is good for you"—it isn't— but in times of duress which is an interesting time for me as a writer because you can see more things—my characters are always in some huge crisis situation, I push them all the way out as far as they will go, as far as I can. But either because or in spite of the duress, the relationship between Black men and Black women in those days was much more a comradeship than the romantic love it got to be later as a result of the infiltration from the other culture. I know my mother and father, my grandmother and grandfather, and the people that lived around me, they thought they were doing something important. And I don't know if they "loved" each other or not, but they took careful care of one another and there was something clear and common about what they were doing. They worked with each other. Sometimes they complained about things, but you always knew that there was some central thing that was bigger than they were, that they were doing. It had to do with raising children, with being morally coherent people. Maybe that's a boring little life, but it seemed to me that was what was strong about it. Because of the dual responsibility that Black women had—when they were left, they didn't collapse. They didn't have crutches in the first place, so with nothing but themselves to rely on they just had to carry on. And that, I think, is absolutely extraordinary and marvelous.

Contemporary hostility to men is bothersome to me. Not that they are not deserving of criticism and contempt, but I don't want a freedom that depends largely on somebody else being on his knees. I also think that part of the women's complaint has to do with enormous expectations. The women like to say they are not dependent on love—as we said before—but there's so little left to love anyway— otherwise why make the man into opera, they make them into opera. What I'm trying to say is there was a time when you could love god, or your race, or your brother, or your sister, or your mother, but all those things have been taken from us in a way, because if you love god they think you are backward, if you love your mother they think you got some Freudian thing . . . And you could have a friend that you loved. Now if you have a friend that you love somebody will think that you are lesbian or homosexual. So what's left? There's nothing left to love, except the children and the member of the opposite sex. The person on the other end of that gets everything. It's too much; the lover expects so much from the beloved. If you loved five things intensely, no one of them would receive that hysterical responsibility for yourself, emotions would be diversified. That's what's lacking in the echo that I hear in the Black feminist thing, it's not the goals that I object to, it's not any of that, it's just that it seems not to question what's behind that desperate need to love only one person. It's not the comradeship of past generations, it's romantic—love—eternal. When I talked to a very young black girl recently, it seemed to me that she had never heard of anything. They're grown up like they never had grandmothers. Or if they had them, they never paid them any attention. Kill your ancestors, you kill all. There's no future, there's no past, there's just an intolerable present. And it is intolerable under the circumstances, it's not even life. That's the impression I get sometimes. Then sometimes I'm marvellously rewarded by quite the opposite. I went down to X, for example, it's so wonderful to see that young girl who has lived with three or four generations of her own people and had this incredible sense of mission. I loved it.

K: Why is it that all the relationships between men and women in your novels fall apart?

M: I think that is because my mode of writing is sublimely didactic in the sense that I can only warn by taking something away. What I really wanted to say about the friendship between Nel and Sula was that if you really do have a friend, a real other, another person that complements your life, you should stay with him or her. And to show how valuable that was, I showed a picture of what life is without that person, no matter how awful that person might have treated you. And I wanted to say you'll never know who you are, you'll never be a complete person, until you know and remember what Milkman had been knowing and remembering. And that's so important that you know that, that it doesn't matter how long your life is, because at the end of every book there is epiphany, discovery, somebody has learned something that they never would otherwise. But that's the only way I can say, that's the only message, that's the only way I can reveal the message, and it gives my books a melancholy cast, because it's more important to make a reader long for something to work and to watch it fall apart, so that he will know what, why and how and what the dangers are, more important than to show him how they all solved all their problems. That's not the only way, but that's the way I perceive it. It's just knowing what the dangers are, what people forget when love goes wrong, this is what people do, they forget. But if you really love the characters and want them to love each other, you'll remember that. It's incumbent on me to make the characters interesting, make their relationships interesting, otherwise you don't care. If I can really make them living, really make their relationships alive, the reader will remember. It's important that Sula's and Ajax's relationship fall apart for that reason. Because he's lovely, he's wonderful, and he takes her seriously, they have a friendship, and then she does what a lot of us do. It's so good that she wants to make it permanent.

K: Why is it always the woman who wants to make it permanent?

M: I don't like your "always" question—but I will answer these

generalizations as though they were accurate—which they are
not. Sometimes the men do it, I think the man in my new book [*Tar
Baby*] wants to make it permanent, and she doesn't. It could have
been the other way round. It's just that somebody in there is going to
spoil it, because he is prey to, vulnerable to notions of possession. I
love love and marriage, I'm not against it, but the marriage works
because there is something in it to work, not because it's a marriage.

It's almost as though Sula became like Nel, and he loses interest.
Therefore, if that happens to her and if there's enough of Nel in
her to make her do that, if that is true, then that relationship would
fall apart. For me, the message is much more important than the
gratification of . . . Milkman learns so much in a very short time. He
learns how to love somebody, nicely, tenderly, give something in
return. He learns how to take risks about something important, he
gets civilized. So that there should be some reward for that, I know,
but in order to keep people from focusing on the reward, and to focus
on the process, I take the reward away. He may drop dead afterwards, but I did it deliberately, so that you can't speculate on it. I'm
not sure it worked very well, since a lot of people are very annoyed
by my endings. I can't help it.

K: Is it important that the protagonist in *Song of Solomon* is a
man, and if yes, why so?

M: Yes, it had to be a man. Men have more to learn in certain
areas than women do. I want him to learn how to surrender, and to
dominate—dominion and surrender. Well, I think women already
know that surrender part, and can easily learn how to dominate. But
what I wanted was a character who had everything to learn, who
would start from zero, and had no reason to learn anything, because
he's comfortable, he doesn't need money, he's just flabby and
pampered. Well, that kind of character, a sort of an average person
who has no impetus to learn anything—to watch that person learn
something was fascinating to me as opposed to watching the man
who already was that perfection. And to see the decomposition of a
beautiful idea go apart in Guitar. You can see both things happen. So
a male character was better for me. I thought there were more
possibilities. Well, he would learn to be more dramatic, and he
certainly was not bound to learn how to give feelings in the begin-

ning. And the men have more places they can hide and not learn. They don't have to learn anything, they can always be men. So that's why it had to be a man for me. I had no intention in the beginning of starting out with a book about men, I mean I just started with an idea, and then I had to find somebody who can do it. So in this instance it turned out to be a man. In the beginning I was a little scary about that, until I realized how much he had to learn from women, which is part of what he had to learn. This man, Milkman, has to walk into the earth—the womb—in that cave, then he walks the surface of the earth and he can relate to its trees—that's all very maternal—then he can go into the water which is untrustworthy then, he can bathe and jump into the water, then he can get to the air. But those are the stopped physical stations of his process, his rites of passage. I don't recommend he live like Pilate, I thought I would recommend he live like his father, but those two poles of opposition contribute to his education. Pilate is earth. Her brother is property.

Finally, Milkman is able to surrender to the air and ride it at the same time which to me is translatable—no, not translatable, it's sexual, it's the sexual act, the actual penetration of a woman and having an orgasm; I imagine this is one thing that has the simultaneous feeling that a man at that moment might feel as he is doing both things: a) dominating the woman, b) he's also surrendering to her at the same time. So that the rhythm of the book has this kind of building up, sort of in and out, explosion. There's this beat in it, in my books there's always something in the blood, in the body, that's operating underneath the language, it's hard for me to get it in there so that you don't read it. Because I lean very heavily on the reader in the book, I don't say it a lot, I mean you have to rely on the reader to help you to make the images work. But underneath there has to be some other thing, it's like heartbeat, or it's like the human responses that are always on the surface in all humans. And you struggle for it, once you know what it is.

In the love scene between Ajax and Sula, there's no sexual language there at all. What's underneath there is my conviction that everybody has played in the mud—it's a children thing, funky. The children do it, they like it. It's a very satisfying feeling. And Sula has a lot of images of water, so that she imagines the water and the loam who, together, between the two of them, make mud. But there's loam underneath all of it, so even though the word is there and the loam is there, the reader thinks he's going to read about two people fucking. And he does, but none of the anticipated language is there, but something underneath much more primitive is there—that's what I mean.

What is seductive and attractive about First Corinthians and Porter is the language, not any description, she just looks down at his genitals, and he talks to her, it's short. I have to assume that your sex is sexier than mine, so that when you read my work, I can leave a lot to your imagination. Or when Milkman sleeps with that little girl Sweet, the whole scene is sexual activity, what happens in the bed is the least part of it, but she cooks something for him, he washes out her tub, and he washes her hair and she irons his shirt and pants, all of that is part of the love-making, because the element in there that is sensual is the exchange of something; actually touching somebody else's clothes is much sexier than fumbling around between their legs. Really, when you read about it. So, if I ever can get up under it with something that is very simple, then the language can be very quiet, and ought not to be very elaborate, because I have hit something other than what's on top.

K: I think in what you just described about your sexual scenes in your books, you've described how a feminine—as opposed to the general masculine—way of writing about sex could be like.

M: I think that's probably true. I read only one book by a man in which I thought the sex was wonderfully described, one that I remember, and that is in Jimmy Baldwin's book *If Beale Street Could Talk*. The scene I'm remembering is a scene where a man takes a shower . . . There were two people in the sexual scene, and I'm always under the impression whenever I read a man describing sex that there's only one person there—one person's doing the activity, and somebody's receiving it. Only one. But in Jimmy's book, there were two people there, and you felt both of their presences. I don't know why that is—that there seems to be only one person in most love-making scenes—maybe they see it that way.

Writing for me is challenging for a number of reasons, but the actual craft and the aesthetics of it are—what I'd like to do—it's a kind of restoration. I like to write a story in which the story matters and the people matter, you care who drops dead, that's very old-

fashioned novel-writing, with very primitive recognitions. When
people talk about black writing, that's what I think it is. I don't think
it's the language, the dropping g's, I think it's something so much
more earthbound than that, much more in touch with the magic and
the mystery and things of the body.

K: If it comes to language, would you say that there is a difference
between Black women writers and Black men writers?

M: No. It's pretty much the same language. There's a larger
difference between the way black women write and the way white
women write than between the way black men write and the way
white men write. There's a big difference to me, their experiences
are different. I'm not sure all of what they are, but maybe it's just
who writes and who gets published rather than the differences in the
two races, the sexes. It could be. Everybody's supposed to be able to
project the other. I think when women are writing out of that place
that is theirs, which is feminine, they are different from the way men
write out of their place. And that's good.

K: One example that comes to my mind is the description of
sexuality we were talking about. I'm just thinking of Pauline as a very
good description of complicated sexuality, a feminine description.

M: I think I did a little of that also in Pauline in sleeping with
Cholly, when she's comparing it to something quiet, to happiness,
you know, glimpses and pieces of stuff, that are innocent and shy.
It's like the body holds all, not just the man.

K: I was wondering when I read your descriptions of Eva and
Pilate why both were described as physically distinct, Eva missing
one leg, Pilate having no navel.

M: Well, I don't really know. I think what really happened was
that I got interested in a woman producing a woman producing a
woman in a kind of non-male environment, and each generation has a
different problem. I duplicated it almost entirely in Song of Solomon;
I think I was finished with the idea.

Also I needed a reason for them to be self-invented. With Eva her
genuine matriarchy, with Pilate I needed something to make her be
outside the pale, so to speak, and that idea sort of appeared and I
followed it along, perfectly ready to abandon it at any moment, but it
worked. It worked for her, it established the presence of the surreal.

I think, now that I'm reminded of it, that I was very impressed

with a very lyrical scene. My mother and my grandmother lived in
the same town, and I thought that my mother was a powerful person,
and the person more powerful than she was her mother who was
really powerful. And I had the grand experience of having my great-
grandmother come to town. And who can be more powerful than
your great-grandmother? She was an incredible woman, and I saw
my grandmother sitting on the edge of the table swinging her feet like
a little girl in her mother's presence. I remember all of them in the
room, and there was my grandmother being very girlish when she's
with her mother. And I was the fourth—great-grandmother, grandmother, mother, and me, and the scene, the event, must have made
an enormous impression. Now the men in my family were very huge
presences, and the women were very accommodating but very
independent. But there must have been something about my seeing
that, I guess, if one is interested in the autobiographical. Recently
somebody reminded me of it and said, "Did that have anything to do
with the fact that you produce those women?" I thought that might
be the case, but just the sequence. There was a moment in which I
was aware of all those women and all those generations and having
my grandmother talk about her mother—I think I wasn't in school
yet or had just started—it must have made an enormous impression
on me.

That woman—my grandmother—died before her husband did, my
father died just a few years ago, but my great-grandmother's husband
died when she was just forty. She couldn't read, couldn't read
anything, but she was a midwife, an incredible woman. I knew all
this about her, that people came from all over the state to ask her
advice in matters, and her sister was like her, too. So I kept the
image, it stayed with me. I guess I'm finished with it now. It seems
so complete.

There's another thing I wanted to tell you, some autobiographical
fact that I thought might interest you. My mother's friends and my
mother knew a woman called Hannah Peace, who—I don't know
much about her, except I remember how she looked, not a lot, just
the color of her skin, so dark, rose in it, and the lids of her eyes were
very deep. Now I was little, so she seemed tall to me. And my
mother and her friends, whenever they mentioned her name, and
called her Hannah Peace, it seemed to me in the way they called her

name there was some mixture of awe and approbation, some quality of both in it. Now I've never asked my mother about that lady, and I don't remember seeing her more than two or four times, but it made an impression on me. There was a quality about that, I thought they sort of liked her and—not disliked her—they liked and admired her and disapproved of her. Admiration and disapproval, at the same time. Whenever something was up, they didn't say her name like you say other people's names. So when I was writing Sula, I used the name because I couldn't not use it. It was all caught up with the sound of "Hannah Peace." Then I gave her the personality of somebody else, but it was almost like the way people might say "Sula," the quality of . . .

K: A magical quality?

M: Yes, I gave it to the younger woman. But Hannah Peace was the woman I thought was real. Well, sometimes the real names are so much better than any name you can make up.

K: I was just thinking about that, because some critics suggested that the name "Peace" was a kind of metaphor in the novel.

M: They do the same thing with "Breedlove," and I knew a lot of Black people called Breedlove. I thought it was an ordinary name, like "Sula" seemed to me an ordinary name, "Sula Mae." And the names I pick from real life, everybody thinks they're strange. Now "First Corinthians," just the sound I liked, and I wanted to illustrate both the respect those people have for the Bible, as well as the way they manipulate it. My mother's name is Ramah, which was chosen that way. That's a city, and she would fuss and say, "The least they could have done was choose a person instead of a city." For me, it was that gesture of getting something holy, but at the time, you don't really look to choose a person. It's not about literary associations, it really is about—the fatality of it, the chance.

K: The scene where Pecola compares herself to dandelions reminded me of a scene in *Maud Martha* where the protagonist also compared herself to flowers. There seem to be a lot of natural images in Black women's literature. Would you agree that the image of flowers is a common image?

M: It certainly is in most cases, I imagine. Maybe not. I was just thinking it's absent in Toni Cade, but it isn't in the recent things she writes. There's some kind of longing or affinity for nature that exists maybe in just the women. But I think it probably has to do with the longing that's kind of a prehistoric verdict for what I did . . . with the earth, in addition to the obvious literary devices. What is more interesting or equally interesting to me is a kind of sense of a woman I'd almost say sexless in the sense of not being limited to that that is in some Black women's writing, not just in the term of anathema. If you can imagine what it must have been like, historically, before men found out that they made children when they thought that women just had them, when they thought that women created life, till they figured out that they created life and they made a male god. And assuming that society was egalitarian—because women produced both women and men, so therefore they were not given to discrimination—and assuming that society then was not a male-headed society, but the women and their children, bedding with whomever they wished—that scenario seems to me to be operating heavily in my work. I was delighted to see those references in Toni Cade's *The Salt Eaters*, she talked about mud mothers . . . Sometimes people call these people spirits, feminine spirits, not in the sense of goddesses, not in the sense of wood-nymphs, but much more pre-historic kinds of figures. "Gathering" women, gathering, I think of flowers and of trees, women who know medicine and roots, root-workers who are not hunting perhaps—maybe they are—but they have to know a poison-leaf from a non-poison leaf. Ajax's mother is like that. That kind of wisdom which is discredited in almost every corner of the civilized, progressive world.

But it seems to me a kind of clawing to get back to something grown, something adult, maybe even something meaningful. If women are to—I suppose, this is speculation on my part, it just occurred to me this moment—perhaps if women are to become full, complete, the answer may not be in the future, but the answer may be back there. And that does interest me more than the fully liberated woman, the woman who understands her past, not the woman who merely has her way. Because that woman did know how to nurture, *and* how to survive. Pilate's closer to that than anybody, she was earthy in that sense, and sort of magical and sweet, but it did not make her wolfish, and she's not a ball-breaker, or emasculating, you know what I mean?

In fact, in becoming free, people go to emasculation, they even

imitate the worst of their male masters. Or you can get some total
woman, feminine, trying to make herself an expert woman in the
sense of seducing men and being married. But there's another root,
and that's what interests me. It's a question of who the women
respect, who the Black women respect, in their own imagination, in
their own conscience. And it seems to me that the most respectable
person is that woman who is a healer and understands plants and
stones and yet they live in the world. Those people are always
strange, when they get to the city. These women know what time it is
by looking at the sky. I don't want to reduce it to some sort of heavy
know-how, but it's paying attention to different sets of information,
and that information certainly isn't useful in terms of a career. But
it's the kind of information that makes you gravitate toward the . . .
It's a quality that normally one associates with a mammy, a black
mammy. She could nurse, she could heal, she could chop wood, she
could do all those things. And that's always been a pejorative word, a
bad thing, but it isn't. That stereotype is bad only when people think
it's less. You know what I mean? Those women were terrific, but
they were perceived of as beastly in the very things that were wonderful about them.

K: So you wouldn't be so interested in creating a woman character
who'd combine different roles, roles you said weren't conflicting
ones for Black women, like a woman who'd have a job and children
and be a lover?

M: You mean a contemporary woman? Well, this woman in the
novel I'm writing now, she's sort of 1976, she's alert.

K: Does she have a job?

M: No. A job is not anything that stimulates anybody to write
about it. I've never been able to get very interested in writing about
any event that I'd lived through. It didn't seem to have the right
color. It's sort of blank. My imagination is more interesting than my
life.

But I did write a story which is more contemporary, more of the
time. And I would suggest that by what I have done (in my new
book) is put a woman who is very modern in the sense of—she likes
herself, she's interested in fulfilling herself—in the context of those
other requirements to see what she chooses to be. To see if she
would choose to be entirely modern or if she chooses to rely on that

past . . . Or I would write a story in which a woman actually becomes a person who does both, except that that might be too heavy, too heroic.

K: Could you comment on the way your novels end, like in *Sula*, where Nel comes to understand her life at the end of the book?

M: There is an ending that is an ending, you just see it, it just closes. And happy and unhappy is irrelevant, you just know that something has come full circle, something has clicked, a door is shut. Life is like that . . . I want to get as close to that as possible, a kind of breathless stop in the fall. You don't know on any day whether what's happening to you is the most important thing. So you just go along with it. But the reader has to feel it coming to an end: instead of making it work out for readerly reasons, it has to close on its own. It's sort of like a painting in a way. There's a moment at which it's finished, now there's the possibility that another stroke, you know, might make it more acceptable . . . Or even in music, you know, it closes and leaves you something. Knowing that, you're prepared for the close, and whether it shakes you or quiets you, depends on what the thing was itself.

I thought that was true of *Song of Solomon*, it was a celebration. And I thought that *Sula* was always smiles, but hovering there was something very sad, tearful. It was a kind of a cry.

In the beginning, *Sula* started with Shadrack, the first sentence was, "Except for World War II." But then I couldn't begin it that way. I found that out later, as I finished the book.

The beginnings are hard for me, there's too much I had to do in the beginning. Get the reader's trust, and you open a door, you have to close that door. And it's hard. But I always know the endings, because I feel that, I know it. And I really thought that this love story which was going to be just terrific, you know—real love between two attractive people, and you want them to fall in love—I just knew they'd go off into the sunset. They haven't yet. I don't strive for sad endings, and I don't strive for obscure ones. I just know that's it, and anything I write after that would be another book.

The Visits of the Writers
Toni Morrison and Eudora Welty
Kathy Neustadt / 1980

From the *Bryn Mawr Alumnae Bulletin* Spring 1980: 2–5. The following excerpt does not include the section on Eudora Welty's visit.

You are involved in so many demanding activities: editing, teaching, writing, mothering. Are these conflicting enterprises?

They are not for me. Time is the problem, not the activities. Apparently it's a facility that I have to tune out the chaos and routine events if I'm thinking about the writing. I never have had sustained time to write, long periods or a week away to do anything—I never had that. So I would always write under conditions that probably are unbearable when people think of how one writes. I never applied to go to those wonderful artist retreats. My wish sometimes was that if someone would just take care of the children for a little while, then I wouldn't have to go any place: I could just stay where I was.

It has to do with what I feel about writer's block, which I take very seriously. The block comes when I don't understand what's happening in the writing, when the solution is not there yet. When it *is* there, then other things really fall away of their own accord. There is such a compulsion to it that anything else that I'm doing looks as though it's under water, and then there's this dazzling thing that I'm thinking or writing. And my effort is not to erase the conflict between editing and writing but to pay *full* attention to the editing and to pay *full* attention to the teaching, because if I'm really in stride, then I have to hang onto these other things. I don't think that I'm the kind of person who can write without that kind of mix.

I was going to ask you if you could ever imagine just writing.

No, never. I once went with a friend to the country, and we said we would just stay a week or two and write, and both of us brought back blank pieces of paper. I just looked at the deer, you know; nothing happened.

When I started working on a different schedule at Random House,

there was a two-week period in there which was a little odd. I hadn't
been home at that time of day for years. I didn't know what the
mailman looked like, and the house had entirely different sounds. I
was distracted by the place, which I was seeing for the first time—not
a day off or a holiday, but a long period of being home regularly
without having to travel from place to place, without having anything
else to do. It was startling, and I didn't work at all.

*You were talking in class about the course you have taught on
black women writers, where there really aren't any secondary
sources to go to. Do you find that being a writer yourself helps you
teach this new writing better, makes you better able to guide the
students?*

Yes, that's a difficult thing to do though. I think it is beneficial to
the students; I really do. But one thing that has interested me is how
enormously timid the students are about risking any criticism on
things where there are only primary sources. They talk an awful lot
about pioneering criticism, but they are really unwilling to pass
judgment on paper about a book that has only a few little reviews to
examine. They don't mind having a body of work that they can
respond to: secondary sources, criticism, a teacher's evaluation. But
I was astounded that it took so long for them to feel willing to take
risks in evaluating a book that they loved but hadn't heard anybody
pass judgment on. But this is important for women because so much
of what has already been written *by* women—even when it's Jane
Austen—has been distorted, is awkward, so that they may have to
not only rewrite, re-evaluate, revise what has already been said;
there are whole areas in which they will have to do all of it because
there may not be anybody else to do it. They might as well start now,
and they might as well start in my class.

I just wanted them to distrust whatever there was available, and to
distrust the novelist as well. Forget about what I say in an interview—it might be anything—but trust the tale and start with what
you have. It was difficult to do that. I think that the fact that I'm a
writer makes it attractive to me to work this way. I think that if I
were simply or exclusively a teacher, I might not have found that
valuable or a valuable way to think about something.

The problem was also to move into and around literary criticism.
In a course like that, you have to spend so much time getting away

from sociology. Whenever you have any subject about women, even if it's poetry, short stories, or whatever, half of it is always sociology or some other -ology before you get to simply see what is beautiful, and why, and what the criteria are, the criteria for that book.

When you teach aspiring writers, what do you think their biggest problems are?

Identifying error. Or identifying the bad writing that they do. The problem is, first, to know when you are not writing well and, then, to be able to fix it. It's craftsman-like problems.

I do not teach passion and vision and all of those big, wonderful things which are absolutely necessary for extraordinary writing: I have to assume that my students have vision, passion, integrity, brilliant ideas. But many people possess those things, and the problem is moving from there to the writing, to getting a character off the boat and onto the shore. It's like a magician, you know: when you watch him on the stage you see the rabbit and the lights and the beautiful colors, but the skill is in the false bottom and the dexterity of his fingers. That's what I teach: how to handle it so that the reader is only aware of the rabbit that comes out of the hat and doesn't see the false bottom. That's craft—and hard work.

Can the passion, the art, be taught in any way?

I don't really think so. I think people would disagree, but I don't think so. I think it's possible to talk to students and to get them—help them—to open a door or remove cataracts.

But you have to at least sense that there's a door or a vision there?

Yes, and that's the mysterious part, the ineffable part. You really don't know why somebody has it, somebody doesn't. But whatever it is, I'm sure that it's going this way—outward. The problem then becomes distance. That's what I meant when I said identifying error. Students are frequently unwilling to rewrite, because rewriting suggests to them that what they wrote the first time is *wrong,* and they don't like that feeling. But it's not that, it's just that writing is a process and you are cleaning up the language.

It's not that you're changing it: you're doing it better, hitting a higher note or a deeper tone or a different color. The revision for me is the exciting part; it's the part that I can't wait for—getting the

whole dumb thing done so that I can do the real work, which is
making it better and better and better.

You have said that you started with one idea for The Bluest Eye
*and then changed your mind and rewrote the whole thing. It seems
like an enormous task.*

That was thrilling to do. But if I had approached it like, "Oh, my
God, I did it *wrong*, now I have to do it right," I would never have
done it at all. It's a process of discovery. I feel an enthusiasm for it.
It's not like getting a paper back that you have to do over; it's
different.

*Then the idea in the teaching is to make the students feel that the
changes are part of a bettering process.*

That's right. That's hard. The only way that I was ever successful
in doing it—the way that informs the courses that I teach—was not to
use their stuff, the students' work. I bring to the class manuscripts
that I have bought, or somebody has bought and published, that are
unedited, and I make them do it. They have to identify where it is
that the author has gone wrong, where the characters are too thin,
the setting and so on—I caution them not to get overenthusiastic
about this, but they never listen. They are *ruthless* when it comes to
evaluating other people's things. Then I don't go back to the authors
for changes, I go to the students. "You thought the dialogue was flat;
well, *puff* it up!" They start to see what it takes to make a distinction
between this person's dialogue and that one's—they don't talk the
same. "What would this person see?" "This kind of character would
not notice that." So they make the changes, and that's what the
grading is based on.

If it were an ideal course, it would go on to their own writing,
because my assumption is—and I'm certain that it is true—once you
get into the habit of fixing, you can fix your own. I remove from them
this emotional connection of defending constantly; everything that
someone says about your work may not be right, but I say you must
pay attention to it. If I am restless about it, something *is* wrong. I
may not know what it is; what I say is wrong may not be right; but
pay attention to my unease, or anybody's unease.

When I'm talking to students who want to write professionally, I
try to draw from simple analogies: the carpenter who is going to

make a perfect chair has to know about wood, trees, the body and how it looks when it is in a sitting position. He should know something about the industry first of all. And then he should pick the right wood for color, look at the quality—in other words, it's a job of craftsmanship. You approach it in a responsible, intelligent way. What has happened, I think—and I would like to place blame somewhere, but I shift so often—is that writing has become almost a celebrity thing in the sense that people don't want to *write*; they want to *be authors*. And that's quite different.

About this notion of celebrity, you were saying that you had never thought of yourself as a writer, had never even thought of The Bluest Eye *as a novel when you were writing it. Now, with three novels behind you, do you think of yourself as a writer?*

I now think of myself as a writer. I didn't realize it on my own though. It was after *Sula* was published; I was talking to my editor (Robert Gottlieb of Knopf) one day, and he said, "This is what you are going to be when you grow up. This is it." I said, "A writer?" He said, "That's right. Of all those other little things you do, this is it. This is what you are." It wasn't that long ago, and I've had to think about it. In my life, I've never known what I was doing from one minute to the next; I was just working, I didn't have a "career." I grew up in a time when people didn't think like they do now, about what they are going to be and do. I wanted to be a whole person, I wanted to be a good person, I wanted to be all those big things, and none of that had anything to do with a job. It was quite apart from the work that I was doing—I respected the work, but I didn't live there. So when someone said to me, "This is what you are going to be when you grow up; you are now grown up and this is your job," it really came as a huge idea. It was like I had never heard it before.

But when I am writing, if I have in mind that I am writing a *novel* or that *they* are going to read it, it does something to the voice: the voice is not intimate. You read stuff and you know that the author is talking to somebody right there, next to you, but not you. The impetus for writing *The Bluest Eye* in the first place was to write a book about a kind of person that was never in literature anywhere, never taken seriously by anybody—all those peripheral little girls. So

I wanted to write a book that—if that child ever picked it up—would look representational. And so, what you do is focus on that kind of intimacy. If you do it well enough, it becomes accessible to lots and lots of people. If you're writing for lots and lots of people, you have these vague, lumpy books.

I was writing for some clear, single person—I would say myself, because I was quite content to be the only reader. I thought that everything that needed to be written had been written: there was so much. I am not being facetious when I say I wrote *The Bluest Eye* in order to read it. And I think that is what makes the difference, because I could look at it as a reader, really as a reader, and not as my own work. And then I could say, "This doesn't make me feel right," and I could change it. That's what I mean by the distance. People always say that to be a good writer you have to read: that sounds like they're collecting ideas and information. But what it ought to mean is that you have to be able to read what you write critically. And with distance. And surrender to it and know the problems and not get all fraught. There must be tons of "first novels," written and unwritten.

The other problem is beginnings. My beginnings are not beginnings; I just start. Sometimes I have to write the beginning after the book is done. Well, that seems like a natural thing, but many people don't go forward because the beginning isn't right; they just leave it until they get it right. I write what's there, what I *know* is there. If I have to rewrite it or change it, I'm not fearful about that any more. I always know the story, the plot. The difficulty is with the intricate problems of language.

What was the impetus for writing The Bluest Eye? *Had you written before?*

Not really. Just little nothings. I think it was the situation which I was in at that time that was conducive to writing. I was in a place where I knew I was not going to be for a long time; I didn't have any friends and didn't make any, didn't want any because I was on my way somewhere else. So I wrote as a thing to do. If I had played the piano, I think I would have done that—but I didn't have a piano and don't play. So I wrote.

By the time *The Bluest Eye* was published, I had already begun

Sula. If all the publishers had disappeared in one night, I would have written anyway. I like the fact that other people like what I write, and I suppose that if the publishers had disappeared, I would have written it and xeroxed it and passed it around. But writing was a thing that I could not *not* do at that point—it was a way of thinking for me. It still is; I don't have any choice about that.

So much of the writing in Song of Solomon *is like folklore, oral lore. Did you grow up listening to voices like that?*
Yes. Stories. There were two kinds of education going on: one was the education in the schools which was print-oriented; and right side by side with it was this other way of looking at the world that was not only different than what we learned about in school, it was coming through another sense. People told stories. Also there was the radio; I was a radio child. You get in the habit of gathering information that way, and imagining the rest. You make it up. It was horrible to see *pictures* of Hamlet and Cinderella—it was awful. I hate to see pictures of *my* characters, good or bad—although I always compliment the artists.

I never use characters from my life. I may have matched pieces, but it's usually something vague. The song of Solomon: there's a song like that in my family. I don't know all the lyrics but it starts with a line like "Green, the only son of Solomon," and then some words I don't understand, but it is a genealogy. I made up the lyrics in the *Song of Solomon* to go with the story. And my mother was named out of the Bible, the way they were in the book. So stuff like that.

I remember seeing a friend of my mother's when I was four or five years old, and I don't know anything about that woman except her name and the way she looked. But there would be a flood of things that I attached to her, and I suppose that I could say that I used her for part of a character. I don't know a thing about that lady except what her name was, but what I remember is the way they said her *name*, the way the women *said* her name, so I knew as a child that she was different. They said it with such *stuff*—they had some strong reaction to her that was part awe and part disapproval and part affection. I don't know a thing about that lady, and I haven't asked anybody about her, but I remember her face, and mostly this part

around the eyes. So those are shreds, but that's all you need to build
somebody like Sula or Hannah.

In Song of Solomon *the main character is a man, and you seemed
to have no trouble getting inside of him. Do you think that men and
women in general can write about each other honestly?*
They ought to be able to do it. It shouldn't be a problem—it's just
a question of perception. You know, it's like we were saying in
class yesterday, about that question that always disturbs me, that
question of identification with black writers and about being able to
understand the book *in spite* of that. It's always a bothersome idea.
But Nadine Gordimer writes about black people with such astound-
ing sensibilities and sensitivity—not patronizing, not romantic, just
real. And Eudora Welty does the same thing. Lillian Hellman has
done it. Now, we might categorize these women as geniuses of a
certain sort, but if they can write about it, it means that it is possible.
They didn't say, "Oh, my God, I can't write about black people"; it
didn't stop them. There are white people who do respond that way
though, assuming there's some huge barrier. But if you can relate to
Beowolf and Jesus Christ when you read about them, it shouldn't be
so difficult to relate to black literature.

I am curious about one thing: it seems to me that of the white
writers who write about black people well, most of them are women.
All the people that I have mentioned are also from the South, South
Africa, born in totally racist places, and that's a fascinating idea.
They are all extraordinary women; their perceptions are so unlike
what are supposed to be the perceptions of the community in which
they live and, of course, who they are. So when they make that leap,
they make it totally.

I feel the same way about writing about men. It takes some relaxed
sensibility, that's all. Trying to imagine it. Think about it. I look at
my children—boy children—and they are different from me. And
they are impelled by different things. Instead of saying something
general about it, I would say, "I wonder what that is?" and then try
to see the world the way they might see it. So that you enter the
world instead of hovering over it and trying to dominate it and make
it into something. You have to have that kind of absence of hostil-

ity—absence of anything. You should do it for every character, and if a character is very old or very young or very rich or very poor or black or white or male or female, your ability to do it is the marked difference between writing on the surface and writing underneath.

Toni Morrison

Charles Ruas / 1981

From *Conversations with American Writers*. New York: Mc-Graw Hill, 1984: 215–43.

Toni Morrison began writing fiction in her maturity, and from the first she expressed the themes that she would explore and develop in her subsequent work. She has written a body of work that is unified by continuity and development.

She was born Chloe Anthony Wofford in 1931 in Lorain, Ohio, which is the setting of her earliest novels. She attended Howard University and received a B.A. in English in 1953, and a master's degree from Cornell in 1955. She taught English at Howard University, and worked as a textbook editor prior to writing fiction. But these are jobs she has continued, even as an established novelist. She is an editor at Random House, and is in great demand as a lecturer and teacher.

Toni Morrison published her first novel, *The Bluest Eye*, in 1969, followed by *Sula* (1973). Her reputation was established with *Song of Solomon* (1977), which was awarded the National Book Critics' Circle Award and the National Book Award for best novel. In 1981 she published the controversial *Tar Baby*.

In *The Bluest Eye*, a small Midwestern community is depicted through the eyes of a little girl, Claudia, during a cycle of four seasons. Her best friend, Pecola, prays for blue eyes, a special mark, the way her mother finds refuge in the immaculate kitchen, where she can forget her cross—Pecola—and her "Crown of Thorns"—Cholly, her alcoholic husband. In a drunken moment Cholly Breedlove assaults his daughter. Claudia's answered prayer has the effect of an implosion that destroys her family and by extension heralds the eventual disappearance of the community.

Sula tells of the passionate and lawless Sula, the last of a matriarchal family. Nel, the narrator, is her complementary opposite, brought up in a strict Baptist household where every stirring of her

imagination is disciplined. Sula's energy propels her out into the
world, but the world drives her back into the community. Sula
destroys her family and Nel's marriage, and she becomes an outcast.

Song of Solomon presents Macon Dead the slumlord and his
bootlegging sister, Pilate, who are pitted in a duel that is carried into
the third generation by the affair between his son, Milkman, and
her granddaughter, Hagar. Within the conflicts of the black community, Toni Morrison introduces a secret society dedicated to retaliat-
ing, murder for murder, every crime against the black community.
Yet this society misinterprets Milkman's quest for his African origins
as a betrayal of their secret mission.

With *Tar Baby* the conflict between the races explodes, revealing
all the underlying interrelationships between white masters and black
servants. The Tar Baby is the black couple's niece (and adopted
daughter), educated by their employers to a privileged position that
places her midway between the two worlds. At the start of the novel,
Valerian Street and his wife, Margaret, have retired from their
confection industry in Philadelphia and are preparing for Christmas
in their Caribbean retreat, "L'Arbe de la Croix." Their old butler,
Sydney, and the cook, Ondine, uprooted and as yet unsettled in the
tropics, await their adopted daughter, Jadine, as well as the son of
the house. Suddenly, an intruder in the house creates a panic that
dislocates each character and reveals a pattern of dependence,
exploitation, and complicity between master and servants, servants
and children, husbands and wives.

Jadine runs off to New York with Son, the young black intruder,
only to be confronted by their incompleteness as individuals and as a
couple. She will not compromise with his backward black world,
and he cannot live in her white world. He becomes the rabbit caught
by and sinking with the Tar Baby. Here Toni Morrison dramatizes his
choice of death by Eros, or death by Psyche. The novel has a
circular construction based on the cycle of nature and the spiritual
relationships of the characters to the laws of nature.

These conversations occurred in Toni Morrison's office at Random
House. She is an impressive, strong woman, with an open counte-
nance and a sonorous, melodious voice. Her eyes are amber-colored,
of changing golden hue, and her face is extremely expressive, with

sudden shifts in tone and mood. Her sense of humor is dominant, and she mimics in expression and voice the different people and characters in her conversation. But when she is deep in thought, her eyes almost close, her voice grows quieter and quieter, lowering almost to a whisper, and the quality of her conversation approaches that incantatory flow which is akin to the lyric moments of her written style. Her response to the questions are direct and forthright; she is eloquent about her beliefs and kindly in her analysis of people. She reserves her mocking humor and caustic wit for comment about herself.

Toni Morrison used the interview to explore and clarify her own thoughts in the light of the interviewer's reading of the text. The conversation took place in February 1981, prior to the publication of *Tar Baby*. Eight months later, after the reaction to the novel had abated somewhat, we picked up our conversation where we had left off, only to discover once again that there were at the close still other topics not touched upon, such as her reading of certain classics and her abiding interest in new black authors, as well as what is for her the central issue of the black writer's feeling sometimes that his or her work exists in a framework and conveys an experience so unfamiliar to most of the reading public as to seem like a translated text.

PART I

CR: What made you begin writing *The Bluest Eye?*

TM: I don't know. I never wanted to grow up to be a writer, I just wanted to grow up to be an adult. I began to write that book as a short story based on a conversation I had with a friend when I was a little girl. The conversation was about whether God existed; she said no and I said yes. She explained her reason for knowing that He did not: she had prayed every night for two years for blue eyes and didn't get them, and therefore He did not exist. What I later recollected was that I looked at her and imagined her having them and thought how awful that would be if she had gotten her prayer answered. I always thought she was beautiful. I began to write about a girl who wanted blue eyes and the horror of having that wish fulfilled; and also about the whole business of what is physical beauty and the pain of that yearning and wanting to be somebody else, and how devastating that was and yet part of all females who were peripheral in other people's lives.

CR: Since your first novel is such a mature statement, clearly you are steeped in literary tradition, but I assume also in the great black novelists of the past.

TM: I was preoccupied with books by black people that approached the subject, but I always missed some intimacy, some direction, some voice. Ralph Ellison and Richard Wright—all of whose books I admire enormously—I didn't feel were telling *me* something. I thought they were saying something about *it* or *us* that revealed something about *us* to *you*, to others, to white people, to men. Just in terms of the style, I missed something in the fiction that I felt in a real sense in the music and poetry of black artists. When I began writing I was writing as though there was nobody in the world but me and the characters, as though I was talking to them, or us, and it just had a different sound to it.

CR: When you say that you feel these writers are explaining something "to me," are you referring to the fact that their work is morally informed?

TM: There is a mask that sometimes exists when black people talk to white people. Somehow it seems to me that it spilled over into the fiction. I never thought that when I was reading black poetry, but when I began to write. When I wrote I wanted not to have to explain. Somehow, when black writers wrote for themselves I understood it better. What's that lovely line? When the locality is clear, fully realized, then it becomes universal. I knew there was something I wanted to clear away in writing, so I used the geography of my childhood, the imagined characters based on bits and pieces of people, and that was a statement. More important to me was making a statement on a kind of language, a way to get to what was felt and meant. I always hated with a passion when writers rewrote what black people said, in some kind of phonetic alphabet that was inapplicable to any other regional pronunciation. There is something different about that language, as there is about any cultural variation of English, but it's not saying "dis" and "dat." It is the way words are put together, the metaphors, the rhythm, the music—that's the part of the language that is distinctly black to me when I hear it. But the only way for me to do it when I was writing was to have this kind of audience made up of people in the book.

CR: When I began *Song of Solomon* I thought, the King James Bible is the spine of this style.

TM: The Bible wasn't part of my reading, it was part of my life. In coming to writing I wrote the way I was trained, which was [*laughs*] scholarly bombast, so that I had to rewrite a lot. Getting a style is about all there is to writing fiction, and I didn't realize that I had a style until I wrote *Song of Solomon*. Yes, there's a formality and repetition in it, and I like that risk. I like the danger in writing when you're right on the edge, when at any moment you can be maudlin, saccharine, grotesque, but somehow pull back from it [*laughs*], well, most of the time. I really want this emotional response, and I also want an intellectual response to the complex ideas there. My job is to do both at the same time, that's what a real story is.

CR: You never had thought of yourself as a writer, yet you're certain of your artistic aims. Is it based on your reading as well?

TM: When I said I wrote my first novel because I wanted to read it, I meant it literally. I had to finish it so that I could read it, and what that gave me, I realize now, was an incredible distance from it, and from that I have learned. If what I wrote was awful, I would try to make it like the book I wished to read. I trusted that ability to read in myself.

CR: But tell me about the subject of your novels. In *The Bluest Eye*, for example, although Claudia is the narrator you switch the narrative point of view from first to third person. Yet it's the unfolding drama of Pecola which is the center of the book.

TM: I had written the book without those two little girls at first. It was just the story of Pecola and her family. I told it in the third person in parts, in pieces like a broken mirror. When I read it, there was no connection between the life of Pecola, her mother and father, and the reader—myself. I needed a bridge—the book was soft in the middle, so I shored it up. I introduced the two little girls, and chose an "I" for one of them, so that there would be somebody to empathize with her at her age level. This also gave a playful quality to their lives, to relieve the grimness. I had to go back and restructure all of the novel, and I introduced a time sequence of the seasons, the child's flow of time. I culled—from what I thought life was like in the thirties and forties—the past, whatever the past is. Once I realized that, I knew that I could not *not* write the book any more. After I had written it and "stopped"—that's the way I thought then—I still didn't know if I was a writer, but I knew that I always wanted to have writing to do.

With *Sula* I was obsessed with the idea, and totally enchanted by it. I was fearful that with *Sula* I was being bookish. It got hermetic and tight, which as a writer I now say. It may have been correct to have written *Sula* that way, but I know that when I wrote *Song of Solomon* it was more open and looser. That is more dangerous than writing in which every sentence has to be exactly right or you'll shoot yourself. I always thought that *Sula* was the best idea I ever had, but the writing was on its own.

CR: Were there family influences that eventually made you turn to writing?

TM: Life is very short—they couldn't think of that. When I graduated from high school, it was a huge thing. My mother had graduated from high school, but not my father. They assumed that all my life I should work. And I guess they assumed that I should get married. It never occurred to me that I could get married and not work. What was needed was skill. I had an uncle who had gone to college, and I was surrounded by people who had done extraordinary things under duress in order to survive. I didn't know it, but I think I had a feeling that I probably wrote well, because when I was very little and we were asked to write stories in classes, I just remember that I knew the teacher didn't believe I wrote those stories. I thought that other people didn't write well because they weren't interested.

Speaking of being a writer, when I mentioned to my editor, Bob Gottlieb, after I finished *Song of Solomon*, that I was thinking of working less, he said, "Well, you should really make up your mind that this is what you are going to be when you grow up." [*Laughs.*] I said, "A writer?" Because I was convinced I could never be without a job: I'm the head of a household, I teach, I'm an editor, I write. I never equated writing with money, as a living. When he said that, I thought for the first time maybe I could just go home and write, as a job.

CR: These different jobs are important to you for reasons other than financial stability. I know you've devoted yourself as an editor to bringing out some very fine young black writers. Does being the head of a household become part of your identity as a writer?

TM: In terms of being a writer it's very stabilizing, being the head of a household. I don't find it a deprivation. It also means that when I go to write, I go there with relish, because of the requirement of working at several jobs at the same time.

CR: Do you withdraw to a room, your own, or do you write in your head before sitting down to work?

TM: I type in one place, but I write all over the house. I never go to the paper to create. The meat and juice and all that I work out while I'm doing something else, and it makes completing the chores possible, so I'm not staring off into space. Well, I might, but I also do the chores.

CR: In *Song of Solomon* the symbolism is different from psychological portrayal of the passionate characters, and different from the dream sequences or the lyrical moments. These different types of writing make me ask about the different aspects of your creative consciousness.

TM: I look for the picture in some instances. In order to get at the thing at once, I have to see it, to smell it, to touch it. It's something to hold on to so that I can write it. What takes longest is the way you get into the heart of that which you have to describe. Once I know, then I can move. I know that if the action is violent, the language cannot be violent; it must be understated. I want my readers to see it, to feel it, and I want to give them things even I may not know about, even if I've never been there. Getting to that place is problematic, that's the process. I remember how long it took me to write about the town that Milkman goes to, when he finally gets there. It took me months, and I could not begin. I could see it, but I wanted to write without going through long, involved descriptions of that village. Then I remembered the women walking without anything in their hands, and that set the scene.

CR: Your characters have dreams and waking dreams, but, also, spirits will come to speak to the characters. You differentiate that from the religious, which is often narrow and hard.

TM: As a child I was brought up on ghost stories—part of the entertainment was storytelling. Also, I grew up with people who believed it. When they would tell you stories about visions, they didn't tell them as though they were visions. My father said, "Oh, there's a ring around the moon, that means war." Indeed there was a war in 1941. I remember his saying that; now, whether he was also reading the newspapers or not, I don't know.

My grandmother would ask me about my dreams and, depending on the content of them, she would go to the dream book, which would translate dreams into a three-digit number. That was the number you played in the numbers game. You dream about a rabbit, or death, or weddings, and then color made a difference—if you dreamed about dying in a white dress or a red dress—and weddings always meant death and death always meant weddings. I was very interested because she used to hit a lot on my dreams for about a year or two.

CR: You mean she actually won money based on your dreams?

TM: She won [*laughs*], yes, she won. Then I stopped hitting for her, so she stopped asking me. It was lovely to have magic that could turn into the pleasure of pleasing one's grandmother and was also profitable. My dream life is still so real to me that I can hardly distinguish it from the other, although I know what that is. It's just as interesting to me and an inexhaustible source of information. I was very conscious of trying to capture in writing about what black life meant to me, not just what black people do but the way in which we look at it.

CR: Then the cycle of seasons, of birth and death, and the nature spirits that you use to structure your novels form your sense of the cosmology and of the psyche?

TM: It's an animated world in which trees can be outraged and hurt, and in which the presence or absence of birds is meaningful. You have to be very still to understand these so-called signs, in addition to which they inform you about your own behavior. It always interested me, the way in which black people responded to evil. They would protect themselves from it, they would avoid it, they might even be terrified of it, but it wasn't as though it were abnormal. I used the line "as though God had four faces instead of three. . . ." Evil was a natural presence in the world. What that meant in terms of human behavior was that when they saw someone disgraceful, they would not expel them in the sense of tarring and killing. I think that's a distinct cultural difference, because the

Western notion of evil is to annihilate it. That may be very cleansing, but it's also highly intolerant.

CR: To return to your novels, your concepts are always so clear. Each novel has a circular construction. Does the idea come to you whole?

TM: I always know the ending; that's where I start. I don't always have a beginning, so I don't always know how to start a book. Sometimes I have to rewrite different beginnings. *Sula* began with Shadrack, so I had to write the part that precedes it. I always know the ending of my novels because that's part of the idea, part of the theme. It doesn't shut, or stop there. That's why the endings are multiple endings. That's where the horror is. That's where the meaning rests; that's where the novel rests. I suppose there is a strong influence of Greek tragedy, particularly the chorus, commenting on the action.

For me, it's also the closest way I can get to what informs my art, which is the quality of response. Being in church and knowing that the function of the preacher is to make you get up, you do say yes, and you do respond back and forth. The music is unplanned and obviously not structured, but something is supposed to happen, so the listener participates. The chorus participates both by meddling in the action and responding to it, like the musical experience of participation in church.

I try to bring the essentials to a scene, so the reader, for example, can bring his own sexuality to that scene, which makes it sexier. Your sexuality is sexier than mine because it's yours. All I have to do is give you the lead, you bring your own perception, and you are in it. I don't have to use clinical language, I can say, "Son parted the hair on her head and ran his tongue along the part."

CR: You begin *Tar Baby* with Valerian Street, a retired candy executive, rather than with Jadine, who is the Tar Baby.

TM: But he is the center. He's not the main character, but he certainly is the center of the world. I mean, white men run it. He is the center of the household—toppled, perhaps, but still the center of everybody's attention—and that's pretty much the way it is. He is a rather nice man, not a wicked man. He has his serious flaws, as all of the characters have serious limitations, as all people do: trying to come to terms with each other, give up a little something, behave properly, and live in the world decently, maybe even love something, just trying to pick something out that's worth holding on to and worth loving. Sometimes it's a person, sometimes it's a house, or a memory. They are what they are and rub against one another in that way. I chose, literally, the skeleton as the story of the Tar Baby. I had heard it and it just seemed to me overwhelmingly history as well as prophecy, once I began thinking about it, because it bothered me madly.

CR: Joel Chandler Harris, who recorded it, said that it was an African story told him by "Uncle Remus."

TM: I never read the story, but it was one of the stories we were told, and one of the stories my mother was told, part of a whole canon of stories. It's supposed to be a funny little child's story. But something in it terrified me. What frightened me was the notion of the Tar Baby. It's a lump of tar shaped like a baby, with a dress on and a bonnet. It's a sunny day and the tar is melting, and the rabbit is getting stuck and more stuck. It's really quite monstrous. The rabbit approaches it and says good morning and expects it to say good morning back. He anticipated a certain civilized response—he was a little thief—and when it didn't happen he was outraged and therefore got stuck and went to his death. Of course, as in most peasant literature, that sort of weak but cunning animal gets out of it by his cleverness. So I just gave these characters parts, Tar Baby being a black woman and the rabbit a black man. I introduced a white man and remembered the tar. The fact that it was made out of tar and was a black woman, if it was made to trap a black man—the white man made her for that purpose. That was the beginning of the story. Suppose somebody simply has all the benefits of what the white Western world has to offer; what would the relationship be with the rabbit who really comes out of the briar patch? And what does the briar patch mean to that rabbit? Wherever there was tar it seemed to me was a holy place. "Tar Baby" is also a racial slur, like "nigger," and a weapon hostile to the black man. The tragedy of the situation was not that she *was* a Tar Baby, but that she wasn't. She could not know, she could not hold anything to herself. That's what I mean by the prophecy: the twentieth-century black woman is determined in trying to do both things, to be both a ship and a safe harbor.

CR: All of the characters function very comfortably in their self-involved dilemmas until Valerian humiliates Sydney and Ondine and they explode against him and Margaret.

TM: The interdependence of employee and employer is clear, but the human dependencies of such relationships are not because of the artifice of jobs and wages. When you take that structure away, what you have left is very close interrelationships, sometimes seething rages; but you don't until you remove it and see what the relationship really is.

CR: Ondine feels morally superior to Margaret, and there's a complicity between them stronger than hatred.

TM: It's my view that one of the things that black women were able to do in many situations was to make it possible for white women to remain infantile. Margaret has been thoroughly crippled by her husband, who kept her that way, and Ondine helped. In a sense, such women are not innocent victims, but they really are victims of a kind of giant romantic stupidity.

CR: The complicity between the women—that is, about child abuse—is a theme that runs through all your novels.

TM: Certainly since *Sula* I have thought that the children are in real danger. Nobody likes them, all children, but particularly black children. It seems stark to me, because it wasn't true when I was growing up. The relationships of the generations have always been paramount to me in all of my works, the older as well as the younger generation, and whether that is healthy and continuing. I feel that my generation has done the children a great disservice. I'm talking about the emotional support that is not available to them any more because adults are acting out their childhoods. They are interested in self-aggrandizement, being "right," and pleasures. Everywhere, everywhere, children are the scorned people of the earth. There may be a whole lot of scorned people, but particularly children. The teachers have jobs, not missions. Even in the best schools, the disrespect for children is unbelievable. You don't have to go to the exploitation, the ten-year-old model and child porn—that's the obvious. Even in the orderly parts of society it is staggering. Children are committing suicide, they are tearing up the schools, they are running away from home. They are beaten and molested; it's an epidemic. I've never seen so many movies in which children are the monsters, children are the ones to be killed.

CR: Now you see a more impersonal attitude of, No room, no time for children.

TM: They have no apprenticeship. Children don't work with adults as we used to, and there is this huge generation gap. When my grandfather got senile in his nineties, he would walk off, not know where he was, and get lost. My job as a little girl was to find Papa, and we would. Some adult told us to go and we would bring him back, settle him on the porch, bring him walnuts or what have you. I remember I had to read the Bible to my grandmother when she was dying, and somebody assigned me to do that. They were caring for her, and I was involved in the death and decay of my grandmother. Obviously my mother cared for me, and I would do that for her; that is the cycle. It's important that my children participate in that. They have to take my mother her orange juice, and I don't have to tell them, because that's their responsibility. She can get them to do all sorts of things I can't. That's part of knowing who they are and where they came from. It enhances them in a particular way, and when they have children of their own it won't be this little nuclear you and me, babe.

CR: Sadly enough, I agree with you. But in your own novel, after the moral failure of the older generation is revealed, Jadine, it turns out, doesn't love Sydney and Ondine, who are passionate about her, any more than she cares for Valerian and Margaret.

TM: She is an orphan in the true sense. She does not make connections unless they serve her in some way. Valerian she speaks of because he did a concrete thing for her—he put her through school—but she is not terribly interested in his welfare. Ondine and her uncle Sydney are people she uses a little bit.

She is cut off. She does not have, as Thérèse [a spiritualist] says, her ancient properties; she does not have what Ondine has. There's no reason for her to be like Ondine—I'm not recommending that—but she needs a little bit of Ondine to be a complete woman. She doesn't have that quality because she can avoid it, and it's not attractive anyway. The race may need it, human beings may need it, she may need it. That quality of nurturing is to me essential. It should not, certainly, limit her to be only Thérèse with the magic breasts. There should be lots of things: there should be a quality of adventure and a quality of nest.

CR: That's adaptation for survival. This problem is true throughout society.

TM: This civilization of black people, which was underneath the white civilization, was there with its own everything. Everything of that civilization was not worth hanging on to, but some of it was, and nothing has taken its place while it is being dismantled. There is a new, capitalistic, modern American black which is what everybody thought was the ultimate in integration. To produce Jadine, that's what it was for. I think there is some danger in the result of that production. It cannot replace certain essentials from the past. That's what I meant when I said she cannot nurture and be a career woman. You can't get rid of the pie lady and the churches unless you have something to replace them with. Otherwise people like Son are out there, strung out. There is nowhere for them to go. I could have changed it around and it could have been a man in Jadine's position and a woman in his. The sexes were interchangeable, but the problem is the same.

CR: You describe Jadine as feeling lean and male, and since she is a character of will and decision, is there a male/female conflict within her? Does she unconsciously identify will power with being male?

TM: It has to do with being contemporary. The contemporary woman is eager; her femininity becomes sexuality rather than femininity, because that is perceived as weak. The characteristics they encourage in themselves are more male characteristics, not because she has a fundamental identity crisis, but because she wants to be truly free. Part of that is perceived as having the desirable characteristic of maleness, which includes self-sufficiency and adventurousness. For instance, Ondine is a tough lady in an older sense of that word, like pioneers, but she is keenly aware of her nurturing characteristics, whereas someone in Jadine's generation would find that a burden, and not at all what her body was for. She does not intend to have children. In that sense it's not an identity crisis in terms of male/female sexuality and personality. The impetus of the culture is to be feminized, and what one substitutes for femininity is sexuality.

CR: Then, with all of her education and cultivation, femininity for Jadine is the outward image; she is a model. Her focus is on herself, she's essentially narcissistic.

TM: Yes, absolutely. She is really about herself. The thing that happens to her in Paris, the woman spitting at her—even in her semi-dream state, Jadine knows what happened: somebody assaulted her image of herself.

CR: When she is in love with Son and returns with him to what you call his "briar patch," Jadine is alienated from his people.

TM: She feels left out from that environment. She is not afraid of the male world, but she is afraid of the female world. It's interesting to see such women who have gone away put into that situation. I have seen them extremely uncomfortable in the company of church ladies, absolutely out of their element. They are beautiful and they are competent, but when they get with women whose values are different and who judge competence in different areas, they are extremely threatened. It's not just class; it's a different kind of woman.

CR: But Son, for all his qualities, has no place in the black world, and is not equipped to face the white world.

TM: He has that choice. Either he can join the twentieth century as a kind of half-person like Jadine, or he can abandon it. He doesn't want to change. It's a no-win situation. He really wanted to go down, down, and come back up again—that he could control. He can't do it his way. Perhaps the rites of passage are wrong for him. There used to be a way in which people could grow up. Now it's free-floating—you're just out there.

CR: But he is the person in this book who is able to love totally, without reservation or condition. In each of your novels there's a character capable of selfless love, whose identity comes from loving another.

TM: I'm trying to get at all kinds and defintions of love. We love people pretty much the way we are. I think there's a line, "Wicked people love wickedly, stupid people love stupidly," and in a way we are the way we love other people. In *Song of Solomon* the difference between Pilate's selfishness and Hagar's is that Hagar is not a person without Milkman, she's totally erased. Pilate had twelve years of intimate relationship with two men, her father and her brother, who loved her. It gave her a ferocity and some complete quality. Hagar had even less and was even more frail. It's that world of women without men. But in fact a woman is strongest when some of her sensibilities are formed by men at an early, certainly at an important age. It's absolutely necessary that it be there, and the farther away you get from that, the possibility of distortion is greater. By the same token, Milkman is in a male, macho world and can't fly, isn't human, isn't complete until he realizes the impact that women have made on his life. It's really a balance between classical male and female forces that produces, perhaps a kind of complete person.

CR: In your novels the women feel responsible for the failures of the men. Is Jadine also responsible for what Son can and cannot do?

TM: Well, it's a dual thing. On one level, obviously, she is. She is the thing that he wants and he can't live with or without, as he immediately knew as soon as he saw her. This was the love he could not afford to lose; therefore he should not have it in the first place. But there is some complicity in him, also. He is derailed by this romantic passion and his sensibilities are distorted; he can't make judgments any more. When he looked at the photos that she took of his people, he saw what she saw and it could not revive what he had, and that's testimony to his frailty. All those images he carried around in his head and in his heart should have survived her, but they didn't. He can't even get to the briar patch by himself, and he no longer knows where he was born and bred. Because it's in her world view, it takes Thérèse to give him a choice. She gives him this mystical choice between roaming around looking for Jadine and putting himself in danger that is not dignified, versus the possibility of joining these rather incredible men in the rain forest. I want him to be left with a wide-open choice at the end. I also wanted to suggest which one he chose by his asking her a second time, "Are you sure?" could be "Are the men there?" Or, it could mean, "Are you sure this is the island?" She says, "Yes, this is the place," and then she talks about the men, and he asks her again, "Are you sure?" She doesn't answer and he doesn't hear. When he climbs off the rocks and stands up—nature has always been very sweet to him anyway, giving him fruit—the trees sort of step back to make a way, and then to have him go lickety-split is to suggest the rabbit returning to the briar patch.

CR: I thought he was being betrayed by Thérèse, who was leading him to his death or his death wish. In your first novel, the matriarch seeing her son, a veteran of the war, turning into a writhing fetus of pain from drug addiction, decides to put him out of his misery and sets him on fire out of compassion and love. But what you have just said makes me understand that the lawless characters you portray—Sula, Solomon, and Son—belong in that other order of nature spirits, expressing a code of behavior that is aristocratic because it is accountable only to the spirit of nature, which is of African origin. My remaining question is whether Jadine is a character who will be forced to make that connection with the briar patch, even though love doesn't take her outside herself.

TM: She has a glimmering on the plane she thinks that *she* is the safety she has longed for, that there is no haven, and being the safety you have longed for is not only taking care of yourself; you are the safety of other people. She thinks maybe that's what Ondine meant—there is the aunt metaphor about the life of a woman in that stark warrior sense—but she is going back to Paris to start from zero. She will have to, I think the word is "tangle," with the woman in yellow. She thinks she is leaving Ondine and all of that crowd, and she has to, but the issues are still there. She now knows enough—she hasn't opened the door, but she knows where the door is.

PART II

CR: Where do you see yourself now? After *Tar Baby*, where would you place yourself in terms of your work as a novelist?

TM: Still in process, and I think that, if I'm lucky at all, it will always be that way. I want to learn more and more about how to write better. That means to get closer to that compulsion out of which I write. I want to break away from certain assumptions that are inherent in the conception of the novel form to make a truly aural novel, in which there are so many places and spaces for the reader to work and participate. Also, I want to make a novel in which one of the principles of the discipline is to enlighten without pontificating. It accounts for the wide-open nature of the ending of my books, where I don't want to close it, to stop the imagination of the reader, but to engage it in such a way that he fulfills the book in a way that I don't. I try to provide every opportunity for that kind of stimulation, so that the narrative is only one part of what happens, in the same way as what happens when you're listening to music, what happens when

you look at a painting. I would like to do better at this one thing and
to try to put the reader into the position of being naked and quite
vulnerable, nevertheless trusting, to rid him of all of his literary
experience and all of his social experiences in order to engage him in
the novel. Let him make up his mind about what he likes and what he
thinks and what happened based on the very intimate acquaintance
with the people in the book, without any prejudices, without any pre-
fixed notions, but to have an intimacy that's so complete, it human-
izes him in the same way that the characters are humanized from
within by certain activity, and in the way in which I am humanized
by the act of writing.

CR: By contrast to real life, for you the work of art permits this
sanctuary.

TM: Exactly. It's a haven, a place where it can happen, where you
can react violently or sublimely, where it's all right to feel melancholy or frightened, or even to fail, or to be wrong, or to love
somebody, or to wish something deeply, and not call it by some
other name, not to be embarrassed by it. It's a place to feel pro-
foundly. It's hard to get people to trust those feelings in such a way
that they're not harmful to other people.

CR: The function of fiction for you is extending those boundaries.
I also have a strong sense of the continuity of your work. Does the
writing of one work lead to the next? Your four novels form a
coherent body of work.

TM: When I thought about what seemed next in an evolutionary
sense, the most obvious way was to move from a very young girl to
adult women in the second book, and then a man in the third book,
and then a man and a woman in the fourth book. It was a simple
progression, and because of the time in which they were placed, each
one seemed to demand a certain form. I could not write a contemporary love story, so to speak, in the same meandering told-story form
that's in *Solomon*. *Solomon* seemed to be very much a male story
about the rites of passage, and that required a feeling of lore. In *Tar
Baby* the lore is there but in a more direct, bold way than it ever was
in *Song of Solomon*. Extraordinary people have things happen that
are not literally possible in *Song of Solomon,* such as the absence of
a navel on a woman. In *Tar Baby* that was done without even trying
to make any explanation, so that I ran the risk of having nature itself

bear witness, be the cause of everything that's going on. There are so many secrets in *Tar Baby*—everybody, with the possible exception of Sydney, has a secret that they don't want anyone else to know. Those secrets are revealed to other characters sometimes, but always to the reader. It begins with the most fundamental secret of all, which is that while we watch the world, the world watches us. It is the sort of secret that we all knew anyway when we were children, that the trees look back on us. So I put all of that on the surface of the novel in a way that is open to animism or anthropomorphism, whatever the labels are. Although the lore has gotten stronger, the narrative structure is more conventional and more accessible.

CR: Do you understand why the mythological aspect of your works puzzled people? It existed in certain characters in *The Bluest Eye* and *Sula*, and in *Song of Solomon* it's secret mythic history, but in *Tar Baby* it has suddenly manifested itself in the landscape.

TM: Well, one of the reasons it was not bewildering in the earlier books is, they may have decided that those books were distant in time so it's as if they were reading *Beowulf*. All three of those books are closed, back worlds; even though *Solomon* does come up to 1963, it's sort of back there somewhere. Also, it's a quest for roots, and spirituality. But in 1980, to take a person who was, after all, the kind of person that we ought to be, a fully integrated, fearless young woman, and to put that person—us—right next to the women hanging in the trees, may have been difficult because it means what I meant it to mean—those forces are still there now. It's not something that old people talk about, it is not back then, it is now—a violation of the earth, and the earth's revenge.

CR: Critics who didn't understand it seemed to suggest that it was a way out. I became conscious of the fact that the mythic element became a paradox, whereby going into the mythic the characters embraced death, but perhaps it was regeneration.

TM: I meant both. The risk of getting in touch with that world is that some part of you does die. You relinquish something, and what you give up is the person that you have made. But something else is revitalized. It's scary to contemplate, like the contemplation of death and change in the unknown. You discover you don't know it, and that's why it's so frightening. It is not codified the way the mythological world probably is codified. When Jadine is sinking in

quicksand, she's terrified, and all the while above her terrifying
creatures are watching. But they are benevolent and they are thinking
religiously. Whenever butterflies or trees or anything speaks or
thinks, what they think is really quite loving. But people either ignore
that part of perception, or cosmology, or life, or when they confront
it they won't comment. I suppose if one had a visitation of some sort,
it would be too terrifying to think about. Some forms of it lie in
madness, and you're frightened of that because it looks like you
might not get back. Even though there may be some incredible
knowledge revealed, we want to hang on to what we know. That view
of the world may be so narrow and so pitiful and so shabby and so
lonely that we die of starvation because we are not feeding off it, yet
this other, very rich perception may terrify us. But, more to the point
of your question, I thought of the origin of the myth, the story, as
being both history and prophecy, meaning it would identify danger
but it would also hold the promise that if one fully understood it one
would be free or made whole in some way.

   CR: But *Song of Solomon* does end in death. When I read *Tar
Baby* I understood Son's going towards the spirit world as also
rushing to his death.

   TM: Well, in *Song of Solomon* I really did not mean to suggest that
they kill each other, but out of a commitment and love and selfless-
ness they are willing to risk the one thing that we have, life, and
that's the positive nature of the action. I never really believed that
those two men would kill each other. I thought they would, like
antelopes, lock horns, but it is important that Guitar put his gun
down and does not blow Milkman out of the air, as he could. It's
important that he look at everything with his new eyes and say, "My
man, my main man." It's important that the metaphor be in the
killing of this brother, that the two men who love each other nevertheless have no area in which they can talk, so they exercise some
dominion over and demolition of the other. I wanted the language to
be placid enough to suggest he was suspended in the air in the leap
towards this thing, both loved and despised, and that he was willing
to die for that idea, but not necessarily to die. Son's situation in *Tar
Baby* is different, in that he is given a choice, to join the twentieth
century or not. If he decides to join the twentieth century, he would
be following Jadine. If he decides not to join the twentieth century

and would join these men, he would lock himself up forever from the future. He may identify totally and exclusively with the past, which is a kind of death, because it means you have no future, but a suspended place.

CR: Nor is it a wisdom or a power gained that can be brought back to the world, since the characters merge with the mythic landscape of the novel.

TM: No, he can't bring that back to the real world. I felt very strongly then—maybe that's what the next book is—that the book alone is the place where you can take that information, but in Son's situation and in Jadine's, it is literally a cul-de-sac. The choice is irrevocable, and there is no longer any time to mistake the metaphor. It seemed to me the most contemporary situation in the world. We are in a critical place where we would either cut off the future entirely and stay right where we are—which means, in an imaginative sense, annihilate ourselves totally and extend ourselves out into the stars, or the earth, or sea, or nothing—or we pretend there was no past, and just go blindly on, craving the single thing that we think is happiness. I was miserable and unsettled when I wrote the book, because it's a depressing and unlovely thought. I don't think it is inevitable. The ideal situation is to take from the past and apply it to the future, which doesn't mean improving the past or tomorrow. It means selecting from it.

CR: In the novels, you're evolving the mythology of black culture. Is it a mythology that you're retrieving out of a sense of urgency because you feel that there's a crisis in the culture? Has it already disappeared, or is it on the brink of being lost?

TM: The mythology has existed in other forms in black culture—in the music, gospels, spirituals, jazz. It existed in what we said, and in our relationships with each other in a kind of village lore. The community had to take on that responsibility of passing from one generation to another the mythologies, the given qualities, stories, assumptions which an ethnic group that is culturally coherent and has not joined the larger mainstream keeps very much intact for survival. The consequences of the political thrust to share in the economy and power of the country were to disperse that. Also, the entertainment world and fashion have eaten away at all of those moorings, so that the music isn't ours any more. It used to be an underground, personal thing. It's right that it should be larger now. It's done a fantastic thing, it's on the globe, it's universal. We can do it, and that's important. But what that means is, something else has to take its place. And that something else I think I can do best in novels. The mythology in the books can provide what the other culture did. It provides a transition, a way to see what in fact the dangers are, what are the havens, and what is the shelter. That is true for everybody, but for people who have been culturally parochial for a long time, the novel is the transition. The novel has to provide the richness of the past as well as suggestions of what the use of it is. I try to create a world in which it is comfortable to do both, to listen to the ancestry and to mark out what might be going on sixty or one hundred years from now. Words like "lore" and "mythology" and "folk tale" have very little currency in most contemporary literature. People scorn it as discredited information held by discredited people. There's supposed to be some other kind of knowledge that is more viable, more objective, more scientific. I don't want to disregard that mythology because it does not meet the credentials of this particular decade or century. I want to take it head on and look at it. It was useful for two thousand years. We also say "primitive," meaning something terrible. Some primitive instincts are terrible and uninformed, some of them are not. The problem is to distinguish between those elements in ourselves as human beings, as individuals, and as a culture, that are ancient and pure or primitive—that are there because they're valuable and ought to be there—and those that are primitive because they're ignorant and unfocused.

CR: A matriarch is at the center of each of your novels. Within black culture, do you feel that women bear the burden of living in a society where the men are more severely discriminated against?

TM: There's some problem with defining what men go through in the culture of black people, or any group of people who have really to work. Men identify with their ability to work and take care of the people they are responsible for. People are what they do rather than who they are. Now the work has been drained off, and that's the economy in which we live. Also, work is being split into little pieces, so you don't do a whole job but you do part of it. You feel lucky to have any part in it at all. That is devastating for the maleness of a man. So the woman have the domestic burden of trying to keep things going, on the one hand, and also protecting the male from that knowledge by giving him little places in which he can perform his male rituals, his male rites, whether it's drunkenness, arrogance, violence, or running away. It is a certain kind of fraudulent freedom, and destructive perhaps. The man is not free to choose his responsibilities. He is only responsible for what somebody has handed him. It's the women who keep it going, keep the children someplace safe.

It's very interesting, because black women slaves in this country were not, by and large, domestics in the house, with the headrag. They worked out in the fields, and they had to get to the end of a row at the same time as, if not faster than, the men, because there was this terrible totalitarian oppression of black men and women as laborers. There was no question of "You can't haul this sack, you can't cut down this tree, you can't ride this mule," because women were laborers first, and their labor is what was important. They were never permitted—even by their own men, because of the circumstances—to develop this household nurturing of the man. They had this history of competition with men in a physical way, meaning work, which was always there, always. And out of that comes a sense of comradeship among that other generation. I remember my parents and my grandparents—I always knew somehow they were comrades. They had something to do together. That does not exist now, because the work distribution is different. The man can't find work befitting what he believes to be his level, so it changes the relationship between the two. What is valuable about that past is not the fact that women had to work themselves into the grave so early, but this little idea of what it meant to have a comrade. It's not the mode of work, but the relationship of the work. A woman had a role as important as the man's, and not in any way subservient to his, and he didn't feel threatened by it, he needed her.

CR: This perspective you have comes from your own background. I remember you once mentioned that your grandfather remembered the days of emancipation.

TM: There are so many little feathers of stories about that. I never looked at it very closely, because there was so much misery way back then, but I remember he was a little boy under five, and all he heard was that emancipation was coming, and there was a great deal of agitation about that. Because he could feel the excitement, the fear, the apprehension as well as the glee, he knew something important was happening. Emancipation is coming! Nobody explained it to him—and he thought it was some terrible monster. And on the day when he knew it was coming he just went and hid under the bed. [*Laughs.*] Oh, poor baby. And then there were these other people I heard them discuss—their charm and traditions—they were Indians who were married to some slave people in my family. Some of them never made the transition from slavery. They were given land that was then taken away from them by the rapacious part of the culture that they could neither stand up to nor live with. Then there were others who were survivors, who got away with it, and made out in a flexible way. These things were talked about—the family, the neighbors, the community. They talked a great deal about Jesus—they selected out of Christianity all the things they felt applicable to their situation—but they also kept this other body of knowledge that we call superstitions. They were way stations in their thinking about how to get on with it and a reason to get up the next morning.

CR: I was wondering how you view the historical period of slavery. There are two cultural traditions. One is the Old Testament, tenet of the trial that forges an identity. The other is that of the Greek tragedies, that your most heroic people will be destroyed or enslaved. Solomon in flight is an Icarus figure.

TM: The heroic is hidden in the lore. The archetypes have this sort of glory, such as the triumph of this flying African. There's also the pity of the consequences of that heroism, so there's a mixture of terror and delight. In those figures and in those stories, the movement is away from the Brer Rabbit stories, being a kind of wit rather than power, but prior to that there are stories of wonder workers. I remember the story of a woman who was a worker on a plantation. She was sassy, she spoke up, was always being beaten and resold. She was powerful: at one point she was chained to a tree and lashed, and she let it happen. Then something snapped, I guess, and she pulled the tree out of the ground and with it beat the man and his dog. [*Laughs.*] That moment shows a really superhuman effort when we just say, "The hell with it," and let it out. The consequences of that woman's life, of course, were sad. There are hundreds of those stories, and they linger on. They were nourishing stories.

CR: In spirit this folklore is similar to the parables of the church, the hymns where there's the testing and the suffering.

TM: Being able to endure it. The connection with time in a large sense was the most important thing, to get through this because afterwards you can join all those others before you, and it would not be like this. The daily or weekly sessions in church were not only to give each other strength. It was the one place where you could cry, among other people who were also crying and whom you trusted to help you. With everybody else there, you were not afraid or ashamed to do it. You knew that afterwards you still had to get up and face it, but now somehow you could.

CR: You describe the bonding of the community in the church as the theatre of life.

TM: The society was there, the art was there, the politics were there, the theology was there, everything was there. That was the place where all of it was acted out, within a framework that was acceptable to them. There is so much in Christianity that makes it a very interesting religion, because of its scriptures and its vagueness. It's a theatrical religion. It says something particularly interesting to black people, and I think it's part of why they were so available to it. It was the love things that were psychically very important. Nobody could have endured that life in constant rage. They would have all gone mad, and done what other cultures have done when they could not deal with the enemy. You just don't deal with it. You do something that destroys yourself, or else you give up. But with the love thing—love your enemies, turn the other cheek—they could sublimate the other things, they transcended them. I do remember, there were all these things that those people felt they were too good to be, that they were above doing. They didn't commit suicide, they didn't stone people, they just didn't—they were better than that. What made them better was this very pure, very aristocratic love that made them the most civilized people in the world. That was their dignity, how they transcended. And that part appealed to them.

I suppose if they had been untampered with, they could have made out with the vestiges of that African religion that they brought, because it survived in some forms, in ways in which they worked, sang, talked, and carried on. Even now, Africans have a way of saying, at least to people like me, that they feel that other people's religions are an enhancement, something they could incorporate. Some aspects of Christianity are very exclusive rather than inclusive: it tells you who can or can't be in, and what you have to do in order to be in. But the openness of being saved was one part of it—you were constantly being redeemed and reborn, and you couldn't fall too far, and couldn't ever fall completely and be totally thrown out. It was always open for you, and there was something you could do to testify or change your way of life, and it would be fine. Everybody was ready to accept you. And also that transcending love, that quality, which is why the New Testament is so pertinent to black literature—the lamb, the victim, the vulnerable one who does die but nevertheless lives. And of course there was that wonderful, very strange Job, not his original wealth, but his steady, sustained ''I will not do that, I will not do that,'' all the way through, and then finally the recompense. That's your test of inner faith.

CR: What you're describing is the core of the culture after emancipation, which is in your earlier novels. But it existed within its own boundaries in a hostile society. Can you foresee an end to this prejudice?

TM: I really don't know. I write about what it must have been like when we just got here. There couldn't have been another slave society in the world with a Fugitive Slave Law. It could not work with the Greeks and Romans, because they all looked pretty much alike. But with the black people, skin give them away. You could keep up the remnants and the vestiges of slavery far longer than it ever would have lasted if they had enslaved . . . suppose they had decided to buy Irish people and just spread them all about, as they did of course. Then when they stopped doing it you could sort of tell by the name or tell by the religion, but you couldn't have laws—Jim Crow laws. With black people, because of the physical difference, they could be seen as slaves, and subsequently are now viewed as the visible poor. We are perceived as the lowest of the classes because we can be identified that way. It wouldn't make any difference what we wore, or what neighborhood we lived in, we're still visible as that. The visibility has made the prejudices last longer. It's not because one is black that the prejudice exists. The prejudice exists because one can identify the person who was once a slave or in the lower class, and the caste system can survive longer. In Nazi Germany they found a way to identify the Jews by putting a label on them to indicate who they were. You know what I'm saying: they needed a mark. But here you have people who are black people.

CR: Do you think that the prejudices will erode away, or do you think they are always going to renew themselves?

TM: No, I think all your people think that because they're taught to. I think that it will last as long as the economy remains this way.

The Language Must Not Sweat: A Conversation with Toni Morrison

Thomas LeClair / 1981

From the *New Republic* 184 (21 March 1981): 25–29.

Toni Morrison's *Song of Solomon* was published in 1977 to unreserved praise; American readers had found a new voice. The plot of the novel, a young man's search for a nourishing folk tradition, was familiar from other Afro-American books, but Morrison's fireside manner—composed yet simple, commanding yet intimate—gives the novel a Latin American enchantment. Reading backward through *Sula* (1973) to Morrison's first novel, *The Bluest Eye* (1969), one sees her trying out different versions of what she calls her "address," rehearsing on more modest subjects the tone and timbre that give original expression to the large cultural materials in *Song of Solomon*.

How and why she arrived at that special voice were the questions that brought me to Toni Morrison's busy office at Random House (where she is an editor) just after she finished *Tar Baby*. Although our interview was interrupted several times, when Toni Morrison started talking about writing she achieved remarkable concentration and intensity. This—not editorial business or author small talk—was clearly where she lived. No matter what she discussed—her loyalty to the common reader, her eccentric characters, her interest in folklore—her love of language was the subtext and constant lesson of her manner. She *performs* words. Gertrude Stein said poetry was "caressing nouns." Toni Morrison doesn't like to be called a poetic writer, but it is her almost physical relation to language that allows her to tell the old stories she feels are best.

Thomas LeClair: You have said you would write even if there were no publishers. Would you explain what the process of writing means to you?

Toni Morrison: After my first novel, *The Bluest Eye*, writing became a way to be coherent in the world. It became necessary and possible for me to sort out the past, and the selection process, being disciplined and guided, was genuine thinking as opposed to simple response or problem-solving. Writing was the only work I did that was for myself and by myself. In the process, one exercises sovereignty in a special way. All sensibilities are engaged, sometimes simultaneously, sometimes sequentially. While I'm writing, all of my experience is vital and useful and possibly important. It may not appear in the work, but it is valuable. Writing gives me what I think dancers have on stage in their relation to gravity and space and time. It is energetic and balanced, fluid and in repose. And there is always the possibility of growth; I could never hit the highest note so I'd never have to stop. Writing has for me everything that good work ought to have, all the criteria. I love even the drudgery, the revision, the proofreading. So even if publishing did grind to a halt, I would continue to write.

LeClair: Do you understand the process more and more with each novel that you write?

Morrison: At first I wrote out of a very special place in me, although I did not understand what that place was or how to get to it deliberately. I didn't trust the writing that came from there. It did not seem writerly enough. Sometimes what I wrote from that place remained sound, even after enormous revision, but I would regard it as a fluke. Then I learned to trust that part, learned to rely on that part, and I learned how to get there faster than I had before. That is, now I don't have to write 35 pages of throat-clearing in order to be where I wish to be. I don't mean that I'm an inspired writer. I don't wait to be struck by lightning and don't need certain slants of light in order to write, but now after my fourth book I can recognize the presence of a real idea and I can recognize the proper mode of its expression. I must confess, though, that I sometimes lose interest in the characters and get much more interested in the trees and animals. I think I exercise tremendous restraint in this, but my editor says "Would you stop this *beauty* business." And I say "Wait, wait until I tell you about these ants."

LeClair: How do you conceive of your function as a writer?

Morrison: I write what I have recently begun to call village literature, fiction that is really for the village, for the tribe. Peasant literature for *my* people, which is necessary and legitimate but which

also allows me to get in touch with all sorts of people. I think long
and carefully about what my novels ought to do. They should clarify
the roles that have become obscured; they ought to identify those
things in the past that are useful and those things that are not; and
they ought to give nourishment. I agree with John Berger that peasants don't write novels because they don't need them. They have a
portrait of themselves from gossip, tales, music, and some celebra-
tions. That is enough. The middle class at the beginning of the
industrial revolution needed a portrait of itself because the old portrait didn't work for this new class. Their roles were different; their
lives in the city were new. The novel served this function then, and it
still does. It tells about the city values, the urban values. Now my
people, we "peasants," have come to the city, that is to say, we live
with its values. There is a confrontation between old values of the
tribes and new urban values. It's confusing. There has to be a mode
to do what the music did for blacks, what we used to be able to do
with each other in private and in that civilization that existed underneath the white civilization. I think this accounts for the address of
my books. I am not explaining anything to anybody. My work bears
witness and suggests who the outlaws were, who survived under
what circumstances and why, what was legal in the community as
opposed to what was legal outside it. All that is in the fabric of the
story in order to do what the music used to do. The music kept us
alive, but it's not enough anymore. My people are being devoured.
Whenever I feel uneasy about my writing, I think: what would be the
response of the people in the book if they read the book? That's my
way of staying on track. Those are the people for whom I write.

As a reader I'm fascinated by literary books, but the books I
wanted to write could not be only, even merely, literary or I would
defeat my purposes, defeat my audience. That's why I don't like to
have someone call my books "poetic," because it has the connota-
tion of luxuriating richness. I wanted to restore the language that
black people spoke to its original power. That calls for a language
that is rich but not ornate.

LeClair: What do you mean by "address"?

Morrison: I stand with the reader, hold his hand, and tell him a
very simple story about complicated people. I like to work with, to
fret, the cliché, which is a cliché because the experience expressed in

it is important: a young man seeks his fortune; a pair of friends, one good, one bad; the perfectly innocent victim. We know thousands of these in literature. I like to dust off these clichés, dust off the language, make them mean whatever they may have meant originally. My genuine criticism of most contemporary books is that they're not *about* anything. Most of the books that are about something—the books that mean something—treat old ideas, old situations.

LeClair: Does this mean working with folklore and myth?

Morrison: I think the myths are misunderstood now because we are not talking to each other the way I was spoken to when I was growing up in a very small town. You knew everything in that little microcosm. But we don't live where we were born. I had to leave my town to do my work here; it was a sacrifice. There is a certain sense of family I don't have. So the myths get forgotten. Or they may not have been looked at carefully. Let me give you an example: the flying myth in *Song of Solomon*. If it means Icarus to some readers, fine; I want to take credit for that. But my meaning is specific: it is about black people who could fly. That was always part of the folklore of my life; flying was one of our gifts. I don't care how silly it may seem. It is everywhere—people used to talk about it, it's in the spirituals and gospels. Perhaps it was wishful thinking—escape, death, and all that. But suppose it wasn't. What might it mean? I tried to find out in *Song of Solomon*.

In the book I've just completed, *Tar Baby*, I use that old story because, despite its funny, happy ending, it used to frighten me. The story has a tar baby in it which is used by a white man to catch a rabbit. "Tar baby" is also a name, like nigger, that white people call black children, black girls, as I recall. Tar seemed to me to be an odd thing to be in a Western story, and I found that there is a tar lady in African mythology. I started thinking about tar. At one time, a tar pit was a holy place, at least an important place, because tar was used to build things. It came naturally out of the earth; it held together things like Moses's little boat and the pyramids. For me, the tar baby came to mean the black woman who can hold things together. The story was a point of departure to history and prophecy. That's what I mean by dusting off the myth, looking closely at it to see what it might conceal. . . .

LeClair: Do you think it's risky to do this kind of writing?

Morrison: Yes, I think I can do all sorts of writing, including virtuoso performances. But what is hard for me is to be simple, to have uncomplex stories with complex people in them, to clean the language, really clean it. One attempts to slay a real dragon. You don't ever kill it, but you have to choose a job worth the doing. I think I choose hard jobs for myself, and the opportunity to fail is always there. I want a residue of emotion in my fiction, and this means verging upon sentimentality, or being willing to let it happen and then draw back from it. Also, stories seem so old-fashioned now. But narrative remains the best way to learn anything, whether history or theology, so I continue with narrative form.

LeClair: In the kind of fiction you have described, isn't there a danger that it will be liked for something it is not? Are you ever worried about that?

Morrison: No. The people who are not fastidious about reading may find my fiction "wonderful." They are valuable to me because I am never sure that what they find "wonderful" in it isn't really what is valuable about it. I do hope to interest people who are very fastidious about reading. What I'd really like to do is appeal to both at the same time. Sometimes I feel that I do play to the gallery in *Song of Solomon*, for example, because I have to make the reader look at people he may not wish to look at. You don't look at Pilate. You don't really look at a person like Cholly in *The Bluest Eye*. They are always backdrops, stage props, not the main characters in their own stories. In order to look at them in fiction, you have to hook the reader, strike a certain posture as narrator, achieve some intimacy.

LeClair: As an editor, you look for quality in other's work. What do you think is distinctive about your fiction? What makes it good?

Morrison: The language, only the language. The language must be careful and must appear effortless. It must not sweat. It must suggest and be provocative at the same time. It is the thing that black people love so much—the saying of words, holding them on the tongue, experimenting with them, playing with them. It's a love, a passion. Its function is like a preacher's: to make you stand up out of your seat, make you lose yourself and hear yourself. The worst of all possible things that could happen would be to lose that language. There are certain things I cannot say without recourse to my language. It's terrible to think that a child with five different present

tenses comes to school to be faced with those books that are less
than his own language. And then to be told things about his language,
which is him, that are sometimes permanently damaging. He may
never know the etymology of Africanisms in his language, not even
know that "hip" is a real word or that "the dozens" meant something. This is a really cruel fallout of racism. I know the standard
English. I want to use it to help restore the other language, the lingua
franca.

The part of the writing process that I fret is getting the sound
without some mechanics that would direct the reader's attention to
the sound. One way is not to use adverbs to describe how someone
says something. I try to work the dialogue down so the reader has to
hear it. When Eva in *Sula* sets her son on fire, her daughter runs
upstairs to tell her, and Eva says "Is?" you can hear every grandmother say "Is?" and you know: a) she knows what she's been told;
b) she is not going to do anything about it; and c) she will not have
any more conversation. That sound is important to me.

LeClair: Not all readers are going to catch that.

Morrison: If I say "Quiet is as kept," that is a piece of information
which means exactly what it says, but to black people it means a big
lie is about to be told. Or someone is going to tell some graveyard
information, who's sleeping with whom. Black readers will chuckle.
There is a level of appreciation that might be available only to people
who understand the context of the language. The analogy that occurs
to me is jazz: it is open on the one hand and both complicated and
inaccessible on the other. I never asked Tolstoy to write for me, a
little colored girl in Lorain, Ohio. I never asked Joyce not to mention
Catholicism or the world of Dublin. Never. And I don't know why I
should be asked to explain your life to you. We have splendid writers
to do that, but I am not one of them. It is that business of being
universal, a word hopelessly stripped of meaning for me. Faulkner
wrote what I suppose could be called regional literature and had
it published all over the world. It is good—and universal—because it
is specifically about a particular world. That's what I wish to do. If
I tried to write a universal novel, it would be water. Behind this
question is the suggestion that to write for black people is somehow
to diminish the writing. From my perspective, there are only black
people. When I say "people," that's what I mean. Lots of books

written by black people about black people have had this "universality" as a burden. They were writing for some readers other than me.

LeClair: One of the complaints about your fiction in both the black and white press is that you write about eccentrics, people who aren't representative.

Morrison: This kind of sociological judgment is pervasive and pernicious. "Novel A is better than B or C because A is more like most black people really are." Unforgivable. I am enchanted, personally, with people who are extraordinary because in them I can find what is applicable to the ordinary. There are books by black writers about ordinary black life. I don't write them. Black readers often ask me, "Why are your books so melancholy, so sad? Why don't you ever write about something that works, about relationships that are healthy?" There is a comic mode, meaning the union of the sexes, that I don't write. I write what I suppose could be called the tragic mode in which there is some catharsis and revelation. There's a whole lot of space in between, but my inclination is in the tragic direction. Maybe it's a consequence of my being a classics minor.

Related, I think, is the question of nostalgia. The danger of writing about the past, as I have done, is romanticizing it. I don't think I do that, but I do feel that people were more interesting then than they are now. It seems to me there were more excesses in women and men, and people accepted them as they don't now. In the black community where I grew up, there were eccentricity and freedom, less conformity in individual habits—but close conformity in terms of the survival of the village, of the tribe. Before sociological microscopes were placed on us, people did anything and nobody was run out of town. I mean, the community in *Sula* let her stay. They wouldn't wash or bury her. They protected themselves from her, but she was part of the community. The detritus of white people, the rejects from the respectable white world, which appears in *Sula* was in our neighborhood. In my family, there were some really interesting people who were willing to be whatever they were. People permitted it, perhaps because in the outer world the eccentrics had to be a little servant person or low-level factory worker. They had an enormous span of emotions and activities, and they are the people I remember when I go to write. When I go to colleges, the students say

"Who are these people?" Maybe it's because now everybody seems
to be trying to be "right."

LeClair: Naming is an important theme in *Song of Solomon*.
Would you discuss its significance?

Morrison: I never knew the real names of my father's friends. Still
don't. They used other names. A part of that had to do with cultural
orphanage, part of it with the rejection of the name given to them
under circumstances not of their choosing. If you come from Africa,
your name is gone. It is particularly problematic because it is not just
your name but your family, your tribe. When you die, how can you
connect with your ancestors if you have lost your name? That's a
huge psychological scar. The best thing you can do is take another
name which is yours because it reflects something about you or your
own choice. Most of the names in *Song of Solomon* are real, the
names of musicians for example. I used the biblical names to show
the impact of the Bible on the lives of black people, their awe of and
respect for it coupled with their ability to distort it for their own
purposes. I also used some pre-Christian names to give the sense of a
mixture of cosmologies. Milkman Dead has to learn the meaning of
his own name and the names of things. In African languages there is
no word for yam, but there is a word for every variety of yam.
Each thing is separate and different; once you have named it, you
have power. Milkman has to experience the elements. He goes into
the earth and later walks its surface. He twice enters water. And he
flies in the air. When he walks the earth, he feels a part of it, and that
is his coming of age, the beginning of his ability to connect with the
past and perceive the world as alive.

LeClair: You mentioned the importance of sound before. Your
work also seems to me to be strongly visual and concerned with
vision, with seeing.

Morrison: There are times in my writing when I cannot move
ahead even though I know exactly what will happen in the plot and
what the dialogue is because I don't have the scene, the metaphor to
begin with. Once I can see the scene, it all happens. In *Sula*, Eva is
waiting for her long lost husband to come back. She's not sure
how she's going to feel, but when he leaves he toots the horn on his
pea-green Model-T Ford. It goes "ooogah, ooogah," and Eva knows
she hates him. My editor said the car didn't exist at the time, and I

had a lot of trouble rewriting the scene because I had to have the color and the sound. Finally, I had a woman in a green dress laughing a big-city laugh, an alien sound in that small-town street, that stood for the "ooogah" I couldn't use. In larger terms, I thought of *Sula* as a cracked mirror, fragments and pieces we have to see independently and put together. In *Bluest Eye* I used the primer story, with its picture of a happy family, as a frame acknowledging the outer civilization. The primer with white children was the way life was presented to the black people. As the novel proceeded I wanted that primer version broken up and confused, which explains the typographical running together of the words.

LeClair: Did your using the primer come out of the work you were doing on textbooks?

Morrison: No. I was thinking that nobody treated these people seriously in literature and that "these people" who were not treated seriously were me. The interest in vision, in seeing, is a fact of black life. As slaves and ex-slaves, black people were manageable and findable, as no other slave society would be, because they were black. So there is an enormous impact from the simple division of color—more than sex, age, or anything else. The complaint is not being seen for what one is. That is the reason why my hatred of white people is justified and their hatred for me is not. There is a fascinating book called *Drylongso* which collects the talk of black people. They say almost to a man that you never tell a white person the truth. He doesn't want to hear it. Their conviction is they are neither seen nor listened to. They also perceive themselves as morally superior people because they do *see*. This helps explain why the theme of the mask is so important in black literature and why I worked so heavily with it in *Tar Baby*.

LeClair: Who is doing work now that you respect?

Morrison: I don't like to make lists because someone always gets left out, but in general I think the South American novelists have the best of it now. My complaint about letters now would be the state of criticism. It's following post-modern fiction into self-consciousness, talking about itself as though it were the work of art. Fine for the critic, but not helpful for the writer. There was a time when the great poets were the great critics, when the artist was the critic. Now it seems that there are no encompassing minds, no great critical audi-

ence for the writer. I have yet to read criticism that understands my
work or is prepared to understand it. I don't care if the critic likes or
dislikes it. I would just like to feel less isolated. It's like having a
linguist who doesn't understand your language tell you what you're
saying. Stanley Elkin says you need great literature to have great
criticism. I think it works the other way around. If there were better
criticism, there would be better books.

A Conversation with Toni Morrison

Judith Wilson / 1981

From *Essence* July 1981:84–86, 128.

Toni Morrison's appearance on the cover of *Newsweek* magazine this past March could be considered something of a literary milestone, given that only a handful of writers have been so honored—and never before a Black writer.

When told she was to achieve this "coup of the cover," Morrison, a 50-year-old Black novelist, editor and divorced mother of two sons, reacted with customary skepticism. "The day you put a middle-aged, gray-haired colored lady on the [cover of the] magazine, I will know the revolution is over!" The exaggeration is typical of her wry sense of humor. In fact, Toni Morrison's media triumph marks the end of an era in which Black literature was most often thought of as Black male literature.

Morrison is not only one of America's most gifted writers but also a particularly vocal champion of Black *women* writers, a concern matched by an emphasis on the Black female experience in her own fiction.

Toni Morrison's first novel, *The Bluest Eye* (1970), encouraged many of us to speak for the first time about the enormous damage to the psyche that results from trying to adopt an alien standard of beauty. Her second book *Sula* (1973), explored another well-kept secret: the difference between Black women's friendships with one another and their emotional ties to Black men. However, Morrison's first look at things from a Black *male* point of view with her third book *Song of Solomon*, won far more attention than her previous works.

Song of Solomon, published in 1977, made the front page of *The New York Times Book Review*, received a National Book Critics Circle Award, was offered as a Book-of-the-Month Club main selection (the first Black author on the list since Richard Wright's *Native*

Son) and became a best-seller in its paperback edition. This family saga focused on the fate of a male character, and the book's image of Black manhood provided a literary mate to Morrison's insights into the Black female psyche.

Her latest works, *Tar Baby* (excerpted in the May issue of ESSENCE) is the book that put Morrison on *Newsweek*'s cover, "The Dick Cavett Show," the "Today" show and *The New York Times* best-seller list in less than a month after its publication. The book is her first departure from a self-contained world of Black community and family life.

Set on a fictitious Caribbean isle, the plot revolves around four couples—one white, three Black. At the heart of the story is the relationship between Jadine Childs, high-fashion Black model trained and educated in Paris and Son Green, a Black American on the run from the law. They form the centerpiece for a spiraling web of relationships—between Black women and Black men; between different generations, classes and races; between the West and the Third World.

Some white critics who were formerly Morrison's loyal fans seemed startled by *Tar Baby*—it's as though someone they trusted suddenly whipped out a gun and yelled "Power to the people!" But Toni Morrison's new "militancy" should not have been a surprise— the signals were there all along.

ESSENCE contributing editor Judith Wilson interviewed Toni Morrison in the offices of her publisher, Alfred E. Knopf. Dressed in her softly tailored style, Morrison is a warm, sensuous woman who speaks in the same magic language of poetry she brings to her writing. Here she discusses some of her consuming passions—our responsibilities as Black women to our children and elders, our relationships with men and, of course, her own vision of writing.

Essence: In *Tar Baby* you set up a conflict between Jadine's kind of freedom and her idea of the kind of woman to be, and her Aunt Ondine's reminder about the duties of daughterhood. Can women like Jadine, who have options Black women never had before, reconcile freedom with responsibilities—to elders, men, children?
  Morrison: We have to.
  Essence: How?

Morrison: It has to be done; otherwise, we are dead. If you kill the ancestors, you've just killed everything. It's part of the whole nurturing thing. My mother took care of me when I could not go to the bathroom or feed myself. When she gets in that position, I have to do that for her. And my children have to see that; they have to participate in it. If the race is to survive, it has to take care of its own—that's not an agency's job.

Nobody really lives where they were born anymore. So you have little children who knock old people in the head—because they don't know 'em. And it's too bad, because the children are losing something valuable. They're losing their childhood.

In *Tar Baby*, Son loves those pie ladies from his hometown. They are his past. They are anchors for him—just the notion of them at those church suppers. They're the people who tell you to uncross your legs and meddle you all your life and raise you, in that sort of tribal way in which every adult raises every child. Which is really what I think it takes, 'cause I don't think one parent can raise a child. I don't think two parents can raise a child. You really need the whole village. And, if you don't have it, you'd better make it.

Son loved those women, but Jadine found them "backwards." She perceived his relationship with them as spoiling—"They spoiled you and kept you infantile," she says—which she is not about. She has lost the tar quality, the ability to hold something together that otherwise would fall apart—which is what I mean by the nurturing ability. That's what one surrenders, or can surrender, in order to do this other thing—in order to go and get a degree in art history, learn four languages and be in the movies and stuff. That sounds like I'm putting it down; I'm not. I'm only saying that the point is to be able to do both.

Essence: Isn't that asking for Superwoman?

Morrison: Since it was possible for my mother, my grandmother and her mother to do what they did, which to me is scary, really scary—snatching children and roaming around in the night; running away from the South and living in Detroit, can't read or write; in a big city trying to stay alive and keep those children when you can't even read the road signs—now, *these* are hard things to do. And if they can do that, surely I can work at Random House and cook—I

mean, what is it after all? You know, the worst that can happen is
that I get fired and have to do something else.

I know I can't go to those women [mothers and grandmothers] and
say, "Well, you know, my life is so hard. I live in New York and it's
just . . ." They don't want to hear that! They were boiling sheets and
shooting pheasant and stuff, then they got married to people and
had children and fights. And the world was different then—white
people were not punished for killing Black folks.

That's all history means to me. It's a very *personal* thing—if their
blood is in my veins, maybe I can do this little part right here. I don't
want to meet them people nowhere—ever!—and have them look at
me and say, "What were *you* doing back there?"

Essence: That sense of tradition colors your writing style. By
leaving the conclusion of *Tar Baby* open-ended, you suggest a continuity between past and present, a stream of history that's still in
motion.

Morrison: It's a very classic, peasant story. Peasant stories don't
pass any judgments. The village participates in the story and makes it
whatever it is. So that accounts for the structure, the sort of call-and-
response thing that goes on—the narrator functions as chorus. And
this book is really kind of crazy 'cause nature functions as the
chorus. That's what's in my mind when I'm trying to put together the
bits and pieces of a style that has not only its own sound but its own
purpose and its own legitimate cultural sources.

There is an enormous variety of stuff that can be done within that
mode, and it's interesting that I can distinguish style in Black women
writers now faster than I can in the Black male writers.

Essence: Why is that?

Morrison: I think the men have been addressing white men when
they write. And it's a legitimate confrontation—they're men telling
white men what this is. But the women are not trying to prove
anything to white men. No woman writer is writing in that direction.
She's writing to, probably, other people like herself. So she has to
rely on this other quality, of mode and style, in order to get her
message across. She may have all sorts of political statements in it,
but the address is different. When I think of women's writing, that's
all I ever think about—I think of Black women writers. The others
[white women] seem to be doing something very confession-oriented.

Essence: Do you consider yourself a "success" at this point?

Morrison: Well, there is a demonstrable public success that's there, which is tame. Somebody asked me, "What's next? Is there anything?" And I said, "Yes, there's eminence." And they said, "What's eminence?" And I said, "Eminence is when you don't have to be on the cover of *Newsweek* and you don't have to go on a lecture tour. . . ."

But I feel no success with my sons, I feel no success as an editor—because nothing has been completed. Anything may happen at any moment. If I'm a hundred and they [her sons] are 70, I would still go to them if they break a hip. And with the editing thing, there is so much to be done and I can only do so little. I should have—I would like to have—my own line [of books]. It should be done. Somebody in a major publishing house should do it. I can't—it requires more days and more energy than I have.

Essence: Why don't you feel satisfied with what you've accomplished as an editor?

Morrison: The books didn't sell. When I publish Toni Cade Bambara, when I publish Gayl Jones, if they would do what my own books have done [in sales], then I would feel really fantastic about it. But the market can only receive one or two [Black women writers]. Dealing with five Toni Morrisons would be problematic. I'm not talking about quality of work—who writes better than I do and stuff. I'm just talking about the fact that, in terms of new kinds of writing, the marketplace receives only one or two Blacks in days when it's not fashionable. That's true of literature in general, but it's particularly true for Black writing.

I can't rely on a huge, aggressive Black buying audience. But I think that will all change. You see, Black people don't just read, they have to *absorb* something. I've tried to write books so that whoever reads them absorbs them—so that the process of reading them means you have to take it in. That's a slower way to do it, but people participate in the books heavily. Two thousand people bought *The Bluest Eye* in hardback and maybe 12,000 or 15,000 bought *Sula*. Then it tripled for *Song of Solomon*. And maybe it will triple again for *Tar Baby*.

But the point is that once there can be a commercial success of a book that is clearly, relentlessly Black—and I don't care if they

handle it as just "this one little colored girl up here today"—it opens
a door. So no one can ever say again it can't be done. It's an old
technique that Black people use—you know, the first one in the pool,
the first one in the school.

My mother, when she would find out that they were not letting
Black people sit in certain sections of the local theater, would go and
sit in the white folks' section, go see *Superman* just so she could
come out and say, "I sat there, so everybody else can too." It's that
tradition.

Which is why I don't like that "But you're not a Black writer,
you're a plain old writer." I hate that. It's depoliticizing you, and I
understand all those other ramifications of what that's supposed to
mean—but that's *their* problem, not mine.

Essence: Tar Baby outlines political issues to a degree that your
previous works never seemed to do. Why has your writing taken this
new course?

Morrison: I don't think *Tar Baby* is more political than anything
else I've written. The politics of the other books were greater,
but they were addressed only to Black people—it was obvious that it
was a domestic affair.

This book *required* white people because of the tar baby story. In
the original story, the tar baby is made by a white man—that has to
be the case with Jadine. She has to have been almost "constructed"
by the Western thing, and grateful to it. But the political statement
isn't as great to me as it is in *Song of Solomon*.

Essence: Both *Tar Baby* and *Song of Solomon* end in an ambiguous
way, with a Black male character engaged in some sort of magical
act. Some readers seem uncomfortable with that sort of mythic
solution. They seem to want to see a Black man who succeeds in
real-life terms. Does that sort of complaint trouble you at all?

Morrison: I know what that hunger is. It would be nice, I think—
for therapy and for hope and all of that—to have a nice book in
which you have two attractive people and they resolve their situation
and hold hands and walk off into the sunset. I tried, I wished for
that happy ending for *Tar Baby*. But there's something that, to me, is
more vital than that—which is some kind of exploration of what the
difficulty is in the first place. The problem has been put in the wrong
place, as though it's a sexual battle, not a cultural one.

Racism hurts in a very personal way. Because of it, people do all sorts of things in their personal lives and love relationships based on differences in values and class and education and their conception of what it means to be Black in this society.

Essence: Since Jadine decides to return to Paris at the end of the book and constantly defends her white patrons and their cultural values, she seems like the "heavy" in the battle between her and Son. Are you saying that women like her, who are privileged, with a college education and a lucrative career, should feel guilty about themselves in comparison with men who are poor like Son?

Morrison: No Black woman should apologize for being educated or anything else. The problem is not paying attention to the ancient proprieties—which for me means the ability to be "the ship" *and* "the safe harbor." Our history as Black women is the history of women who could build a house *and* have some children, and there was no problem.

What we have known is how to be complete human beings, so that we did not let the education keep us from our nurturing abilities. And that was not because those old women went to Dartmouth! It's because they were in the fields as comrades to their men—they had to get to the edge of the row at the same time. They were not in some house just popping out babies. They were working all of the time— hard labor—and they were handling those households.

To lose that is to diminish ourselves unnecessarily. It is not a question, it's not a conflict. You don't have to give up anything. You *choose* your responsibilities. And I don't want an A-plus for it—it's just doing what a grown-up person does.

A grown-up—which, I think, is a good thing to be—is a person who does what she has to do without complaining, without pretend- ing that it's some enormous, heroic enterprise. One doesn't have to make a choice between whether to dance or to cook—do both. And if *we* can't do it, then it can't be done!

We have a special insight that can find harmony in what is nor- mally, in this country, perceived as conflict.

Essence: Is "bringing things together" the reason for your particular style of writing?

Morrison: Definitely. Black people rely on different sets of infor- mation, and we explain things in different ways. I mean, there was

the education in schools and there was *our* education—and it was
different. When we talked about what we dreamed, that was real—it
wasn't a Freudian anything! So, that's the effort—to put it together.

I'm trying to do what I call a Black style—not *the* Black style, but
a Black style—very much in the way that if you say "a Black
musician," that's not pejorative; it's a clarifying statement. If you
know something about music, you know something about its sound.
People say, "Don't you want to be just a plain old writer?" No!

Essence: How do you create a Black literary style?

Morrison: Some of the writers think it's dropping *g*'s. It's not—it's
something else. It's a putting together of all sorts of things. It's
cleaning up the language so that old words have new meanings. It has
a spine that's very biblical and meandering and aural—you really
have to hear it. So that I never say "She says softly." If it's not
already *soft*, you know, I have to leave a lot of space around it so a
reader can hear that it's soft.

Essence: Until *Tar Baby*, all of your novels were set in the Midwest, which seems atypical in terms of what we think of as the Afro-
American experience. Do you feel there's a distinction between
Black language or culture in the Midwest and in other parts of the
country?

Morrison: I know the Midwest and I'm from it [Lorain, Ohio]. My
feeling is that Black culture survives everywhere pretty much the
same way. If I go to California and see my aunt, or if I go to
Carterville, Ga., or if I go up here on Riverside Drive [in New York
City], there will always be the same thing. There are similarities
between anybody's Links party and anybody's church supper and
anybody's barbecue. I can move anywhere in there and hear the
same thing.

The first time I went south, it was staggering! It was like going
home.

Essence: Do you have any future plans?

Morrison: The future for me is always my children—whether I can
stay healthy long enough to be there or be available to them. That's
pretty much all I think about when I think about the future.

I don't have a story to write now, but I'm not anxious about that.
It's there and it will make itself manifest at some point. I trust that.

The next book will have different hurdles. Whatever it is, it'll be different from the last one. But they will always be about the same thing—you know—about that whole world of Black people in this country.

An Interview with Toni Morrison

Nellie McKay / 1983

From *Contemporary Literature* 24.4(1983):413–29.

In life and in art, the outstanding achievements of writer Toni Morrison extend and enlarge the tradition of the strength, persistence, and accomplishments of black women in America. In life, her immediate models are first, her grandmother who, in the early part of this century, left her home in the South with seven children and thirty dollars because she feared white sexual violence against her maturing daughters; and second, her mother who took "humiliating jobs" in order to send Morrison money regularly while she was in college and graduate school. Her artistic precursors are equally impressive. The first black person in America to publish a book was a woman—Phillis Wheatley—a slave, whose *Poems on Various Subjects, Religious and Moral* appeared in 1773. The single most substantial fictional output of the much celebrated Harlem Renaissance of the 1920s was the work of a woman, Jessie Fauset, who published four novels between 1924 and 1933. In 1937, Zora Neale Hurston's Janie, in *Their Eyes Were Watching God*, heralded the coming of the contemporary black feminist heroine to American literature. Morrison is aware of both the burdens and the blessings of the past. "In all of the history of black women," she told me during our interview, "we have been both the ship and the harbor. . . . We can do things one at a time, or four things at a time if we have to."

Toni Morrison was born in Lorain, Ohio, in the 1930s. Southern roots extend up and out from both branches of her family background. Her mother's parents traveled North from Greenville and Birmingham, Alabama, by way of Kentucky, in a flight from poverty and racism. There her grandfather worked in the coal mines. The search for a better education for their children provided the incentive that propelled them to Ohio. Morrison's father came from Georgia, and the racial violence with which he grew up in that state had a lasting impact on his vision of white America. The most valuable legacy he left his daughter was a strong sense of her own value on her own terms.

Black lore, black music, black language, and all the myths and rituals of black culture were the most prominent elements in the early life of Toni Morrison. Her grandfather played the violin, her parents told thrilling and terrifying ghost stories, and her mother sang and played the numbers by decoding dream symbols as they were manifest in a dream book that she kept. She tells of a childhood world filled with signs, visitations, and ways of knowing that encompassed more than concrete reality. Then in adolescence she read the great Russian, French, and English novels and was impressed by the quality of their specificity. In her writing she strives to capture the richness of black culture through its specificity.

Morrison's first novel, *The Bluest Eye*, was published in 1970. The book examines the experiences of a young black girl as she copes with the ideal of beauty and the reality of violence within the black community. Within the novel Morrison demonstrates that even with the best intentions, people hurt each other when they are chained to circumstances of poverty and low social status. "Violence," says Morrison, "is a distortion of what, perhaps, we want to do." The pain in this book is the consequence of the distortion that comes from the inability to express love in a positive way.

In *Sula*, her second novel (1974), the main theme is friendship between women, the meaning of which becomes illuminated when the friendship falls apart. The indomitable Peace women, especially Eva and Sula Peace, grandmother and granddaughter, are two of the most powerful black women characters in literature. Sula, counterpart to the Biblical Ishmael, her hand against everyone, and everyone's hands against her, is an unforgettable and anomalous heroine.

In *Song of Solomon*, the fictive world shifts from that of black women in their peculiar oppression to that of a young black man in search of his identity. But Milkman Dead lives in a world in which women are the main sources of the knowledge he must gain, and Pilate Dead, his aunt, a larger-than-life character, is his guide to that understanding. *Song of Solomon* won Toni Morrison the prestigious National Book Critics Circle Award in 1977.

Tar Baby, her fourth novel, was published in 1981. The action moves from the Caribbean, to New York, to a small town in Florida.

A Sorbonne-educated, successful black model and a young black
male who rejects middle-class American values are at center stage in
a work that examines the relationships between men and women, as
well as between blacks and whites, that are possible in the conditions
of contemporary society.

Toni Morrison is a major twentieth-century black woman writer.
She is a member of the American Academy and Institute of Arts and
Letters, and an active member of the National Council on the Arts.
In addition to her position as Senior Editor at Random House, she
teaches, lectures nationally and internationally, and is a single
mother with two sons. "How do you do all of these things?" I asked
her. "Well, I really only do two things," she said. "It only looks like
many things. All of my work has to do with books. I teach books,
write books, edit books, or talk about books. It is all one thing. And
the other thing that I do is to raise my children which, as you know, I
can only do one minute at a time."

Q: In exploring black women's writings, I have a strong sense that in
the time which predates contemporary literature, black women
found ways to express their creativity in a society that did everything
to repress it and them. Alice Walker's tribute to her mother's artistry
in her flower garden is a good example of this. Paule Marshall talks
about the stories that her mother and her mother's friends told
around the kitchen table after work. Both Walker and Marshall
explain these phenomena as the sources of their own "authority" to
create. The mothers of these women could not express themselves in
the printed word, but they did in other ways, and in so doing used
their imaginative powers to confirm their identities. Are there ways in
which you feel joined to these early black women who, deliberately
denied a public voice in American society, managed anyhow to
express themselves inventively, creatively, imaginatively, and artistically?

A: Yes, I do feel a strong connection to "ancestors," so to speak.
What is uppermost in my mind as I think about this is that my life
seems to be dominated by information about black women. They
were the culture bearers, and they told us [children] what to do. But
in terms of story-telling, I remember it more as a shared activity
between the men and the women in my family. There was a comrade-

ship between men and women in the marriages of my grandparents, and of my mother and my father. The business of story-telling was a shared activity between them, and people of both genders participated in it. We, the children, were encouraged to participate in it at a very early age. This was true with my grandfather and grandmother, as well as with my father and mother, and with my uncles and aunts. There were no conflicts of gender in that area, at the level at which such are in vogue these days. My mother and my father did not fight about who was supposed to do what. Each confronted whatever crisis there was.

Q: So, within your family, women's creativity was a natural part of family life as a whole.

A: Yes. That is why the word "comrade" comes to mind in regard to the marriages I knew. I didn't find imbalance or unevenness in these relationships. I don't think that my mother's talents were hidden from males or white society, actually—they were very much on display. So I don't feel a tension there, or the struggle for dominance. The same was true for my grandparents—my mother's parents—whom I knew. I remember my great-grandmother, too. Her husband died before I was born, but I remember that when my great-grandmother walked into a room her grandsons and her nephews stood up. The women in my family were very articulate. Of course my great-grandmother could not read, but she was a midwife, and people from all over the state came to her for advice and for her to deliver babies. They came for other kinds of medical care too. Yes, I feel the authority of those women more than I do my own.

Q: If it is generally true that contemporary black women writers consistently look back to their mothers and grandmothers for the substance and authority in their voices, I suspect that this is an important and distinguishing element of black women's approach to their art. In contrast, many white women writers say that they are *inventing* the authority for their voices pretty much from scratch in an effort to break the silence of Shakespeare's sisters. Black women writers—having the example of authoritative mothers, aunts, grandmothers, great-grandmothers—have something special to contribute to the world. They have a distinctive and powerful artistic heritage. It is not white, and it is not male.

There is something else I would like to ask you. I have been

wondering if there is a deliberate line of development in your work.
How do you see your own growth and development as a successful
writer?

A: Sometimes I see connections, but that is in hindsight. I am
unaware of them at the time of writing. Still, it seems to me that from
a book that focused on a pair of very young black girls, to move to a
pair of adult black women, and then to a black man, and finally to a
black man and a black woman is evolutionary. One comes out of the
other. The writing gets better, too. The reading experience may
not, but the writing gets better. I am giving myself permission to
write books that do not depend on anyone's liking them, because
what I want to do is write better. A writer does not always write in
the ways others wish. The writer has to solve certain kinds of
problems in writing. The way in which I handle elements within a
story frame is important to me. Now I can get where I want to
go faster and with more courage than I was able to do when I began
to write.

Q: Your canvasses have gotten larger. You began with a closed
community, the community of Lorain, Ohio. Then you sent Sula out
into the world from Medallion. Milkman goes from North to South,
and Jadine and Son have the United States, Paris, and the West
Indies in which to find themselves. They participate in a very large
world.

A: I found that I had to leave the town in *Song of Solomon*
because the book was driven by men. The rhythm of their lives is
outward, adventuresome. Milkman needs to go somewhere, although
he hangs around that town for a long time—not listening to what he
hears, not paying any attention to what it is. In *Tar Baby*, I wanted to
be in a place where the characters had no access to any of the escape
routes that people have in a large city. There were no police to call.
There was no close neighbor to interfere. I wanted the characters all
together in a pressure cooker, and that had to be outside of the
United States. Of course it could have been on a remote farm, too.
But it seemed easier to isolate them in a kind of Eden within distance
of some civilization, but really outside of it. So when they find a
"nigger in the woodpile," there's nothing they can do about it. And
when they are upset because they think that he is going to rape them,
there is no place to go. Then they, the lovers, can look for a place to

live out their fantasies, in one of two places: in New York and/or in
Eloe. They alone manage to get to the United States. Everyone else
is confined to the island by Valerian who has dominion over everything there. I wanted to examine that kind of fiefdom. And I wanted
them to be in an ideal place. What makes such vacation spots ideal is
the absence of automobiles, police, airplanes, and the like. When a
crisis occurs, people do not have access to such things. The crisis
becomes a dilemma and forces the characters to do things that
otherwise would not be required of them. All the books I have
written deal with characters placed deliberately under enormous
duress in order to see of what they are made.

Q: Can you tell us something about how you handle the process of
writing? What is it like to have characters whose actions you cannot
always predict?

A: I start with an idea, and then I find characters who can manifest aspects of the idea—children, adults, men or women.

Q: Do you tell them what to do?

A: I give them a circumstance that I like and try to realize them
fully. I always know the endings. It seems clear to me that if I begin a
book with a man flying off the roof of a hospital, then somebody's
going to fly at the end, especially since the book comes out of a black
myth about a flying man. What I don't know when I begin is how the
character is going to get there. I don't know the middle.

Q: You work that through with the character?

A: Yes. I imagine the character, and if he or she is not fully
imagined, there is awkwardness. Obviously, I can force characters to
do what I want them to do, but knowing the difference between my
forcing them and things coming out of the givenness of the situation I
have imagined is part of knowing what writing is about. I feel a kind
of fretfulness when a writer has thought up a character, and then for
some reason made the character execute certain activities that are
satisfying for the author but do not seem right for the character. That
happens sometimes. Sometimes a writer imagines characters who
threaten, who are able to take the book over. To prevent that, the
writer has to exercise some kind of control. Pilate in *Song of Solomon* was that kind of character. She was a very large character and
loomed very large in the book. So I wouldn't let her say too much.

Q: In spite of keeping her from saying much, she is still very large.

A: That's because she is like something we wish existed. She represents some hope in all of us.

Q: I've wondered if Pilate is the step beyond Sula. Sula had limitations, in her inability to make the human connection. She was not able to love anyone. Pilate realizes the fullness of love in a positive way.

A: Not Sula, but Eva. Pilate is a less despotic Eva. Eva is managerial. She tells everybody what to do, and she will dispute everybody. Pilate can tell everybody what to do, but she's wide-spirited. She does not run anybody's course. She is very fierce about her children, but when she is told by her brother to leave, she leaves, and does not return. She is wider scaled and less demanding about certain things. She trusts certain things. She does behave in a protective way with her children, but that's purely maternal. That strong maternal instinct is part of her other-worldliness. Eva was this-worldly. She wanted to arrange everybody's life and did so—and was generally liked. That is the connection I see between the two women in those books.

Q: There are some issues surrounding Pilate's granddaughter, Hagar, that have been disquieting for readers. Hagar dies because Milkman rejects her, and she is unable to cope with that. Milkman goes on to fulfill the role of the transcendent character in the novel. Aren't there disturbing implications in this type of plot—the young woman dying so that the young man can learn and rise?

A: There is something here which people miss. Milkman is willing to die at the end, and the person he is willing to die for is a woman.

Q: But what of Hagar?

A: Hagar does not have what Pilate had, which was a dozen years of a nurturing, good relationship with men. Pilate had a father, and she had a brother, who loved her very much, and she could use the knowledge of that love for her life. Her daughter Reba had less of that, but she certainly has at least a perfunctory adoration or love of men which she does not put to very good use. Hagar has even less because of the absence of any relationships with men in her life. She is weaker. Her grandmother senses it. That is why Pilate gives up the wandering life. Strength of character is not something one can give another. It is not genetically transferred. Pilate can't give Hagar her genes in that sense, can't give her that strength; and Hagar does not take what she has available to her anyway. The first rejection she ever has destroys her, because she is a spoiled child.

I could write a book in which all the women were brave and wonderful, but it would bore me to death, and I think it would bore everybody else to death. Some women are weak and frail and hopeless, and some women are not. I write about both kinds, so one should not be more disturbing than the other. In the development of characters, there is value in the different effects.

Q: The men in your novels are always in motion. They are not "steady" men. Where are the stable black men?

A: But it is not true that all those men are "unsteady." Claudia's father is stable, Sidney is stable, and there are lots of stable black men in my books. On the other hand, I'm not obliged to write books about stable black men. Who is more stable than Milkman's father?

Q: But we don't admire Milkman's father.

A: Why not? The people in these novels are complex. Some are good and some are bad, but most of them are bits of both. I try to burrow as deeply as I can into characters. I don't come up with all good or all bad. I do not find men who leave their families necessarily villainous. I did not find Ajax villainous because he did not want Sula. Milkman was ignorant. That was his problem. He wanted to be comfortable, and he didn't want to go anywhere, except to chase something that was elusive, until he found out that there was something valuable to chase. It seems to me that one of the most fetching qualities of black people is the variety in which they come, and the enormous layers of lives that they live. It is a compelling thing for me because no single layer is "it." If I examine those layers, I don't come up with simple statements about fathers and husbands, such as some people want to see in the books.

There is always something more interesting at stake than a clear resolution in a novel. I'm interested in survival—who survives and who does not, and why—and I would like to chart a course that suggests where the dangers are and where the safety might be. I do not want to bow out with easy answers to complex questions. It's the complexity of how people behave under duress that is of interest to me—the qualities they show at the end of an event when their backs are up against the wall. The important thing about Hagar's death is the response to it—how Pilate deals with the fact of it—how Milkman

in his journey caused real grief. One can't do what he did and not
cause enormous amounts of pain. It was carelessness that caused
that girl pain. He has taken her life. He will always regret that, and
there is nothing he can do about it. That generally is the way it is—
there is nothing that you can do about it except do better, and don't
do *that* again. He was not in a position to do anything about it
because he was stupid. When he learns something about love, it is
from a strange woman in another part of the country. And he does
not repeat the first mistake. When he goes South with Pilate he is
ready to do something else. That is the thrust of it all. A woman once
got very angry with me because Pilate died. She was very incensed
about it. I told her that first, it was of no value to have Guitar kill
someone nobody cared anything about. If that had been the case it
would not show us how violent violence is. Some character that we
care about had to be killed to demonstrate that. And second, Pilate is
larger than life and never really dies in that sense. She was not born,
anyway—she gave birth to herself. So the question of her birth and
death is irrelevant.

Q: Can you say something about Milkman's relationship to Pilate?

A: Milkman's hope, almost a conviction, has to be that he can be
like her.

Q: One of the things that I observe about your novels is that no
one who reads them ever seems to forget them. When the reading is
done, one is not through with the book. The themes are haunting;
they do not go away.

A: I am very happy to hear that my books haunt. That is what I
work very hard for, and for me it is an achievement when they haunt
readers, as you say. That is important because I think it is a corol-
lary, or a parallel, or an outgrowth of what the oral tradition was,
which is what we were talking about earlier in relationship to the
people around the table. The point was to tell the same story again
and again. I can change it if I contribute to it when I tell it. I can
emphasize special things. People who are listening comment on it and
make it up, too, as it goes along. In the same way when a preacher
delivers a sermon he really expects his congregation to listen, participate, approve, disapprove, and interject almost as much as he does.
Eventually, I think, if the life of the novels is long, then the readers

who wish to read my books will know that it is not I who do it, it
is they who do.

Q: Do what?

A: Who kill off, or feel the laughs, or feel the satisfactions or the
triumphs. I manipulate. When I'm good at it, it is not heavy-handed.
But I want a very strong visceral and emotional response as well as a
very clear intellectual response, and the haunting that you describe is
testimony to that.

Q: Your concern is to touch the sensibilities of your readers.

A: I don't want to give my readers something to swallow. I want to
give them something to feel and think about, and I hope that I set it
up in such a way that it is a legitimate thing, and a valuable thing.

I think there is a serious question about black male and black
female relationships in the twentieth century. I just think that the
argument has always turned on something it should not turn on:
gender. I think that the conflict of genders is a cultural illness. Many
of the problems modern couples have are caused not so much by
conflicting gender roles as by the other "differences" the culture
offers. That is what the conflicts in *Tar Baby* are all about. Jadine and
Son had no problems as far as men and women are concerned. They
knew exactly what to do. But they had a problem about what work to
do, when and where to do it, and where to live. Those things hinged
on what they felt about who they were, and what their responsibilities were in being black. The question for each was whether he or she
was really a member of the tribe. It was not because he was a man
and she was a woman that conflict arose between them. Her problems as a woman were easily solved. She solved them in Paris.

Q: But in Paris she was not happy either?

A: Because of her *blackness!* It is when she sees the woman in
yellow that she begins to feel inauthentic. That is what she runs away
from.

Q: Is that woman the roots—the past?

A: The time is not important. It is that she is a real, a complete
individual who owns herself—another kind of Pilate. There is always
someone who has no peer, who does not have to become anybody.
Someone who already "is."

Q: She walks in and out of the novel without saying a word, yet
she leaves such a powerful impact behind her!

A: Such people do. The genuine article only has to appear for a moment to become memorable. It would be anticlimactic to have a conversation with her, because that person is invested with all the hopes and views of the person who observes her. She is the original self—the self that we betray when we lie, the one that is always there. And whatever that self looks like—if one ever sees that thing, or that image—one measures one's other self against it. So that with all of the good luck, and the good fortune, and the skill that Jadine has—the other is the authentic self. And as for Son, he has a similar loss. He loved Eloe, and he loved all those people, but he wasn't there. Eloe is the kind of thing that one takes when one leaves, and harbors it in the heart.

Q: Later, when he looks at the pictures, Jadine destroys it for him.

A: Maybe it wasn't real anyway. If it were, she could not destroy it with a camera. He did not live in that world either. Maybe there was just a little bit of fraud in his thinking as he did since he was away. So you can't really trust all that he says.

Q: One of the things that this conversation with you seems to emphasize is that it is wrong to see your characters in any kind of limited symbolic way. But even so, I've been wondering if Son represents black culture, the black community that seems lost to our modern way of life.

A: He represents some aspects of it. But it is the combinations in characters that are the best part of writing novels—the combinations of virtue and flaw, of good intentions gone awry, of wickedness cleansed and people made whole again. If you judge them all by the best that they have done, they are wonderful. If you judge them all by the worst that they have done, they are terrible. I like the relationship between Sidney and Ondine. He is, in the jargon of the seventies, a good old Uncle Tom. But I feel enormous respect for him. He is a man who loved work well done. He is not befuddled and confused about who he is. And when all the world seems as though it is horrible, he takes over. He does not want to do so, but if Valerian is not going to run things, he will. There is the touching and tenderness between him and his wife. They have an abiding trust in one another. There is Ondine's sorrow for having sacrificed her whole life for this child, Jadine, and still she has not given her the one thing she needed most: the knowledge of how to be a daughter. I liked Sidney's willingness to blow Son's head off if he behaved badly. These people do not respect bad behavior, no matter where it comes from. And they are different from Son. The fact that he does not like them does not mean that I do not.

Q: Sidney is a "Philadelphia Negro." Do you love all of your characters?

A: Always!

Q: Do you identify with any one of them?

A: No, that would not be a good position to take.

Q: Would such a position create a problem for you in writing?

A: Yes. I love them and I cherish them, and I love their company as long as I am with them. The point is to try to see the world from their eyes, and I think that is probably what causes readers some dismay. I like to do what I think actors do on stage. My work is to become those characters in a limited way, to see what they see, not what I see. I need to see how they see the world. Each one speaks his or her own language, has an individual set of metaphors, and notices certain things differently from other people. If I have a scene such as the one in which Nel and Sula are talking [when Nel visits the sick Sula], I let them talk, but they may not be talking to each other. Each has something else on her mind. That is part of the excitement of being incarnate, as it were, in the flesh. We have to learn more about the other person. Sometimes we have perfect conversations, as with Sidney and Ondine. They don't have to feed each other whole sentences. But sometimes people need whole paragraphs of arguments, as Son and Jadine do, in order to explain themselves, except when they are doing something specific. They don't need to talk about lust. There are differences in the way people talk to each other when they are hanging on some sort of hook, and they are trying to touch and to reach. But what prevents them from achieving that is all the baggage that they bring with them through life. We have to understand that. And there are revelations that take place. The characters have revelations, large or small, which might not have happened but for the preceding information in the book.

Q: What happens to your characters under such circumstances?

A: They learn something. Nel pursues something at the end that she did not know before. So does Milkman. So does Jadine. So does the narrator of *The Bluest Eye*. And in most of these circumstances

there is a press towards knowledge, at the expense of happiness
perhaps.

Q: Is Jadine ever going to know who she is?

A: I hope so. She has a good shot at it a good chance. Now she
knows something that she did not know before. She may know why
she was running away. And maybe, the biggest thing that she can
learn, even if she never gets back to Son, is that dreams of safety are
childish.

Q: Can you tell me why you ended *Tar Baby* with "lickety-split"?

A: I wanted it to have the sound of the Tar Baby story, which is
lickety-split towards or away from or around the briar patch. But I
also wanted to suggest that this journey is Son's choice—although he
did not think it up. Thérèse did. He said he had no choice, so she
manipulated his trip so that he had a choice. On his way back to
Valerian's house in order to get the address so he can find Jadine,
there is a strong possibility that he joins or is captured by the
horsemen—captured by the past, by the wish, by the prehistoric
times. The suggestion in the end, when the trees step back to make
way for a certain kind of man, is that Nature is urging him to join
them. First he crawls, then he stands up, he stumbles, then he walks,
and last, he runs, and his run is lickety-split, lickety-split, which has
a movement of some confidence, and also suggests the beat of a
rabbit running.

Q: And he is surrounded by water and darkness.

A: There is a birth in the beginning of the book. Close to the
opening of the book, Son is going towards the island through the
water. In the last part of the book he is doing the same thing, going
towards the island through the water. Neither of these sections has a
chapter head—they are parentheses around the book. In the first
one, the suggestion was birth because the water pushes and urges
him away from the shore, and there is the ammonia-scented air. He
comes out of it as from a womb. In the last part there is a similar
kind of birth, except that this time he is being urged by the water to
go ashore. This time he stands up and runs, and there is cooperation
with the land and the fog.

Q: Is there anything that you would like especially to add to the
things that you have already said today?

A: Everything I really have to say is in my books. I can clarify and

illuminate some small things. Critics of my work have often left
something to be desired, in my mind, because they don't always
evolve out of the culture, the world, the given quality out of which I
write. Other kinds of structures are imposed on my works, and
therefore they are either praised or dismissed on the basis of something that I have no interest in whatever, which is writing a novel
according to some structure that comes out of a different culture. I
am trying very hard to use the characteristics of the art form that I
know best, and to succeed or fail on those criteria rather than on
some other criteria. I tend not to explain things very much, but I long
for a critic who will know what I mean when I say "church," or
"community," or when I say "ancestor," or "chorus." Because my
books come out of those things and represent how they function in
the black cosmology. Sula's return to Medallion can be seen as a
defeat for her in the eyes of some critics, because they assume that
the individual, alone and isolated, making his or her way, is a triumphant thing. With black people, her return may be seen as a triumph
and not a defeat, because she comes back to where she was at the
beginning. As much of a pariah as she is in that village, she is
nevertheless protected there as she would not be elsewhere. I am
yearning for someone to see such things—to see what the structures
are, what the moorings are, where the anchors are that support my
writings.

Q: I think I understand what you mean. Black writers and black
critics share similar frustrations in this area. There is a tension
between what comes from inside of the critic (that which is a function of black culture) and what comes from outside of him or her
(that which has been imposed on the individual by the larger world).
At the beginning of this conversation I noted that black writers ply
their trade out of a multiplicity of intersecting traditions. All of black
life in Western culture shares in this, and sometimes I like to believe
that it is the richness that derives from this conglomeration that
makes black people special. There is joy and there is pain; there are
successes and failures; but always there is tension, a tension that is
the struggle for integrity.

A: I am always aware of those tensions. It is as easy to explain as
saying that if I am going to do the work that I do, I can't do it on my
home street. I live in and among people who may misunderstand

me completely. Also, one's grades are given on other people's scales. So it is always a balancing act. My plea is for some pioneering work to be done in literary criticism, not just for my work, but for all sorts of people's work, and now that the literature exists, there can be that kind of criticism. Our—black women's—job is a particularly complex one in that regard. But if we can't do it, then nobody can do it. We have no systematic mode of criticism that has yet evolved from us, but it will. I am not *like* James Joyce; I am not *like* Thomas Hardy; I am not *like* Faulkner. I am not *like* in that sense. I do not have objections to being compared to such extraordinarily gifted and facile writers, but it does leave me sort of hanging there when I know that my effort is to be *like* something that has probably only been fully expressed perhaps in music, or in some other culture-gen that survives almost in isolation because the community manages to hold on to it. Sometimes I can reflect something of this kind in my novels. Writing novels is a way to encompass this—this something.

Q: You are looking for a special relationship between the literature and the criticism of black writers—a relationship that will enable the literature to be heard as it really is—a criticism that will illuminate whatever story black people have to tell from its inside.

A: Black people have a story, and that story has to be heard. There was an articulate literature before there was print. There were griots. They memorized it. People heard it. It is important that there is sound in my books—that you can hear it, that I can hear it. So I am inclined not to use adverbs, not because I am trying to write a play, but because I want to try to give the dialogue a certain sound.

Q: It is not difficult to detect that sound.

A: Yes, you hear that. What you hear is what you remember. That oral quality is deliberate. It is not unique to my writing, but it is a deliberate sound that I try to catch. The way black people talk is not so much the use of non-standard grammar as it is the manipulation of metaphor. The fact is that the stories look as though they come from people who are not even authors. No author tells these stories. They are just told—meanderingly—as though they are going in several directions at the same time. I had to divide my books into chapters because I had to do something in order for people to recognize and understand what I was doing. But they don't necessarily have to have that form. I am not experimental, I am simply trying to recreate something out of an old art form in my books—the something that defines what makes a book "black." And that has nothing to do with whether the people in the books are black or not. The open-ended quality that is sometimes a problematic in the novel form reminds me of the uses to which stories are put in the black community. The stories are constantly being retold, constantly being imagined within a framework. And I hook into this like a life-support system, which for me, is the thing out of which I come. It is an easy job to write stories with black people in them. I look beyond the people to see what makes black literature different. And in doing this my own style has evolved. It is not the only style, but it is a style by which I recognize my own work. Another writer, another black writer, such as Toni Cade Bambara, has another style. She has a very clear style, and there is no question that it is black. She could write about anything—birds, stamps—it would still sound that way. Gayl Jones has another style. So it is not a question of *a* black style, but it is a question of recognizing the variety of styles, and hanging on to whatever that ineffable quality is that is curiously black. The only analogy that I have for it is in music. John Coltrane does not sound like Louis Armstrong, and no one ever confuses one for the other, and no one questions if they are black. That is what I am trying to get at, but I don't have the vocabulary to explain it better. It can be copied, just like the music can be copied. But once one has it, it is distinguishable and therefore recognizable for itself. If it is written, it can be learned—but to be learned, it has to be in print.

I also want my work to capture the vast imagination of black people. That is, I want my books to reflect the imaginative combination of the real world, the very practical, shrewd, day to day functioning that black people must do, while at the same time they encompass some great supernatural element. We know that it does not bother them one bit to do something practical and have visions at the same time. So all the parts of living are on an equal footing. Birds talk and butterflies cry, and it is not surprising or upsetting to them. These things make the world larger for them. Some young people don't want to acknowledge this as a way of life. They don't want to hark back to those embarrassing days when we were associated with "haints" and superstitions. They want to get as far as possible into

the scientific world. It makes me wonder, in such cases, if the
knowledge we ignore is discredited because we have discredited it.

Q: Speaking of knowledge, what do you think about the special
kind of knowledge that black women have always had, and how do
you think that is seen in the world?

A: Much of that knowledge is also discredited, and I think it is
because people say it is no more than what women say to each other.
It is called old wives' tales, or gossip, or anything but information.
In the same way, friendship between women is not a suitable topic
for a book. Hamlet can have a friend, and Achilles can have one, but
women don't, because the world knows that women don't choose
each other's acquaintanceship. They choose men first, then women
as second choice. But I have made women the focal point of books in
order to find out what women's friendships are really all about. And
the same thing is true about why I wrote *Song of Solomon* the way I
did. I chose the man to make that journey because I thought he had
more to learn than a woman would have. I started with a man, and I
was amazed at how little men taught one another in the book. I
assumed that all men ever learn about being men they get from other
men. So that the presence of Pilate, and the impact that all the other
women had on Milkman's life, came as a bit of a surprise to me.
But it made it work out right, because there were two sets of information he needed to learn in order to become a complete human being.

Q: He learns one set of information from Guitar, and he learns
another set of information from Pilate, so there is a balance between
what he learns from a man and what he learns from a woman.

A: And that kind of harmony is what makes it possible for him to
do what he does toward the end of the book, and to do something
important instead of figuring how he can live better and more comfortably, and easier.

Q: You have been very open with your feelings about your writings. This is a rare opportunity for me.

A: I'm a bit more open about it now than I was before, because
when I first began writing I assumed a lot of things that were not
true. Then I began to see odd things in odd places—like people
having to talk about Northrup Frye or somebody like that in order to
get through. I don't mean to say that Frye is inapplicable, just to
point out that at some point one has to move with some authority

into one's own structure. But the new structure must be well constructed, and it could not be constructed until there was a library out of which to build something.

Q: We have that now.

A: We can tell it the way it is. We have come through the worst, and we are still here. I think about what black writers do as having a quality of hunger and disturbance that never ends. Classical music satisfies and closes. Black music does not do that. Jazz always keeps you on the edge. There is no final chord. There may be a long chord, but no final chord. And it agitates you. Spirituals agitate you, no matter what they are saying about how it is all going to be. There is something underneath them that is incomplete. There is always something else that you want from the music. I want my books to be like that—because I want that feeling of something held in reserve and the sense that there is more—that you can't have it all right now.

Q: They have an idiom of their own?

A: That's right. Take Lena [Horne] or Aretha [Franklin]—they don't give you all, they only give you enough for now. Or the musicans. One always has the feeling, whether it is true or not, they may be absolutely parched, but one has the feeling that there's some more. They have the ability to make you want it, and remember the want. That is a part of what I want to put into my books. They will never fully satisfy—never fully.

Toni Morrison
Claudia Tate / 1983

From *Black Women Writers at Work*. Ed. Claudia Tate. New York: Continuum, 1983: 117–31. Copyright © 1983 by Claudia Tate. Reprinted by permission of the Continuum Publishing Company.

Toni Morrison was born Chloe Anthony Wofford in 1931 in Lorain, Ohio. She received her B.A. from Howard University and an M.A. from Cornell. She is the mother of two and is a senior editor at Random House.

Morrison's novels are characterized by meticulously crafted prose, using ordinary words to produce lustrous, lyrical phrases and to portray precise emotional perceptions. Her extraordinary characters struggle to understand aspects of the human condition: good and evil, love, friendship, beauty, ugliness, death. While her stories seem to unfold with natural ease, the reader can discern the great care Morrison has taken in constructing them.

Her first novel, *The Bluest Eye* (1969), depicts the tragic life of a young black girl, Pecola Breedlove, who wants nothing more than to be loved by her family and her school friends. She surmises that the reason she is despised and ridiculed is that she is black and, therefore, ugly. Consequently, Pecola sublimates her desire to be loved into a desire to have blue eyes and blond hair; in short, to look like Shirley Temple, who is adored by all. Unable to endure the brutality toward her frail self-image, Pecola goes quietly insane and withdraws into a fantasy world in which she is the most beloved little girl because she has the bluest eye of all.

Morrison's second novel, *Sula* (1974), is about a marvelously unconventional woman, Sula Peace, whose life becomes one of unlimited experiment. Not bound by any social codes of propriety. Sula is first thought to be simply unusual, then outrageous, and eventually evil. She becomes a pariah of her community, a measuring stick of what's evil and, ironically, inspires goodness in those around her.

The Song of Solomon (1977) traces, in an epic way, the self-discovery of Macon Dead III. Macon or "Milkman," as he is called by his friends, sets out on a journey to recover a lost treasure in his family's past, but instead of discovering wealth learns the intricate details of his ancestry. Milkman's odyssey becomes a kind of cultural epic by which black people can recall their often obscured slave heritage.

Morrison's latest novel, *Tar Baby* (1981), is about the evolution of an intimate relationship between an unlikely couple. Jade, a jet-set fashion model, falls in love with a young vagrant only to become estranged soon thereafter. He is not discouraged by their breakup but pursues her with the hope of reconciliation. Through the use of elaborate symbol, Morrison suggests that reconciliation between the black man and the black woman can only occur when they mutually understand they are both victims of racial exploitation.

Claudia Tate: How does being black and female constitute a particular perspective in your work?

Toni Morrison: When I view the world, perceive it and write about it, it's the world of black people. It's not that I won't write about white people. I just know that when I'm trying to develop the various themes I write about, the people who best manifest those themes for me are the black people whom I invent. It's not deliberate or calculated or self-consciously black, because I recognize and despise the artificial black writing some writers do. I feel them slumming among black people.

When I wrote *Sula*, I knew I was going to write a book about good and evil and about friendship. I had to figure out what kind of people would manifest this theme, would have this kind of relationship. Nel would be one kind of person; Sula would be different.

Friendship between women is special, different, and has never been depicted as the major focus of a novel before *Sula*. Nobody ever talked about friendship between women unless it was homosexual, and there is no homosexuality in *Sula*. Relationships between women were always written about as though they were subordinate to some other roles they're playing. This is not true of men. It seemed to me that black women have friends in the old-fashioned sense of the word; perhaps this isn't true just for black people, but it seemed so to me. I was half-way through the book before I realized that friendship in literary terms is a rather contemporary idea. So when I was making up people in *Sula*, it was inevitable I would focus on black women, not out of ignorance of any other kind of people, but because they are of compelling interest to me.

C.T.: Do you consciously select towns like Lorain, Ohio, as settings for your stories?

Morrison: Only *The Bluest Eye*, my first book, is set in Lorain, Ohio. In the others I was more interested in mood than in geography. I am from the Midwest so I have a special affection for it. My beginnings are always there. No matter what I write, I begin there. I may abandon this focus at some point, but for now it's the matrix for me.

Black people take their culture wherever they go. If I wrote about Maine, the black people in Maine would be very much like black people in Ohio. You can change the plate, but the menu would still be the same. The barber shop in Maine would still be the same kind of barber shop as in Ohio; there would be the same kinds of people sitting around. They cook a little bit differently, but I know what the language will be like.

C.T.: Ohio is an interesting and complex state. It has both a southern and a northern disposition. The Ohio River has historically represented freedom. Therefore, the state seems to be especially well suited for staging leaps in *The Song of Solomon* and free falls in *Sula* into freedom.

Morrison: Yes. The northern part of the state had underground railroad stations and a history of black people escaping into Canada, but the southern part of the state is as much Kentucky as there is, complete with cross burnings. Ohio is a curious juxtaposition of what was ideal in this country and what was base. It was also a Mecca for black people; they came to the mills and plants because Ohio offered the possibility of a good life, the possibility of freedom, even though there were some terrible obstacles. Ohio also offers an escape from stereotyped black settings. It is neither plantation nor ghetto.

C.T.: How do you fit writing into your life?

Morrison: Time has never really been a problem for me. I don't do much. I don't go out. I don't entertain. And I get off the telephone. Those activities demand an enormous part of what people call time. In addition, I can do two things at once. Most of the things I do, I know how to do so I don't have to concentrate on them, give them my full attention. And they don't suffer as a consequence. There's very little one does that engages the full mind for a long period of time. In a sense we all produce time. But when we compartmentalize our lives, then we complain about time. We say this is the time we do this; this is the time we do that. Then we feel we have to do things in some sort of sequence.

Writing is a process that goes on all the time. I can find myself in any place, solving some problem in the work that I am at the moment working on. I don't have to summon it. It's just a way of life, so there's never a time when I'm writing a book when it's not on my mind. I live with it. But there are times when I have to sit down and write. The difficulty comes in not having sustained periods of time— four or five hours at a clip. I have more of that now, but the trick is to get to where I want to be very fast in the writing so I can avoid three hours of frustrating, clumsy writing. . . . I have done a lot if I produce six pages during such times.

C.T.: Do you employ particular methods to summon your muse?

Morrison: When I sit down in order to write, sometimes it's there; sometimes it's not. But that doesn't bother me anymore. I tell my students there is such a thing as "writer's block," and they should respect it. You shouldn't write through it. It's blocked because it ought to be blocked, because you haven't got it right now. All the frustration and nuttiness that comes from "Oh, my God, I cannot write now" should be displaced. It's just a message to you saying, "That's right, you can't write now, so don't." We operate with deadlines, so facing the anxiety about the block has become a way of life. We get frightened about the fear. I can't write like that. If I don't have anything to say for three or four months, I just don't write. When I read a book, I can always tell if the writer has written through a block. If he or she had just waited, it would have been better or different, or a little more natural. You can see the seams.

I always know the story when I'm working on a book. That's not difficult. Anybody can think up a story. But trying to breathe life into characters, allow them space, make them people whom I care about is hard. I only have twenty-six letters of the alphabet; I don't have color or music. I must use my craft to make the reader see the colors and hear the sounds.

My stories come to me as clichés. A cliché is a cliché because it's worthwhile. Otherwise, it would have been discarded. A good cliché

can never be overwritten; it's still mysterious. The concepts of
beauty and ugliness are mysterious to me. Many people write about
them. In mulling over them, I try to get underneath them and see
what they mean, understand the impact they have on what people
do. I also write about love and death. The problem I face as a writer
is to make my stories mean something. You can have wonderful,
interesting people, a fascinating story, but it's not about anything. It
has no real substance. I can fail in any number of ways when I write,
but I want my books to always be about something that is important
to me, and the subjects that are important in the world are the same
ones that have always been important.

Critics generally don't associate black people with ideas. They see
marginal people; they just see another story about black folks. They
regard the whole thing as sociologically interesting perhaps but
very parochial. There's a notion out in the land that there are human
beings one writes about, and then there are black people or Indians
or some other marginal group. If you write about the world from that
point of view, somehow it is considered lesser. It's racist, of course.
The fact that I chose to write about black people means I've only
been stimulated to write about black people. We are people, not
aliens. We live, we love, and we die.

A woman wrote a book on women writers, and she has an apology
in the preface in which she explains why the book doesn't include
any black women writers. She says she doesn't feel qualified to
criticize their work. I think that's dishonest scholarship. I may be
wrong but I think so, and I took the trouble to tell her that. I feel
perfectly qualified to discuss Emily Dickinson, anybody for that
matter, because I assume what Jane Austen and all those people have
to say has something to do with life and being human in the world.
Why she could not figure out that the preoccupation of black characters is this as well startled me, as though our lives are so exotic that
the differences are incomprehensible.

Insensitive white people cannot deal with black writing, but then
they cannot deal with their own literature either. It's not a question
of my not liking white criticism. I don't like most black criticism
either. Most criticism by blacks only respond to the impetus of the
criticism we were all taught in college. It justifies itself by identifying
black writers with some already accepted white writer. If someone

says I write like Joyce, that's giving me a kind of credibility I find offensive. It has nothing to do with my liking Joyce. I do, but the comparison has to do with nothing out of which I write. I find such criticism dishonest because it never goes into the work on its own terms. It comes from some other place and finds content outside of the work and wholly irrelevant to it to support the work. You can hear them talking to Northrop Frye, and you can hear his response. You can also hear a novelist talking to *The New York Times* and not to me, the anonymous reader. The criticism may read well, in fact very well, but it's not about the book at hand. It's merely trying to place the book into an already established literary tradition. The critic is too frightened or too uninformed to break new ground.

C.T.: What is your responsibility as a writer to yourself and to your audience?

Morrison: I wrote *Sula* and *The Bluest Eye* because they were books I had wanted to read. No one had written them yet, so I wrote them. My audience is always the people in the book I'm writing at the time. I don't think of an external audience. You can see it when a writer is writing deliberately to educate an audience. You can feel the artifice, not the art, when the writer is getting somebody told.

C.T.: Do black men and women approach subjects differently in their works?

Morrison: I think women probably do write out of a different place. There's some difference in the ways they approach conflict, dominion, and power. I don't find the large differences between male and female writing in terms of intimacy though. But I do think black women write differently from white women. This is the most marked difference of all those combinations of black and white, male and female. It's not so much that women write differently from men, but that black women write differently from white women. Black men don't write very differently from white men.

It seems to me there's an enormous difference in the writing of black and white women. Aggression is not as new to black women as it is to white women. Black women seem able to combine the nest and the adventure. They don't see conflicts in certain areas as do white women. They are both safe harbor and ship; they are both inn and trail. We, black women, do both. We don't find these places, these roles, mutually exclusive. That's one of the differences. White women often find if they leave their husbands and go out into the world, it's an extraordinary event. If they've settled for the benefits of housewifery that preclude a career, then it's marriage *or* a career for them, not both, not *and*.

It would be interesting to do a piece on the kinds of work women do in novels written by women. What kinds of jobs they do, not just the paying jobs, but how they perceive work. When white women characters get depressed about the dishes, what do they do? It's not just a question of being in the labor force and doing domestic kinds of things; it's about how one perceives work, how it fits into one's life.

There's a male/female thing that's also different in the works of black and white women writers, and this difference is good. There's a special kind of domestic perception that has its own violence in writings by black women—not bloody violence, but violence none-theless. Love, in the Western notion, is full of possession, distortion. and corruption. It's a slaughter without the blood.

Men always want to change things, and women probably don't. I don't think it has much to do with women's powerlessness. Change could be death. You don't have to change everything. Some things should be just the way they are. Change in itself is not so important. But men see it as important. Under the guise of change and love, you destroy all sorts of things: each other, children. You move things around and put them in special places. I remember when I was in elementary school, there were all sorts of people in my class: the mentally defective, the handicapped, and us. To improve that situa-tion, the school removed all those people and put them into special classes. Perhaps they were better cared for, but they were not among us. There's an enormous amount a sighted child can learn from a blind child; but when you separate them, their learning becomes deficient. That kind of change is masculine. Women don't tend to do this. It's all done under the guise of civilization to improve things. The impetus for this kind of change is not hatred; it is doing good works.

Black people have a way of allowing things to go on the way they're going. We're not too terrified of death, not too terrified of being different, not too upset about divisions among things, people. Our interests have always been, it seems to me, on how un-alike things are rather than how alike things are. Black people always see differences before they see similarities, which means they probably cannot lump people into groups as quickly as other kinds of people can. They don't tend to say all Polish people are such and such. They look at one person in order to see what he or she is like.

So-called primitive languages always emphasize differences. You have hundreds of words for yam, but no one word for yam—hundreds of words for every variety. That's not a deficiency in the thought process; it reflects an emphasis on distinctions. It may account for why black people, generally speaking, used to have such difficulty thinking in purely racist terms.

C.T.: In *The Bluest Eye* and *Sula* there are evocative, lyrical, verbal compression and expansion. In *The Song of Solomon* there is a linear progression of language, a sense of intrigue with subsequent resolution. Does the selection of a hero as compared to a heroine place demands on the quality of your expression?

Morrison: The first two books were beginnings. I start with the childhood of a person in all the books; but in the first two, the movement, the rhythm is circular, although the circles are broken. If you go back to the beginnings, you get pushed along toward the end. This is particularly so with *The Bluest Eye*. *Sula* is more spiral than circular. *The Song of Solomon* is different. I was trying to push this novel outward; its movement is neither circular nor spiral. The image in my mind for it is that of a train picking up speed; and that image informs the language; whereas with *The Bluest Eye* and *Sula*, the rhythm is very different.

Every life to me has a rhythm, a shape—there are dips and curves as well as straightaways. You can't see the contours all at once. Some very small incident that takes place today may be *the* most important event that happens to you this year, but you don't know that when it happens. You don't know it until much later. I try to reflect this awareness in my work. In a chapter I may talk about what has already happened so the reader knows what I'm about to say has already taken place, but he or she is moving toward something they don't know yet. The best illustration is in the chapter in *Sula* where Hannah accidentally catches on fire. It starts out with what the second strange thing was, then recalls the first strange thing, so you know to expect something. A black person in particular would know, if I'm going to list strange things, to expect something dreadful.

These things are omens. If I'm talking about death, you should know
to expect it because the omens alert you. The strange things are all
omens; you don't know what's going to happen at the time the omens
occur, and you don't always recognize an omen until after the fact,
but when the bad thing does happen, you somehow expected it.
As the reader, you can take comfort in knowing whatever it is has
already happened so you don't have to be too frightened. The author
has already experienced it. It's happened; it's over. You're going to
find out about it, but it's not going to be a big surprise, even though it
might be awful. I may hurt you, but I don't want to tear the rug out
from under you. I don't want to give you total surprise. I just want
you to feel dread and to feel the awfulness without having the
language compete with the event itself. I may want to hold you in a
comfortable place, but I want you to know something awful is going
to happen, and when it does happen you won't be shattered. When it
happens, you expect it, though you did not before.

The language has to be quiet; it has to engage your participation. I
never describe characters very much. My writing expects, demands
participatory reading, and that I think is what literature is supposed
to do. It's not just about telling the story; it's about involving the
reader. The reader supplies the emotions. The reader supplies even
some of the color, some of the sound. My language has to have holes
and spaces so the reader can come into it. He or she can feel
something visceral, see something striking. Then we [you, the
reader, and I, the author] come together to make this book, to feel
this experience. It doesn't matter what happens. I tell you at the
beginning of *The Bluest Eye* on the very first page what happened,
but now I want you to go with me and look at this, so when you get
to the scene where the father rapes the daughter, which is as awful a
thing, I suppose, as can be imagined, by the time you get there, it's
almost irrelevant because I want you to *look* at him and see his love
for his daughter and his powerlessness to help her pain. By that time
his embrace, the rape, is all the gift he has left.

C.T.: Cholly [*The Bluest Eye*], Ajax [*Sula*], and Guitar [*The Song
of Solomon*] are the golden-eyed heroes. Even Sula has gold flecks in
her eyes. They are the free people, the dangerously free people.

Morrison: The salt tasters. . . . They express either an effort of the
will or a freedom of the will. It's all about choosing. Though granted

there's an enormous amount of stuff one cannot choose. But if you own yourself, you can make some type of choices, take certain kinds of risks. They do, and they're misunderstood. They are the misunderstood people in the world. There's a wildness that they have, a nice wildness. It has bad effects in society such as the one in which we live. It's pre-Christ in the best sense. It's Eve. When I see this wildness gone in a person, it's sad. This special lack of restraint, which is a part of human life and is best typified in certain black males, is of particular interest to me. It's in black men despite the reasons society says they're not supposed to have it. Everybody knows who "that man" is, and they may give him bad names and call him a "street nigger"; but when you take away the vocabulary of denigration, what you have is somebody who is fearless and who is comfortable with that fearlessness. It's not about meanness. It's a kind of self-flagellant resistance to certain kinds of control, which is fascinating. Opposed to accepted notions of progress, the lock-step life, they live in the world unreconstructed and that's it.

C.T.: Your writing seems effortless. Of course, I know tremendous work is concealed behind effortless writing. No seams show. The garment has marvelous images. Everyday details become extraordinary when flashed through your perception, your craft.

Morrison: I try to clean the language up and give words back their original meaning, not the one that's sabotaged by constant use, so that "chaste" means what it meant originally. I try to do that by constructing sentences that throw such words into relief, but not strange words, not "large" words. Most large words are imprecise. They are useful because of their imprecision. If you work every carefully, you can clean up ordinary words and repolish them, make parabolic language seem alive again.

Dialogue done properly can be heard. Somebody in London told me I seldom used adverbs in my dialogue, that I never have a character say such-and-such *loudly*. But that he always knew how something is said. When I do a first draft, it's usually very bad because my tendency is to write in the language of everyday speech, which is the language of business, media, the language we use to get through the day. If you have friends you can speak to in your own language, you keep the vocabulary alive, the nuances, the complexity, the places where language had its original power; but in order to get there, I have to rewrite, discard, and remove the print-quality of language to put back the oral quality, where intonation, volume, gesture are all there. Furthermore, the characters have to speak their own language. Novice writers, even when they get a good dialogue style, frequently have everybody talking the same way. If they didn't identify the speaker, the reader wouldn't know. You've got to be able to distinguish among your characters. Sula doesn't use the same language Eva does because they perceive things differently. If the reader feels he or she can visualize a character, in spite of the fact no one has said what the character looks like, that's it! All I have to do as a writer is *know* it in my mind. I don't have to write every piece of it. I give a few clues, some gestures . . .

I try to avoid editorializing emotional abstractions. I can't bear to read any more of those books where there is this hopeless, labored explanation of a simple thing. If you can see the person experiencing the thing, you don't need the explanation. When Eva looks at the back of the man who abandoned her, she doesn't know how she's going to feel. It all comes together when he diddy-bops down the steps, and she hears the laughter of the woman in the green dress. Her emotional clarity crystalizes at that moment. When you think of how it feels to see a man who has abandoned you, to see him after a long period of time, you can go a number of ways to convey it. You could use a lot of rhetoric, but you don't need to do any of that if you simply see it. You see a person who *is* a simile, a metaphor, a painting. A painting conveys it better because then the reader can identify with that feeling, whether or not he or she has ever experienced it. They can feel it because they see the things that person sees. It's a question of how to project character, experience from that viewpoint.

I don't use much autobiography in my writing. My life is uneventful. Writing has to do with the imagination. It's being willing to open a door or think the unthinkable, no matter how silly it may appear. When Pilate [*The Song of Solomon*] appeared without a navel, that didn't seem to make much sense to me either, so I did some casual research. Of course, everybody told me it couldn't happen because it was absurd, impossible. Just because I didn't know where I was going with it didn't stop me from seeing what use it could be to me in terms of developing the character. The fact that I thought of it at all was of interest to me. If I thought about it, it may be valuable. There are a lot of things I think about that are not valuable, but I don't discard them just because they don't "make sense." It's like the tail end of a dream. You wake up and you remember a few little pieces. Those are the pieces you can concentrate on, just the ones you remember. You don't have to worry about the part you can't remember. If the woman doesn't have a navel, then I have to think what that could mean, not just in terms of her development, her life, but in terms of the whole book. I didn't try to think of some strange thing. I was trying to draw the character of a sister to a man, a sister who was different, and part of my visualization of her included that she had no navel. Then it became an enormous thing for her. It also had to come at the beginning of the book so the reader would know to expect anything of her. It had to be a thing that was very powerful in its absence but of no consequence in its presence. It couldn't be anything grotesque, but something to set her apart, to make her literally invent herself. Of course, it has tremendous symbolic ramifications, but that wasn't uppermost in my mind. What I thought was what would happen if a person was not to have a navel, then other things became clearer.

C.T.: When did you know you were a writer?

Morrison: After I had written *Sula*. I've said I wrote *The Bluest Eye* after a period of depression, but the words "lonely, depressed, melancholy" don't really mean the obvious. They simply represent a different state. It's an unbusy state, when I am more aware of myself than of others. The best words for making that state clear to other people are those words. It's not necessarily an unhappy feeling; it's just a different one. I think now I know better what that state is. Sometimes when I'm in mourning, for example, after my father died, there's a period when I'm not fighting day-to-day battles, a period when I can't fight or don't fight, and I am very passive, like a vessel. When I'm in this state, I can hear things. As long as I'm busy doing what I should be doing, what I'm supposed to be doing, what I must do, I don't hear anything; there isn't anything there. This sensibility occurred when I was lonely or depressed or melancholy or idle or emotionally exhausted. I would think I was at my nadir, but it was then that I was in a position to hear something. Ideas can't come to me while I'm preoccupied. This is what I meant when I said I was in a state that was not busy, not productive or engaged. It happened after my father died, thus the association with depression. It happened after my divorce. It has happened other times, but not so much because I was unhappy or happy. It was that I was unengaged, and in that situation of disengagement with the day-to-day rush, something positive happened. I've never had sense enough to deliberately put myself in a situation like that before. At that time I had to be put into it. Now I know how to bring it about without going through the actual event. It's exactly what Guitar said: when you release all the shit, then you can fly.

C.T.: Do you take particular delight in the unusual character, the pariah?

Morrison: There are several levels of the pariah figure working in my writing. The black community is a pariah community. Black people are pariahs. The civilization of black people that lives apart from but in juxtaposition to other civilizations is a pariah relationship. In fact, the concept of the black in this country is almost always one of the pariah. But a community contains pariahs within it that are very useful for the conscience of that community.

When I was writing about good and evil, I really wasn't writing about them in Western terms. It was interesting to me that black people at one time seemed not to respond to evil in the ways other people did, but that they thought evil had a natural place in the universe; they did not wish to eradicate it. They just wished to protect themselves from it, maybe even to manipulate it, but they never wanted to kill it. They thought evil was just another aspect of life. The ways black people dealt with evil accounted in my mind for how they responded to a lot of other things. It's like a double-edged sword. It accounts for one of the reasons it's difficult for them to organize long-term political wars against another people. It accounts for their generosity and acceptance of all sorts of things. It's because they're not terrified by evil, by difference. Evil is not an alien force; it's just a different force. That's the evil I was describing in *Sula*.

Even when I'm talking about universal concepts, I try to see how people, such as myself, would look at these universal concepts, how they would respond to them. Our cosmology may be a little different, as each group's is, so what I want to figure out is how ours is different. How is our concept of evil unlike other peoples'? How is our rearing of children different? How are our pariahs different? A legal outlaw is not the same thing as a community outlaw. That's why I have the Deweys, Shadrack and Sula; they are all variations of the pariah. The town can accept Shadrack much easier than Sula because he's systematized. They know what to expect from him.

A woman who wrote a paper on *Sula* said she thought Sula's community was very unnurturing for her. That's very strange to me because I found that community to be very nurturing for Sula. There was no other place in the world she could have lived without being harmed. Whatever they think about Sula, however strange she is to them, however different, they won't harm her. Medallion is a sustaining environment even for a woman who is very different. Nobody's going to lynch her or call the police. They call her bad names and try to protect themselves from her evil; that's all. But they put her to very good use, which is a way of manipulating her.

C.T.: Have your works been misunderstood?

Morrison: Of course. That's all quite legitimate. Some people get things in your work you never saw. But that's all right. After all, one reads and gets what one can. Sometimes people talk about the work in a way that is closer to my own feeling, interpretation. I don't know if they're any more right than the people who see it another way. I'm sometimes disappointed that something I think is key is missed, but that's a writer's ego surfacing at that point. I always assume that if it didn't impress the reader, that it has something to do with the writing and not with the person reading it. It's my job to make it clearer, to make it dazzling. If it didn't happen, then I was too timid, too subtle, too clumsy—something was wrong. To make it happen is my job, not the reader's.

C.T.: Do you talk about your books before they're finished?

Morrison: I talk about the little I know, which is always a little risky because I might change my mind or it might change itself. I write out of ignorance. I write about the things I don't have any resolutions for, and when I'm finished, I think I know a little bit more about it. I don't write out of what I know. It's what I don't know that stimulates me. I merely know enough to get started. Writing is discovery; it's talking deep within myself, "deep talking" as you say. The publishing is rather anticlimatic, although I'm in the publishing business. I know all the wonderful things that are made possible by publishing something; but for me, on a very personal level, the publishing is really very secondary.

My students ask me when I'm going to make my books into movies. I tell them I'm not terribly interested in that because the film would not be mine. The book is my work. I don't want to write scripts; I don't want artistic "control" of a film. I don't mean that it shouldn't be done, just that I don't have to do it. What's alarming to me is the notion that the book is what you do before the film, that the final outcome is the film.

There's a difference between writing for a living and writing for life. If you write for a living, you make enormous compromises, and you might not ever be able to uncompromise yourself. If you write for life, you'll work hard; you'll do it in a disciplined fashion; you'll do what's honest, not what pays. You'll be willing to say no when somebody wants to play games with your work. You'll be willing to not sell it. You'll have a very strong sense of your work, your self-development.

C.T.: What has been the cost of success for you?

Morrison: I don't subscribe to the definition of success I think you're talking about. For me, whatever the cost is, I don't pay it. Success in those terms is a substitute for value in your life. When you say a successful life, you generally mean a life surrounded by material things. I continue to live my life pretty much as I always have, except I may live a little better now because I can make some choices I wasn't able to before. Having more money than I had a few years ago makes it possible for me to have choices and, therefore, make them. But in terms of meaningful things, relationships with other people, none of that has changed. What changes is not always the successful person; other people change.

C.T.: How do you feel when you've finished a book?

Morrison: I feel something's missing. I miss the characters, their company, the sense of possibility in them. But then I have another idea.

Some people work on several books at one time. I can never do that. So if one's not there, I feel a little lonely, as though I've lost touch, though momentarily, with some collective memory. But each time the waiting period between ideas for books grows shorter and shorter, for which I am grateful.

An Interview with Toni Morrison

Bessie W. Jones and Audrey Vinson / 1985

From *The World of Toni Morrison: Explorations in Literary Criticism* by Bessie W. Jones and Audrey Vinson. Dubuque, Iowa: Kendall Hunt, 1985: 127–51

This interview was taped on November 23, 1981, in Toni Morrison's office at Random House Publishers in New York. The questions represent the collaborative concerns of both Audrey Vinson and me. The reader recognizes each of our specific interests based on the essays which bear our signatures. The interview is the culmination of approximately a year and a half of intermittent correspondence between Miss Morrison and me. The transcript of the tape was edited by Miss Morrison and is published with her approval.

Jones: How do your own experiences growing up in Ohio compare with those in the novels? I suppose I am asking if you consider any of your novels as having autobiographical elements.

Morrison: It is difficult always for me and probably any writer to select those qualities that are genuinely autobiographical because part of what you are doing is re-doing the past as well as throwing it into relief, and what makes one write anyway is something in the past that is haunting, that is not explained or wasn't clear so that you are almost constantly rediscovering the past. I am geared toward the past, I think, because it is important to me; it is living history. I was very, very conscious of that mood and atmosphere of my hometown in the first book, *The Bluest Eye*, and used literal descriptions of neighborhoods and changed the obvious things, the names of people, and mixed things all up, but the description of the house where we lived, the description of the streets, the lake, and all of that, is very much the way I remember Lorain, Ohio, although people go there now and they don't see what I saw. And more importantly, I seem to remember some people, at that time (mind you this is with dazzling hindsight and also from the point of view of a child in which things

171

are very much exaggerated and new and fresh) seemed mysterious to
me and their mystery and their eccentricities were fascinating to me.
And because we were unexamined at that time—Black people were
unexamined and unstudied, at least it appeared so (laughter) to
me, nobody was paying us too much attention in a scholarly sense.
There were no social workers, you know, none of that, so what
we did was unaffected and was not posed. There was enormous
oppression but within that oppressive structure there was an incredible amount of freedom. That is reflected in *The Bluest Eye* and
many of the others as well as my sense of not—even though I never
lived in a Black neighborhood in Lorain, Ohio, because there weren't
any, at that time—it was too small, too poor, to have officially racist
structures. Our family's social life was very much confined to what
we were doing but, you know, the schools, and stores and so on, and
our next door neighbors were white people. There were always
some on the block, or I guess they say there were always some of us
on the block. So I grew up with Black and white children. However,
and it's still astonishing to me, in spite of that proximity white people
did not seem to appear very much in the life of the spirit or the mind.
Which is a way of saying that there were two sorts of education that
were going on—a school education, and another education, and the
one that stuck was the one that was not in the school. Whatever my
people said, that was the real life, subverted, I think, for a lot of
my life when I left home. But you realize that whenever you get in a
crisis situation that's where you go for help. So the philosophy is as
accurate, the mood is as accurate as I can remember it, and some of
it I don't remember. It is sort of like, I don't know, a racial recollec-
tion that I just have to trust even though I cannot claim to know it all.
I did use my sister. I have an older sister, but our relationship was
not at all like the girls in *The Bluest Eye*. But there are scenes in *The
Bluest Eye* that are bits and pieces—my father, he could be very
aggressive about people who troubled us—throwing people out and
so on, my mother's habit of getting stuck like a record on some
problem, going on for days and days and days and then singing in
between, you know, just like a saga. You wake up every morning and
she has had another chapter of the same problem. (Laughter) And,
you know, that curious 30's Depression atmosphere—that was very
much there. The rest is fiction. Once the characters are there and

they begin to be fully realized and have their own voices, then they really begin to move. They are not at all concerned about facts. And it's less and less true in each successive book. I think most first novels are pretty autobiographical in some way because you are frightened to pull from too many places. Later on I was able to use only the odors or the sounds or the smells of the things I needed. But they are curious places. I knew of a woman named Hannah Peace, for example. I didn't know her well. I just remembered the name and remembered vaguely seeing her, and what I most remembered was the way there was a kind of echo when people called her name. I have no idea of anything about that lady—nothing really. But I seem to remember that when other people said her name they were saying something else, and I don't know what that was, but I don't really want to know. I just want the taste of it. So that's the kind of thing that's, you know, sort of genuinely autobiographical.

Jones: I am concerned also about your ties with your Alabama past. Is that through your mother exclusively or do you go back yourself? Do you make that pilgrimage at any time?

Morrison: No—I've been back more frequently than she has. She talks about it with affection, but she never goes. My father used to go back to Georgia every year, but although she remembers it with a great deal of pleasure, she never goes there. There is a huge wing of our family who lived in Greenville and then in Birmingham, and that portion of them that didn't come to Ohio went out to California, and I only recently met some of them whom I had only heard stories about. The song in *Song of Solomon* is a song from that wing of the family in Alabama. The song that my mother and aunts know starts out, "Green, the only son of Solomon." And then there are some funny words that I don't understand. It's a long sort of a children's song that I don't remember. But Green was the name of my grandfather's first son and it was a kind of genealogy that they were singing about. So I altered the words for *Song of Solomon*. Those people were born in Greenville.

Jones: At what time in your life did you form specific judgments about the value of being Black?

Morrison: I came to that as a clear statement very late in life, I think, because I left home, say at 17 and went to school, and the things I studied were Western and, you know, I was terrifically

fascinated with all of that, and at that time any information that came
to me from my own people seemed to me to be backwoodsy and
uninformed. You know, they hadn't read all these wonderful books.
You know how college students are. And, I think, I didn't regard it as
valuable as being Black. I regarded it as valuable as being part of
that family because it was an interesting collection of people who had
done some rather extraordinary things. I don't mean publicly successful things but, you know, just the way in which they handled
crisis situations and life threatening circumstances, so that when I
found myself in critical circumstances I literally remembered those
people and I thought, "Well, if they could do that, I can do this." It
was just that intimate to me. But the consciousness of being Black
I think happened when I left Cornell and went to teach at Texas
Southern University. You see, I had never been in a Black school like
that. I don't mean my awareness was all that intense, but even at
Howard University where I went to school, I remember I asked once
to do a paper in the English Department on Black Characters in
Shakespeare, and they were very much alarmed by that—horrified by
it, thought it was a sort of lesser topic, because Howard wasn't really
like that. It was very sort of middle class, sort of upwardly mobile
and so on. But when I left Cornell and went to Houston, even though
I was only there a year and a half, in the South they always had
Negro History Week; I'd never heard of it. We didn't have it in the
North. (Laughter) But then I began to think about all those books my
mother always had in the house—J. A. Rodgers and all those people—and all those incredible conversations my grandfather had and
all those arguments that would just hurt my head when I listened
to them at the time suddenly had a different meaning. There was a
difference between reading the *Call* and *Post* when it came or the
Pittsburgh Courier and all the Black papers and then going someplace when there was something called the Black press. So I think it
was as a novice teacher, and that was in 1957 or 1958, that I began to
think about Black culture as a subject, as an idea, as a discipline.
Before it had only been on a very personal level—my family. And I
thought they were the way they were because they were my family.

  Jones: In what ways did your college teaching experience enhance
or deter your creative writing?

  Morrison: It deterred it a great deal. (Laughter) I don't think that's the fault of teaching. Some people can teach and write at the same time, write fiction or poetry and do both. I can't do it well; even when I take small jobs it bothers me, only because the mode of thinking is so different. It is analytical. It is taking something apart and examining it, and when I write I am trying to put things together. Also I have to trust something that is ineffable when I write, whereas when I teach I don't trust anything, you know. I try to find out things and I need proof. When I write there is a different side of the brain or a different part of me that's being used, and I find that conflicting. I don't find editing conflicting at all, but I do find teaching because the mode is so different from the mode that I have to be in when I write a novel. So teaching is not helpful to me.

Jones: What kind of writing schedule do you follow? Do you write everyday.

Morrison: If I'm going well, I do. If I'm not going well, I skip it. I don't write just because I have the time. I write when it's there and then I have to make the time because I find if I have a block of time in order to write and I haven't resolved anything or nothing has come, it's a real waste of time. I just write stuff I have to throw away. So I am a little more compulsive about it, I think, and less disciplined. I operate on compulsion.

Jones: I am fascinated by your effective use of irony as an artistic technique. Would you please comment on why you use irony so profusely?

Morrison: I think that's a Black style. I can't really explain what makes the irony of Black people different from anybody else's, and maybe there isn't any, but in trying to write what I call Black literature which is not merely having Black people in or being Black myself, there seems to be something distinctive about it and I can't put it into critical terms. I can simply recognize it as authentic. Any irony is the mainstay. Other people call it humor. It's not really that. It's not sort of laughing away one's troubles. And laughter itself for Black people has nothing to do with what's funny at all. And taking that which is peripheral, or violent or doomed or something that nobody else can see any value in and making value out of it or having a psychological attitude about duress is part of what made us stay alive and fairly coherent, and irony is a part of that—being able to see the underside of something, as well. I can't think at the moment of any specific instances, but I am conscious of all sorts of things—nature and magic and a kind of mother wit as well as a certain kind of cosmology about how Black people during that time apprehended life simply because they didn't trust anybody else's version of it. That's why I can't trust much research when I do novels because most of the information I want is not written. I mean I can't go to most history books. I can go to some now, I suppose, but certain kinds of things I have to either remember them or be reminded of them or something. It's an area of risk that a writer takes.

Jones: I detect many Greek tragic patterns in your novels, especially in *Song of Solomon*. Do you see any relationship between Greek tragedy and the Black experience?

Morrison: Well, I do. I used to be a little confused about it, and I thought it was just because I was a Classics minor that it was important to me. But there was something about the Greek chorus, for example, that reminds me of what goes on in Black churches and in jazz where there are two things. You have a response obviously. The chorus being the community who participates in this behavior and is shocked by it or horrified by it or they like or they support it. Everybody is in it. And it has something also to do with the way in which those stories are told because the reader becomes a participant in the books, and I have to make it possible for the reader to respond the way I would like the chorus to in addition to the choral effects in the book itself. In the last book I wrote I was deliberately trying to make a choral witness out of the whole world of nature so that butterflies say stuff and, you know, the characters were watched by all that there was. Natural phenomena not only commented on actions, they did so with passion. They had opinions about events but they didn't precipitate any action, yet they were very much involved. And the same sort of participation in churches and even when we were sitting around telling stories, the stories were never the property of the teller. They were community property or they were family property and anybody could elaborate on them or change them or retell them. You heard them over and over again. And there was some quality in them that was stark. There was probably also catharsis in the sense of a combination of the restoration of order—order is restored at the end—and the character having a glimmering of some knowledge that he didn't have when the book began. So everybody complains, well, not everybody, but a lot of people complain about my endings, because it looks like they are falling apart. But something important has happened; some knowledge is there—the Greek knowledge—what is the epiphany in Greek tragedy. But in addition to that, it's community oriented, all of this because the door is open. I don't shut doors at the end of books. There is a resolution of a sort but there are always possibilities—choices, just knowing what those choices are or being able to make a commitment about those choices or knowing something that you would never have known had you not have had that experience—meaning the book. You know, whatever that character knows at the end about herself and her friend could not have happened, whatever Nel knows finally about her relationship with Sula, could not have been clear without the experience of the book. Theirs is a very peculiar relationship. Nel discovered what a friend is—someone you really don't have to explain anything to. And Milkman at the end of *Song of Solomon* being so overwhelmed and so strong and so full of courage and affection that he is ready to die. So it shouldn't matter whether he dies, so long as he is ready and can. And at the end of *Tar Baby* I wanted the choice to be there, where it's possible for him to make a choice and only to hint at the choice that he makes because the deed is done. It can't be undone. And in that sense it is Greek in the sense that the best you can hope for is some realization and that, you know, a certain amount of suffering is not just anxiety. It's also information.

Jones: It's interesting how you are anticipating my next question. My next question is all of your novels have characters who are driven by strong moral forces. Does this have anything to do with your own moral vision? Your religious convictions, maybe?

Morrison: Oh well, I have difficulties with institutions always. But I don't have any doubts—religious doubts, and I find that at the bottom line, striving toward that kind of perfection is more interesting, more compelling. The effort to be good is just more interesting, more demanding. And I don't trust any judgment that I make that does not turn on a moral axis. I can't keep it up all the time, but that is the compelling force. I am prepared to do without if it doesn't sit well. Now, I have a family of people who were highly religious—that was part of their language. Their sources were biblical. They expressed themselves in that fashion. They took it all very, very seriously, so it would be very difficult for me not to. But they combined it with another kind of relationship, to something I think which was outside the Bible. They did not limit themselves to understanding the world *only* through Christian theology. I mean they were quite willing to remember visions, and signs, and premonitions and all of that. But that there was something larger and coherent, and benevolent was always a part of what I was taught and certainly a part of what I believe.

Jones: I consider *Tar Baby* to be a moral allegory. Is this a valid interpretation? Would you want to comment?

Morrison: It has allegorical characteristics in the sense that one watches the characters get in trouble and try to get out, and they do represent certain poles, and certain kinds of thought, and certain kinds of states of being, and they are in conflict with each other, struggling for sovereignty or some sort of primacy. And there are lessons in that sense, in the sense that if you do the following things this will happen. It's true of some of the other books, not the first two so much but certainly *Song of Solomon*. If you believe that property is more important than earth, this is what you are like—you are like Macon Dead. If you believe that earth is more valuable than property, you are like Pilate. If you believe that the revolution means some action, some violent action, and you follow that all the way through, if killing is part of it, this is the logical consequence of it. You can become just a killer, a torpedo, with the best intentions in the world. In *Tar Baby*, if your values are like Jadine's, very contemporary, then you lose something if the past is anathema to you. On the other hand, if you are like Son and you are only concerned about the past, and you can't accommodate yourself to anything contemporary, you lose also. Most satisfactory evolutions of relationships with people have some sort of balance. These people are extremes, making some attempt to accommodate, but they cannot, so that there is some danger in that. I don't know. I may have some attitude about which one is more right than the other, but in a funny sense that book was very unsettling to me because everybody was sort of wrong. (Laughter) Some more wrong than others. And, you know, you sometimes want A to win or B to win and sometimes I didn't like anybody in there some of the time and everybody most of the time. If you say you are somebody's friend as in *Sula*, now what does that mean? What are the lines that you do not step across? And maybe this is the final thing, the final stroke. My efforts is to look at archetypes.

Jones: I would like to move to influences. Who are the novelists who you feel have had the greatest influence on your writing and in what way or ways?

Morrison: I can't think of one novelist that I could say that about. It doesn't mean that I haven't been overwhelmed by lots of writers. I suppose there is one writer, although I've never—it's not even the writing, but Camara Laye wrote a book called the *Radiance of the King* and that had an enormous effect on me. I cannot spot any of that in my writing because I don't know anybody who really writes the way I do and whose style I like that much to incorporate. It's the kind of job that only somebody else could do. I couldn't comment on those influences.

Jones: Your novels are very rhapsodic in style. What is your musical background?

Morrison: None. I mean I can't play any musical instruments and I can't sing, but my mother and my aunts play and sing all the time. They don't read music. My mother sings all the time. So, you know, I heard it all the time.

Jones: Do you write poetry?

Morrison: No, I don't.

Jones: Your explicit imagery often conceals a wealth of implicit ideas. In this sense your novels are quite poetic. Do you consider this a stylistic device?

Morrison: Oh yes, the image, the pictures, for me—it's what holds it. I can't move along in a chapter or part unless I can see the single thing that makes it clear—almost like a painting. As a matter of fact, in regard to your question about influences, I always think I am much more influenced by painters in my writing than by novelists. I can feel direct influences of painters. I can't feel them in novelists that I have read. I think the language of Black people is just so full of metaphor and imagery—the way they talk is very concrete, is bright, and has a lots of color in it; has pictures. It's heavily loaded graphic-graphic. In addition to its sound, it has its sight—those two things.

So it certainly has to sound a certain way, but it has to provoke a certain picture, so that if somebody says, "Oh what harm did I ever do you on my knees?" the "on my knees" is not necessary. "What did I ever do but pray for you. What harm have I ever done you on my knees?" The "on my knees" is the picture. She could have been content with just saying "pray for you," but that was not enough. She wants to impress upon him how it looks to be on her knees praying, you see. Or Milkman coming into the town, and I want to say that this is a little country town, but instead of going on for five or six pages I had to see something there that would say that which is a poetic device. So if I have the women walking down the road with nothing in their hands on their way somewhere, then one knows what kind of village that is. You don't do that in the city. You walk around New York without a purse you might get arrested. People'll think you are running from something. Or peacocks, or the birds dying, you know, all of that is palpable—palpable descriptions that not only can I see them and I hope the reader can see them but from what I choose the meaning behind that vision is that nature is askew, or something is coming together, or something terrible is about to happen. You know, whether it's the thing over Sula's eyes which doesn't define her so much as other people because other people have to get themselves together in her presence because she is not helpful in any way; so that they see in her what they wish to see not only in her birthmark but in her because she was wanton, experimental, genuinely dangerous, morally dangerous person.

Jones: Grotesque elements are evident in all of your novels. Why did the grotesque occur to you as an appropriate vehicle for demonstrating the experiences of your characters?

Morrison: Well, I think my goal is to see really and truly of what these people are made, and I put them in situations of great duress and pain, you know, I "call their hand." And, then when I see them in life threatening circumstances or see their hands called, then I know who they are. And some of the situations are grotesque. These are not your normal everyday lives. They are not my normal everyday life, probably not many people's. It's not that I deny that part of life in life. It just doesn't produce anything for me. If I see a person on his way to work everyday doing what he is supposed to do— taking care of his children, then I know that. But what if something really terrible happens, can you still—so that it is always a push towards the abyss somewhere to see what is remarkable, because that's the way I find out what is heroic. That's the way I know why such people survive, who went under, who didn't, what the civilization was, because quiet as it's kept much of our business, our existence here, has been grotesque. It really has. The fact that we are a stable people making an enormous contribution in whatever way to the society is remarkable because all you have to do is scratch the surface, I don't mean us as individuals but as a race, and there is something quite astonishing there and that's what peaks my curiosity. I do not write books about everyday people. They really are extraordinary whether it's wicked, or stupid or wonderful or what have you. That may go back to the other question about using models from Greek tragedy which seems to me extremely sympathetic to Black culture and in some ways to African culture.

Jones: The legitimacy of the irrational seems to be the reverse of the more rational "norm" in your novels. Would you comment on this?

Morrison: Yes, with a race of people who were perceived as irrational simply because they did not always see the world as white people did, they were regarded as irrational (laughter), but they weren't. You know, their experience simply dictated certain things. They don't seem irrational to me. They seem extreme and maybe excessive. But for most of them, there is a kind of wonderful logic to what they do. And their conclusions may appear to be irrational. If you think of the thought processes that Pilate has, the way she arrived at where she was, with the limited information she had and some good common sense, she got to that place which is a wonderful place to be. She is one of the two or three people that I've written about that I envy. You know, a certain amount of wide-spiritedness and so on. Although I can't recommend that anybody choose that life style, it has got to be based on some legitimate information and a careful analysis without benefit of the traditional kind of education that teaches us what the rational is. That's what distinguishes the colonized from the colonists, viewing what is rational and what is not.

Jones: How important are outrage and anarchy in the attempts of your characters to gain or regain their natural heritage?

Morrison: For some of them, very important. That's the way they do it—like Son. For others its anathema like Macon Dead, and Jadine, and Sydney and Ondine. They don't like that. They are proud people and they take pride in their labor. They like to do things well. They have that sort of elegant way of handling things and they've made their peace with that and they know how to get on in the world step by step, by step, by step, by step. They play with the house cards, and they are not like those people who are not playing with the house deck. They are out to change it, fix it, ignore it, cut off their noses, in many instances to spite their own faces. They're just not going to do it. Many men who are outlaws, not so much contemporary type outlaws but the outlaws that I knew in my youth (laughter), were just those kinds of people. They were, oh, I don't know, episodic; they were adventurers. They felt that they had been dealt a bad hand, and they just made up other rules. They couldn't win with the house deck and that was a part of their daring. So they looked at and that was solution to them, whereas other Black people—they were horrified by all that "bad" behavior. That's all a part of the range of what goes on among us, you know. And until we understand in our own terms what our rites of passage are, what we need in order to nourish ourselves, what happens when we don't get that nourishment, then what looks like erratic behavior but isn't will frighten and confuse us. Life becomes comprehensible when we know what rules we are playing by.

Jones: I am very interested in folklore. My doctoral dissertation was on Black folklore. What are some of your sources for the folklore in your novels?

Morrison: Almost always something I heard literally, and the way I heard it. The tar baby story varies from some versions, but that's the way I heard it. It was a woman, a girl, with a bonnet (laughter), and flying Africans, not stories, just people saying you know, flying before they came here. It is usually something that I have literally heard. Now, I did check on certain things about people who fly by reading those old slave narratives. It was fascinating because everybody else had heard of that or saw, or knew somebody who saw it. Nobody said, "I never heard of that," you know. "What do you mean flying African?" So it was already there although it was after the fact. I was willing to go ahead with it as a motivating thing for

Song of Solomon. But the interesting thing about those stories is that
I only use the stories I have heard; it gives my work a certain
authenticity, but I don't stop there. I try to look underneath it and to
see if there is something more because some of that stuff is not only
history, it's prophecy. If you look as I do in an imaginative way, you
find out all sorts of things that are there that have just been pushed
off as children's stories which is absurd. The way people learn—
narrative, you know. Myth is the first information there is, and
it says realms more than what is usually there. But I don't study
folklore—they are family stories and neighborhood stories and
community stories.

Jones: What do you feel is the role of the Black artist in the
unfolding development of Black culture?

Morrison: Well, I think—well, I can't speak about the Black artist.
I can speak about the Black writer. I suppose all artists have either to
bear witness or effect change—improvement—take cataracts off
people's eyes in an accessible way. It may be soothing; it may be
painful, but that's his job—to enlighten and to strengthen. But as a
writer, I think that because things have changed so much and the
communities seem to be so much in flux, or, if they are not, they are
receiving a deluge of ideas from all parts of the world, it's like being
under siege, you know. It takes some effort to keep a family together, a neighborhood together. So since that is the case, the old
stories don't work any more and songs don't work any more, that
folk art that kept us alive. So now I think novels are important
because they are socially responsible. I mean, for me a novel has to
be socially responsible as well as very beautiful. If you don't have
anything new to say about that which is old or fresh to say, then
probably it doesn't need to be written. Fifty years ago, novels were
not important for the Black community. I don't mean just reading
a good story either. I mean a novel written a certain way can do
precisely what spirituals used to do. It can do exactly what blues or
jazz or gossip or stories or myths or folklore did—that stuff that was
a common well-spring of ideas and again the participation of the
reader in it as though it's not alien to him. The people he may not
know, but there is some shared history.

Jones: Has the feminist movement influenced your treatment of
characters?

Morrison: Not yet. Not yet. I guess Jadine was contemporary or feminist because I usually don't write books about now—that was the only book. The other one ended in 1960. This one came up a little closer. It's very difficult to write about a twenty-five year old. They haven't done anything so you can't get anything together. But certainly she would be the recipient of the alertness of the feminine movement now. She would not tolerate, for example, all sorts of things that Son, being a little bit more old-fashioned, rooted, would lay upon her. She was a feminist woman, feminist in that sense. In the long passage in which she is so "I am," "somebody" is thinking about those warrior ants which is her beginning notion of what nurturing ought to be. There is conflict there between what she perceives as woman's probable fate compared to what warrior ants do which are all female which is a life of power, keeping the kingdom going, burying, feeding, you know. It's a tough thing that sort of nourishing, but it's not soft, not girlish. And that is conflicting with what Ondine tells her about what a woman is. A woman has to be a daughter before she can be any kind of woman. If she doesn't have that in mind, if she doesn't know how to relate to her ancestors, to her tribe, so to speak, she is not good for much. Well, that is directly at odds with her forward looking, futuristic self—"I can't be bound." You know, she wants "freedom." So that's something that I was trying to suggest that she might find out about. At least, she's going back to find out with all her faculties more or less intact.

Jones: I maybe should have asked this question earlier, but to me Pilate is the most singular character in all of your novels. What was your inspiration for creating her?

Morrison: Oh, I don't know. Truth is she sort of looks like a lot of people. But she really sort of appeared full-blown. I mean, I don't think I thought her up. It would be hard to just sit around—and you know, she came that way. She came without a navel. And I just thought that was the most ridiculous thing I had ever heard of. But I kept seeing her that way with that flat stomach. And I put it in perfectly prepared to take it out because it looked funny, but it worked that way. Very early I knew that was the case. It did a couple of things. It made her an outsider in a way and invent herself in a way, which accounted for her eccentricity, but also it made it possible for the whole concept of the combination of that which is real and

that which is surreal to work hand in hand because if you can get to
that part and accept that, then, you know, anything might happen
which is what does happen. In order to make the reader swallow the
flying African, which is what one has to do, at least metaphorically, if
not actually. I was trying to think what really would it take to fly.
Let's think about it as a real thing. Then having this aberration
appear early, it not only worked for her character but for the whole
theme of the book. So I had to—I was very happy to use it. Starting
from what is an unsullied development, she has a combination of the
wonder of childhood and is very sage about other things. She is
very sweet and nurturing and also very fierce. And she really does
combine for me, and I think that is what makes her unique, some
male and female characteristics blended well so they work as opposed to Sula who did what men do which is what made her so
terrible. I mean she behaves so terribly. (Laughter) It was so terrible
because it was askew. It was awful. She didn't care anything about
anybody. But Pilate is a loving, caring woman, nevertheless. And she
is so clear about herself. She has total response and total trust of her
own instincts. And once I found the way that she could become and
stay in this world, then she was unlike everybody. Eva was sort of
like that, but she was very managerial, she named people and controlled people. She didn't like for anybody to buck her either. This
woman Pilate is not interested in possession. She has no vanity.

Jones: You've been a dancer, an actress, a teacher, and editor, and
now a novelist. What's next for Toni Morrison? Are you going to
continue your writing? When can we expect another novel? I want to
be the first to hear it.

Morrison: (Laughter) Yes, I have a sort of novel that's humming in
my earlobes and it has no pattern yet. It's just an idea that I want to
develop. I am not ready to commit myself to four years of hardship
right now. (Laughter) So I am trying to let it arrive. I am not going to
go looking for it. But I can tell when something is sort of up in there.

Jones: Is economics the overriding issue in the lives of Black
Americans?

Morrison: Well, I wish it were that simple. It seems as though it is,
but it is something more sinister than that. Poverty is not good for
you, but it doesn't have to be depraved. There is something dis-
jointed—now mind you when I say this I am very much influenced by

living in New York City—but it's like somebody skipped a beat. It's like you used to be born Black, and that meant something. It meant when you saw another Black person you knew all sorts of things right away. And no matter what kind of financial situation they were in, you know, you all went to the same hairdresser and all went to the same beauty parlor. There were some things you could count on, some language, some shared assumptions. That doesn't seem to be true now. Being Black now is something you have to choose to be. Choose it, no matter what your skin color. I used to always feel safe among Black people. I did. I don't anymore, just because they are Black. And that for me is a huge jump. I'm in betwixt this generation of people who could go into any Black neighborhood and be safe. (Laughter) Somebody told me that their grandmother said that she had come to Philadelphia sixty years ago. And she said, "When I saw a Black man, I thought, 'I am safe. Thank God.' But now when I see a Black man, I think I ought to run." Something has happened. You see we are very close now to the society that is around us. I don't mean that the structures that held us together are gone, but there are new things pressing in our lives—new modes, new music, new menus, television, you know, and it's like going to the city. Stevie Wonder has a little song (laughter) "Living Just for the City." It's not enough. So I am a little bit alarmed by the changes. Maybe I shouldn't be. Maybe I should move. (Laughter) You know there are still lovely places. But I even see it in Lorain, Ohio. Just—I keeping thinking—the children are really in danger—our children.

Jones: What is your view regarding the future of the American family?

Morrison: Well, there seems to be some awareness now of its value as a little microcosm. There was a time when everybody left home to go do it—succeed. And parents encouraged that—going out in order to make it. And parents wanted their children to do better than they did. The bad part of that is that they do like Jadine. They just do better and they forget these people. Now, it might be sort of strife-ridden. Now, there seems to be some form of reclamation that's going on with the family's reclaiming itself. Part of that has to do, I think, with the knowledge that it's under stress. Part of it is economics. You know, young married couples always used to live some place else. Now, you know, children are coming home and staying home.

It's not that little nuclear family—everybody striving for that nuclear family way off somewhere, you know. The times are so scary. It's so frightening that people are grouping back together. But I see it even in the people who are away from home. They make up substitute families. You know, work families, commune families or avocation families. Even if you are not with your family you make up another group of people that serve or function almost as your family. So I am optimistic about that, because your family is like a little, tiny world. Most people's families represent practically everything that you can find—out there. So if you can't get along with them you might as well forget it (laughter) because they are all out there in the street. You know, all the wonderful ones, the terrible ones, the lunatics, the sane, the nicies. Go to any family reunion, and there it is. All the old enmities, the old friendships, all that's right there. If you run away from it, you find it duplicated in other situations. You just take the harm out of it.

Jones: Well, the final inevitable question. Ms. Morrison, what advice would you give to the young Black novelists in the eighties?

Morrison: Well—they are in a pretty good position for writing now because there are a lot of good Black writers around, and twenty years ago there were fewer. So they have a lot of good things to read, and that is the only advice I have for any writer is to read. It's like any other craft. You have to know the industry and know what has been done. And then when you read and find something you like, try to figure out why you like it, what they did, and that's how you develop your craft. Not imitation, not even emulation, but just this wide range of reading. And then have that combination of respect for the language and contempt, so you can break it. But you have to know what it is before you can break it. You can't break any rule that you don't know. This is the language that we speak, and one should know all there is to know about it. Everything.

A Conversation: Gloria Naylor and Toni Morrison

Gloria Naylor / 1985

Hudson, river c. 315 mi. long, rising in NE New York in L. Tear of the Clouds near Mt. Marcy in the Adirondacks and flowing generally S., forming N.Y.-N.J. line for c. 17 mi. near its mouth in Upper New York Bay. . . . At New York City Holland and Lincoln tunnels, railroad tunnel, subways, ferries, and George Washington Bridge link N.Y. and N.J. Above New York City river widens at Tappan Zee. On W bank PALISADES stretch N from N.J. Catskill Mts. descend to Hudson Valley. First explored by Henry Hudson in 1609. Major highway for Indians and early settlers. Has many historic, literary, and artistic associations.

(The Columbia Viking Desk Encyclopedia)

There is a blue house that sits on this river between two bridges. One is the George Washington that my bus has just crossed from the Manhattan side, and the other is the Tappan Zee that it's heading toward. My destination is that blue house, my objective is to tape a dialogue between myself and another black American writer, and I stepped on this bus seven years ago when I opened a slim volume entitled *The Bluest Eye*. Where does the first line of any novel—like any journey—actually begin? . . . *Quiet as it's kept, there were no marigolds in the fall of 1941* . . . I encountered those words, crystallized from the stream of a lifetime where they had been flowing through experiences seen and unseen, felt and unfelt, heard and unheard. That sentence was the product of a thousand tributaries before it would ultimately swell with an existence of its own, flowing off to become yet another source to uncountable possibilities.

From grade school I had been told that I had potential, while I only knew that I felt most complete when expressing myself through the

written word. So I scribbled on bits of looseleaf and in diaries—to
hide it all away. I wrote because I had no choice, but that was a long
road from gathering the authority within myself to believe that I
could actually *be* a writer. The writers I had been taught to love were
either male or white. And who was I to argue that Ellison, Austen,
Dickens, the Brontës, Baldwin and Faulkner weren't masters? They
were and are. But inside there was still the faintest whisper: Was
there no one telling my story? And since it appeared there was not,
how could I presume to? Those were frustrating years until I enrolled
in a creative writing seminar at Brooklyn College. My instructor's
philosophy was that in order for us to even attempt to write good
literature, we must read good literature. And so her reading list
included Tillie Olsen, Henry James—and Toni Morrison. I have tried
hard but I can't remember if we read *The Bluest Eye* at the beginning, middle, or end of the semester. Time has been swallowed
except for the moment I opened that novel because for my memory
that semester is now *The Bluest Eye*, and *The Bluest Eye* is the
beginning. The presence of the work served two vital purposes at
that moment in my life. It said to a young poet, struggling to break
into prose, that the barriers were flexible; at the core of it all is
language, and if you're skilled enough with that, you can create your
own genre. And it said to a young black woman, struggling to find a
mirror of her worth in this society, not only is your story worth
telling but it can be told in words so painstakingly eloquent that it
becomes a song.

Now that I saw it could be done, the question was, who had done
it? Intellectually, I accepted that the author of *The Bluest Eye* was a
black woman, and it gave me a measure of pride that *we* had been
here all along, creating American literature. Yet, I stared at the
name, Toni Morrison, on the book's cover and it seemed as far
removed from me as the separate universe I assumed all artists
moved in—they were "different" people. Then a newspaper clipping,
announcing that Toni Morrison would be reading from her latest
novel, *Song Of Solomon*, gave me my first opportunity to see this
ethereal creature. When I walked into that room the striking resem-
blance between this writer and my second cousin jolted me. *She
looked like Jessie.* The caramel skin, wide full mouth, the liquid eyes
capable of lightning jumps from an almost childlike vulnerability to

a piercing assessment of the surrounding climate. The round head
that would tip sharply to the side just before a burst of laughter. I
didn't approach her after that first reading, but then and several times
afterwards, I would simply sit and watch intently—every movement,
every gesture. I knew all of her novels practically by heart then, but I
was waiting—perhaps a bit fearfully—for some evidence that would
shatter the growing revelation that she was a real person. It never
came. And that refrain kept playing itself over and over in my mind
until it shrieked itself along with her into reality—*She looked like
Jessie.* I knew without a doubt that Jessie and I shared the same
blood. And so that meant, somehow, the writer who could create a
Bluest Eye was just like me. I went home one night after one of
her readings, stared into my bathroom mirror, and I began to cry . . .
*After the funeral the well-meaning came to console and offer their
dog-eared faith in the form of coconut cakes, potato pies, fried
chicken, and tears* . . . Where does the first line of a novel actually
begin and end? Through these experiences, so many before and after
them, my own sentence was crystallized.

That had been my encounter with the work and the writer. But
now two books later as my bus pulls up in back of her home, I am
finally going to meet the woman. How can I possibly begin? What do
you say to someone who has played this type of role in your life?

Well, first, you say, "Hello" . . .

It is now many hours later. Across the Hudson, the New York
shore is becoming a hazy blue-gray as evening approaches. The river
moves against her grounds with a hypnotic rhythm that seems to
suspend you a touch above time and place. I settle back into a deep,
wide lounge that accepts my body as the view from her windows
receives my spirit and gently expands it over the waves. It is a
peaceful moment. While I am in the midst of the contentment most
guests experience with attentive hosts, there is an added facet to my
comfort: I have come to the realization that I like this woman. I had
no guarantee of that before today, knowing that the artist and her art,
while inextricably tied, are still two separate entities. And I had
prepared myself so there would have been no harm done had I left
there acknowledging her genius, but now aware that she was someone I would not voluntarily spend another afternoon with. So I

considered it a gift that I would leave with more than an absence of harm—a newly possessed acquaintance with a good human being.

Through the day I have seen that there is so much that is different about us: I'm at the beginning of my career, she's at the height of hers; I am reticent and cautious, she is open and dramatic. We are from two generations, city and small town. I am childless and she is a devoted parent. But we are, after all, women; and so as I turn the tape recorder on, we continue talking as any two women might who happen to be fiercely proud of their identities and dedicated to their work.—GN

GN: So I took the advance from *Brewster Place* and treated myself to a graduation present. First I went to Algeciras, which is in southern Spain, because I had read that Hemingway had sort of made Barcelona his and Baldwin had made Paris his. I even carried along a copy of *Nobody Knows My Name*, expecting to see Europe the way these writers had seen it. After all I'd just written *a* book—you know, I was ready to be continental. But the experience was so different for me. I was harassed a lot on the streets because I was a woman traveling alone. In southern Spain the women don't walk alone. So the men assumed I was a prostitute or that I wanted them to approach me, and it was really difficult. And the freedom that Hemingway and Baldwin experienced I didn't have. Sure, I had it when I sequestered myself away in that boarding house in Cadiz and started working on *Linden Hills*—I was free to write as much as I wanted, but not to roam the streets. And I'm going to be honest—I resented that; I was bitter that I couldn't have the world like they had the world.

TM: It is such an incredible thing to know that in a very strong way, geographically, it is their world because they alone can walk up and down certain places.

GN: But now you said you went to Paris, and I personally didn't have the same type of problem there. Did you?

TM: No. But I never went anywhere to do what you did. I have never had that courage and I have a tough time even now trying to. I guess because I should have done it much younger. My interior life is so strong that I never associate anything important to any other place, which makes me very parochial in that regard. The only reason I never went to Africa was because I didn't have anything to do over there. I didn't want to just go and look. Before I got married I used to go anywhere at the drop of a hat—overnight, I didn't go long distances; but after that I had other things to take into consideration. But I could do it now I guess.

GN: I wasn't married that terribly long to know that there was a difference between B.M. and A.M.—"before marriage" and "after marriage. I didn't have that, so I always loved to go. I met him because I was on the go.

TM: How old were you when you got married?

GN: Thirty. I was twenty-nine when he proposed. I was going to turn thirty in January. Then he proposed over the telephone—long distance *collect* when I was twenty-nine and eleven months old. I was making that twenty-nine to thirty transition, saying to myself, "Well, what have I done with my life? I better go on and get married." It was really fear. Do you know Marcia Gillespie? I met her that November of 1979 because I sent *Essence* one of my short stories and her secretary called me and set up a luncheon appointment—my first literary luncheon. And she just sat down and said, "Sister, if you do anything, keep writing." And that scared me. And so his proposal coming on the heels of that statement sort of gave me a way out of my fear. I didn't have to face the terror of the dream I had lived with all my life coming true—that was untraveled terrain. But marrying somebody—anybody—was very traveled terrain, because I grew up feeling somehow that that was how you made your definition. Although Marcia had offered me the hope of another way to make a definition, his was safe—it was conventional.

TM: That's what I want to explore in this new book. How we choose to put ourselves someplace else, outside, rather than in here, inside.

GN: But don't you think men do it too? I think they do but their sacrifices aren't as pronounced. But almost every human being, I think, has a problem saying, "Well, who in the hell am I? And what is it that nurtures me, and who is that me?"

TM: Men can hide easier because they can always be men. They can be abstract, in a crunch, and they seem to know what maleness is. They have a posture for that. They have a job for that. They have an idea of how to be male and they talk about it a lot. I'm not sure

that they talk to each other about the other thing, personal identity.
Have you ever heard men talk to each other?

GN: Well, they don't talk to me about such things—or in my
presence.

TM: Well, I have heard them when they talk among themselves,
and they don't talk about the vulnerable "me." It must be hard
for men to confide in one another, not incidents that happen to them,
but to confide that other life that's not *male*. That's hard for them,
because they are trained out of it so early in life. When I was growing
up, I listened to my brothers talk to one another and other men when
they thought they were talking outside my hearing, and they don't
talk to each other the same way that I would hear my aunts and my
mother. Only when they get very much older, then they can stop
posturing. . . . It's a terrible burden, because they want to know—
when they're little kids, of course, they say, "Who am I?" And then
somebody says, "Well, you're a man." And they try to figure out
what that is. That's what they shoot for. But if somebody says,
"Well, you're a woman," what does that mean? Well, that usually
means somebody's handmaiden. If you pass the test of being a
woman, as far as a man is concerned, that's something quite different
from what I would mean. And when you think of who are the women
that you admire and what do you admire about them as women, it
would never be what men would think. So many things just go out the
window. It doesn't mean they don't admire it in some sense; they
just don't want to be in its company day after day.

GN: I know what you're saying, but when someone asks me what
women I admire, they're normally women who have turned their
backs on the world; they're women who have been selfish to some
degree, who have gone against the grain. Zora Neale Hurston is an
example. She defied so many of the acceptable conventions for
women during her time, and I never had the courage to do that. I
hope more young women will, but not go about their lives in a
destructive way so they are socially abrasive, but to do it where it's
just self-confirming.

TM: And that's different from what men want when they're
defining you. It's special and it's true that those are the things that
cause other women to admire, not envy, admire, really get a kick out
of each other. I was trying in *Tar Baby* to suggest that quality. It's

neither up nor down, or socially acceptable or unacceptable. It's original. The woman that Jadine sees in the supermarket (the one with no eyelashes) is somehow transcendent and whatever she really was, what she was perceived as by Jadine, is the real chic. The one that authenticates everything. The one that is very clear in some deep way about what her womanhood is. And it can happen at any moment and any woman might do it. For Jadine it was that particular woman who looked that particular way. But she can appear at any moment. And when you see it, it does stay with you even though you may surrender to whatever your culture's version of you is supposed to be. Still, the memory of that one is somehow a basis for either total repression or a willingness to let one's true self surface. I went through a period of thinking that such women were not only selfish, but narcissistic. And the line between those two became difficult to see. When is it vanity and narcissism and being a spoiled brat, and when is it clarity? Self-affirmation? That's the problem. Sometimes when you see a certain woman you know she is not coherent. She may be a person who has all the accoutrements of *self-centeredness*, but is not centered at all. She may be really just piling stuff on—more jewels, you know, sort of a costume idea of a woman. But that is the search. And I think that in these days and these times, black women, if they don't know what it is, then nobody may know what it is at all.

GN: I had such a character in *Linden Hills*. And when I put Willa in that basement my overall idea was to have this very conservative upper-middle class black woman through her discovery of all those remnants from the past wives who'd lived in that house, just get up, walk out of there and say, "No, this is shallow. This is not for me." I wanted her to learn from those lessons in history. But what eventually evolved through all the pain that she went through was the discovery that she liked being where she was—a conventional housewife. And there is this moment when she says not only to the reader, but to *me*—"I was a good wife and a good mother. And I'm not going to apologize to anyone for that." That was a real surprise to me; I hadn't planned on the character doing that. But what her self-affirmation became was acknowledging her conventional position. You see, I used to believe that self-affirmation meant you had to be totally aconventional. But to keep a house, especially the way my mother kept her house—against all odds—is really a creative statement. So a woman's affirmation doesn't have to be an executive chair at IBM or something like that.

TM: Well, those are class differences. That was, I think, some of the major criticism earlier in the women's movement. Did everybody have to want to be the vice-president? What about the typist who really wanted to type? There's a class conflict. It seemed to suggest that you could only feel as though you had come into your own if you walked in the corridors of power in some capitalist mode. That's another one of those unreal, I think also fraudulent, conflicts between women who want to be mothers and women who don't. Why should there be any conflict with that? You could, first of all, do both. And why should I denigrate somebody who wants to stay home and have a garden?

GN: If that's their choice. Maybe the fight was that we didn't think at one time that there was an alternative. But if you realize these are the alternatives and that is what I choose to do, then that's fine.

TM: If that is the choice. . . . You see, the point is that freedom is choosing your responsibility. It's not having no responsibilities; it's choosing the ones you want. So many women have been given responsibilities they don't want. A lady doctor has to be able to say, "I want to go home." And the one at home has the right to say, "I want to go to medical school." That's all there is to that, but then the choices cause problems where there are no problems because "either/or" seems to set up the conflict, first in the language and then in life—as though you can't do two things or do one and then stop it and go do something else. As though there is a schedule somewhere. That's what's happened with the twenty-nine and thirty. "Now I'm thirty: thirty and not married; that's critical."

GN: But then you get married and realize that you didn't want to be married, you just wanted to get married. And after that you just go on.

TM: The romance thing is a little bit of a problem. Being in love with somebody, it's such a fine, fine feeling. It just turns everything up so nicely. The feeling of being in love, whether it's a successful love affair or not, is almost irrelevant. It's just that you're up. Like the volume of a radio turned up.

GN: Everything becomes a lot clearer in the world; if not clearer, it's filtered through a different kind of light.

TM: Our sensibilities are alive. I love love. I like the feeling of it. And I like the way the world looks, the way things sound, the way food tastes. I like that heightened sensibility. Of course you have to distinguish between that and marriage, which is another kind of sensibility. It's nice when it's all in the same thing. But sometimes you just put everything in marriage like that was the entire solution. There are a lot of other things to love, but none of them have currency these days. Loving God, now that's fanatical. Loving your country, your school, your children. It all has some sort of taint that's Freudian. So the only one that's sort of untainted, the one that everybody thinks is strong and self-important, is loving the other person. And very seldom can that other person bear the weight of all of your attention.

GN: Toni, about *Song Of Solomon* in that marvelous scene when Guitar is driving Hagar home after she tried to destroy Milkman and she realizes that she can't kill him. . . . You know, I called one of my girl friends and read that to her over the phone saying, *"Hear this—"* I've read more of your books over the phone to girl friends—Guitar was taking her home and she was going on about, "Well, I can't live. I'm nothing without him." And he says to her, "Hagar, if you say to someone, 'I am nothing without you' what is there in you for them to want?" So being in love is fine, but only when there's a self there who's doing the loving.

TM: Yes, when there's somebody there doing the loving.

GN: Exactly.

TM: You don't think you're nothing without him. He doesn't think so either. That comradeship, that feeling of working with a partner is what's nice in a marriage, when two people are doing something together. And then of course something shifts. Somebody is running it; somebody is calling the shots. Somebody has to give or make it look like he's giving. Then the play or the battle is about power.

GN: And the responsibility to give way seems to always fall on us. I remember the transformation I went through almost immediately after I was married. Unconsciously, I felt as if I needed to ask permission to do something, and I started to get scared when I really listened to myself. And this was a woman who normally never asked anybody about anything when she wanted to do something. But now being married, somehow, I felt I should do that.

TM: That happens even afterwards. Later you realize that you are the one who tells you "no" or "yes."

GN: Eventually I will reach that point—if I'm with a man or not—when I can just say, "Well, *I* am the authority and I am asking myself." I mean, I want to be able to say that to myself inside. Because now I can do it verbally, but I don't believe a word of it. What I guess I really want to do is be a man; that would make it easy. I used to fantasize about that, you know—I guess a lot of women do.

TM: It wouldn't be easier if you were a man, but what would be easier is if you had all the rights and the authority that are male and the adventure, what we equate with adventure, that is male. And to not, as you say the character in your book does not, have to apologize for that. The history of your women and your family and mine has a lot of different colors in it. A lot of different adventures. But, for example, I tried hard to be both the ship and the safe harbor at the same time, to be able to make a house and be on the job market and still nurture the children. It's trying to make life enhanced by additional things rather than conflicted by additional things. No one should be asked to make a choice between a home or a career. Why not have both? It's all possible. Like women doing nine things since the beginning and getting to the end of the row at the same time.

GN: But you know, I think that whole sense of adventure and authority tied into maleness has a lot to do with how books are created and who's creating them—and in what numbers. I had told you before about how you influenced me and how *The Bluest Eye* sitting there gave me a validity to do something which I had thought was really male terrain. And all of my education had subconsciously told me that it wasn't the place for me.

TM: Only men did that.

GN: Yes, men wrote—because what was I reading? When I hit college what was I reading in the Afro-American studies department? Fine, black, male writers. What had I read in high school? White male writers. Sure, there were a few women then, but they were white women and in another century to boot. But for me, where was the *authority* for me to enter this forbidden terrain? But then finally you were being taught to me. But you've told me, Toni, there was no

you there when you were in school. So how did you get the courage
to just say, "Well, yes, I will pick up this pen."

TM: I wonder . . . I think that at that moment I had no choice. If I
had had some choices such as the ones we are talking about, I
wouldn't have done it. But I was really in a corner. And whatever
was being threatened by the circumstances in which I found myself,
alone with two children in a town where I didn't know anybody, I
knew that I would not deliver to my children a parent that was of no
use to them. So I was thrown back on, luckily, the only thing I could
depend on, my own resources. And I felt that the world was going by
in some direction that I didn't understand and I was not in it.
Whatever was going on was not about me and there were lots of
noises being made about how wonderful I was—"black woman you
are my queen." I didn't believe it. I thought it sounded like something I had heard when I was eleven, but the vocabulary was different. There was something in it I just didn't trust. It was too loud. It
was too grand. It was almost like a wish rather than a fact, that the
men were trying to say something that they didn't believe either.
That's what I thought. And so it looked as though the world was
going by and I was not in that world. I used to live in this world, I
mean really lived in it. I knew it. I used to really belong here. And at
some point I didn't belong here anymore. I was somebody's parent,
somebody's this, somebody's that, but there was no me in this world.
And I was looking for that dead girl and I thought I might talk about
that dead girl, if for no other reason than to have it, somewhere in the
world, in a drawer. There was such a person. I had written this little
story earlier just for some friends, so I took it out and I began to
work it up. And all of those people were me. I was Pecola, Claudia.
. . . I was everybody. And as I began to do it, I began to pick up
scraps of things that I had seen or felt, or didn't see or didn't feel,
but imagined. And speculated about and wondered about. And I fell
in love with myself. I reclaimed myself and the world—a real revelation. I named it. I described it. I listed it. I identified it. I recreated it.
And having done that, at least, then the books belonged in the
world. Although I still didn't belong. I was working hard at a job and
trying to be this competent person. But the dead girl—and not only
was that girl dead in my mind, I thought she was dead in everybody's
mind, aside from my family and my father and my mother—that

person didn't exist anywhere. *That* person. Not the name, but the person. I thought that girl was dead. I couldn't find her. I mean, I could see her on the street or the bus, but nobody wrote about her. Which isn't entirely accurate. People had done that. But for me at that time that was *them,* that was not me. People ask, "Is your book autobiographical?" It is not, but it is, because of that process of reclamation. And I was driven there, literally driven. I felt penned into a basement, and I was going to get out of it. I remembered being a person who did belong on this earth. I used to love my company and then I didn't. And I realized the reason I didn't like my company was because there was nobody there to like. I didn't know what happened. I had been living some other person's life. It was too confusing. I was interested primarily in the civil rights movement. And it was in that flux that I thought . . . I guess it was right there. It was my time of life also. The place where those things came to-gether. And I thought that there would be no me. Not us or them or we, but no *me.* If the best thing happened in the world and it all came out perfectly in terms of what the gains and goals of the *Movement* were, nevertheless nobody was going to get away with that; nobody was going to tell me that it had been that easy. That all I needed was a slogan: "Black is Beautiful." It wasn't that easy being a little black girl in this country—it was rough. The psychological tricks you have to play in order to get through—and nobody said how it felt to be that. And you knew better. You knew inside better. You knew you were not the person they were looking at. And to know that and to see what you saw in those other people's eyes was devastating. Some people made it, some didn't. And I wanted to explore it myself. But once having done that, having gone to those places, I knew I'd go there again. So when I said every now and then, "Well, I don't care if they published it or not," I cared, but I didn't care enough to not do it again. If they had all said, as they did, that they couldn't publish that book for various and sundry reasons . . .

  GN: You mean *The Bluest Eye* was turned down before it was finally published?

  TM: Many times. You know the little letters you get back from the editors. They wrote me nice letters. "This book has no beginning, no middle, and no end"; or, "your writing is wonderful, *but . . .*" I wasn't going to change it for that. I assumed there would be some

writing skills that I did not have. But that's not what they were
talking about. They thought something was wrong with *it* or it wasn't
marketable. I guess I do know what they thought, but it was just too
much to think about at that time. And so after I finished that book I
was in some despair because several months passed and I didn't have
another idea. And then I got to thinking about this girl, this woman.
If it wasn't unconventional, she didn't want it. She was willing to risk
in her imagination a lot of things and pay the price and also go astray.
It wasn't as though she was this fantastic power who didn't have a
flaw in her character. I wanted to throw her relationship with another
woman into relief. Those two women—that too is us, those two
desires, to have your adventure *and* safety. So I just cut it up.

GN: You had a Nel and a Sula.

TM: Yes. And then to have one do the unforgivable thing to see
what that friendship was really made out of.

GN: When I taught *Sula* the second semester, we had a huge fight
about that in class. When I talked about Sula and Nel being two faces
to the same coin and that was the epitome of female bonding, the
kids were with me. And they even hung in there when I explained
that their relationship, while falling short of a physical bonding,
involved a spiritual bonding that transcended the flesh and was much
superior than a portrayal of an actual physical bonding would have
been anyway. But then we got to the scene where Sula and Jude are
on the floor together; the kids rebelled—"How could Sula have been
Nel's *best* friend if she took Jude from her?" But then I tried to make
them think about how important Jude really was—which was Sula's
point. "We shared everything else, so he should be low now on the
priority of things we won't share." At first that really shook my
students up, then it made them begin to think—"Yeah, exactly how
important is it?"

TM: You see, if all women behaved like those two, or if the Sula
point of view operated and women really didn't care about sharing
these things, everything would just crumble—hard. If it's not about
fidelity and possession and my pain versus yours, then how can you
manipulate, how can you threaten, how can you assert power? I went
someplace once to talk about *Sula* and there were some genuinely
terrified men in the audience, and they walked out and told me why.
They said, "Friendship between women?" Aghast. Really terrified.

And you wouldn't think anybody grown-up would display his fear
quite that way. I mean you would think they would maybe think it.
But it was such a shocking, threatening thing in a book, let alone
what it would be in life.

GN: But it's always been there to a great degree—in life. We do
share our men. We may not like it very much, but there is a silent
consensus about that and it hasn't really torn us apart as women. I
believe that women have always been close to women. It's much like
that universe you had mentioned before among black women writers,
but it's not only the writers; black women have always had each
other when we had very little else. But what we didn't dare do was to
put it in black and white like you did in *Sula*. And when that's
done—when it's printed—it's threatening. Maybe what was so threatening about it too was that you didn't rant and rave; you made your
point very subtly. The same way you did in *The Bluest Eye*; it wasn't
a fist stuck up into heaven—"Black Power." But how much more
powerful could that statement be than to say, "Look at what happens
when society makes a little girl invisible." And just to whisper . . .
that's what I wanted to tell you about your work. You know how you
can be in a room and the person that talks in a whisper is the one you
always lean toward. Your books just whisper at the reader and you
move in, you move in, and then you finally hear what's being said,
and you say to yourself, "Oh, my God." You did it with *Sula*. Very
quietly you move the reader in until we get to that line, "All along
I thought I was missing Jude." The impact is then tremendous. And I
believe writing is at its best when it's done that way. I just don't
agree with some people that books should make a statement. And
often when I'll go somewhere to read or lecture, someone will
inevitably ask, "Well, what were you trying to *say*?" in this part or
that part. And my response is, "Nothing at all." I don't think art
should be didactic. My art, as I see it, involves a certain honesty to
the world that I'm creating on that page and a measure of integrity to
myself. And if the readers want to extrapolate a message, then they
can do it on their own; I haven't put one in there for them. That's not
my responsibility as a black or as a black woman.

TM: Well, you're absolutely right. There's no question about it.
For two reasons. One, some of these people have been taught to read
very badly. That is, they have been given even great books and then

trained to think of them as resolutions and solutions and then to put them to uses that are nefarious, as though they are reading a "How To" column. They go to a book the way you go to a medicine cabinet. They're not going to it at all the way I go into a book. The other thing is that I think, really and truly, for a black writer to be didactic is really a cardinal sin because the last thing that I would do with black people, if they're anything like I am or like all the black people that I have respect for, is to be that pompous and tell them what to do. They have never taken direction well; they've always participated in whatever it was. Whether it was political or blues singing or jazz or whatever, you have to share that with them. You don't hand out these little slips of paper and say, "You will do the following; this is the message."

GN: But on the other hand, there was something that I was very self-conscious about with my first novel; I bent over backwards not to have a negative message come through about the men. My emotional energy was spent creating a woman's world, telling her side of it because I knew it hadn't been done enough in literature. But I worried about whether or not the problems that were being caused by the men in the women's lives would be interpreted as some bitter statement I had to make about black men.

TM: You open a section of *Women* with his [Eugene's] conversation.

GN: Yes, I did it purposely there. I wanted the reader to see that that young man did care about the death of his child, but he had been so beaten down he couldn't come through for his family. But I'm wondering if that should have been my worry. The chapter still worked well with that section up front, but it *was* my way of making a statement. Showing that side of Eugene helped creatively because it made him a full-fledged character, and if you want your characters to live—to be human—there must be complexity. But, Toni, I'm talking about something else—there was also a pull there to want there to be no doubt about the *goodness* of these male characters. And I just wonder if I should have that pull?

TM: Yes, you should.

GN: But then it was only because they were black male characters and I was a black woman writing it.

TM: That's right. You should have that pull. You should wonder. Am I doing them justice? Is anybody going to misread this?

GN: That's what I ask myself a lot and especially for *Linden Hills* because a huge number of the major characters are male. Do you think other writers go through that? Did you ask yourself that at first, too?

TM: I didn't ask myself. I just loved them so much.

GN: For me, the love had to grow. I eventually began to love the two boys in *Linden Hills*, and as they went along I could applaud them or cry about whatever they did. You know, at first I actually introduced myself—not, "Hi, Willie and Lester, here's Gloria." But, "Hey guys, now here's a woman and I really don't know what it's like to be twenty years old, at that threshold of manhood, but I'm going to try awfully hard." Do you start with that process as well? That introduction of you to them?

TM: Yeah. You have to introduce yourself and you have to know their names. They won't behave if you don't know their names.

GN: I used to write letters to Willie at first. Before we got going together really well. Before he moved into my apartment, I had to sort of court him. And so I wrote him letters.

TM: You have to know who those people are in order to get that information from them. You have to be worthy and they have to have the trust. You can't go plopping in there talking about somebody's interior life from the position of a stranger.

GN: And therefore we can't worry if "x" months down the line, someone gets up in the audience and says, "Well, you didn't have it right."

TM: They have not written those letters to Willie. They do not know what they're talking about. You know.

GN: You know that you've tried. That's all you can say, "To the best of my ability and with all love and good intentions, I tried."

TM: The love shows. That's one thing that's unmistakable. The only time I never did that and didn't even try was in *The Bluest Eye*. That girl, Maureen Peal. I was not good with her. She was too easy a shot. I wouldn't do that now with her. I mean we all know who she is. And everybody has one of those in his or her life, but I was unfair to her. I did not in that book look at anything from her point of view inside. I only showed the facade.

GN: Because a Maureen Peal suffered as much as a Pecola Breed-love did in this society.

TM: That's right. And I never got in her because I didn't want to go there. I didn't like her. I never have done that since. I've always regretted the speed with which I executed that girl. She worked well structurally for the girls and this and that, but if I were doing that book now, I would write her section or talk about her that way plus from inside.

GN: But that was your first novel, and we learn from the first. When your second book was finished—*Sula*—did you begin to really feel like a writer then? Because now after *Linden Hills*, I feel there's a certain validity about what I do if for nothing than the fact that I can say, I write book*s* with an "s." Was creating *Sula* like that for you, too? You felt really legitimate then, or had you felt it all along?

TM: I felt it after I finished *Song Of Solomon*. After I did *Song Of Solomon*, I thought, "This is what I do."

GN: You know, it takes a lot to finally say that. That "Yes, I write. No, Mama, I'll never have a regular job for more than a year. This is what I do."

You know, there are moments with my work when I can achieve the type of atmosphere that's permeating this house and our conversation now. It's as if I've arrived in a place where it's all spirit and no body—an overwhelming sense of calm. But those moments are rare. Usually, I vacillate between an intense love of my work and "What in the hell am I doing this for?" There has to be an easier way to get the type of pain that I'm inflicting upon myself at this desk. But I guess I keep at it because of those times when I can reach that spiritual center. It's like floating in the middle of that river, and waves are all around you . . . I actually begin to feel blessed.

TM: It is a blessing. Any art form that can do that for you is a special thing. People have to have that sense of having moved something from one place to another and made out of nothing something. Having added something to something and having seen a mess and made it orderly or seen rigidity and given it fluidity. You know, something. And writing encompasses for me all there isn't.

GN: Do you ever think that you've been chosen, knowing that you're always going to do this? Because I really feel as if it's sort of like a calling. Not a calling meaning anything special or different, because the men who come up there to clean your road perform a service to this planet just like an artist performs a service. But I really feel that for me it goes beyond just a gift to handle words, but that it was *meant* for me to be writing as opposed to other things that I'm talented enough to do and can do well when I put my mind to it. For example, I do teach and I enjoy it. But there's not the same type of pull—I think I would self-destruct if I didn't write. I wouldn't self-destruct if I didn't teach.

TM: You *would* self-destruct if you didn't write. You know, I wanted to ask you whether or not, when you finished *The Women*, did you know what the next book was? Did you have any idea about it or did you go through that depressed period, postpartum, of wondering whether or not you would have a new idea, or were you sort of serene about it? What was that period like? I'm not talking about the publication date of the book. When you finished *The Women of Brewster Place*, what was the time period and the emotional trek to *Linden Hills*?

GN: Well, two things were going on, Toni. One was that I wanted there to be a *Linden Hills*.

TM: Even before you finished . . .

GN: Yes, because I had a character in *Brewster Place* named Kiswana Browne who lived in Linden Hills. And my next dream—you know, the daydreams about what you want to do, the easy part of writing any book—was that I would love to do a whole treatment of her neighborhood. And at about that time, I was taking this course at Brooklyn College, "Great Works of Literature." And we had read *The Inferno* and I was overwhelmed by the philosophical underpinnings of the poem as well as the characters that Dante created. Then the idea came to me that I could try to sketch out this neighborhood along the lines of *The Inferno*. But it was a while before I could actually sit down and work on the book because there was fear, a little, because this was going to be a *real* novel. *Brewster Place* was really interconnected short stories and that type of work demands a shorter time span, a different emotional involvement. So it was in the summer of 1981 when I began to seriously sketch out what I might like to do with *Linden Hills* and it was a year later when I literally sat down and said, "Here is the emotional involvement. I have the idea and I'm going to go for it."

TM: I can see how you would know because you can see little pieces. Can't you see the trees or a little bit of the brook from Brewster Place? There's a little bit of it sticking up.

GN: But for you yourself?

TM: Well, I've had different kinds of things. I remember after *The Bluest Eye* having an extremely sad six or eight months. And I didn't know what it was because that was the first time I had ever written a novel. And I wasn't even sure when I could write another one because I wasn't thinking about being a novelist then. I just wrote *that* and I thought that would be *that* and that would be the end of *that* 'cause I liked to read it and that was enough. But then I moved from one town to another, for one thing, and I was feeling, for this very sustained period, what can only be described now as missing something, missing the company I had been keeping all those years when I wrote *The Bluest Eye*, and I couldn't just write because I was able to write. I had to write with the same feeling that I had when I did *The Bluest Eye*, which was that there was this exciting collection of people that only I knew about. I had the direct line and I was the receiver of all this information. And then when I began to think about *Sula*, everything changed, I mean, all the colors of the world changed, the sounds and so on. I recognized what that period was when I finished *Sula*, and I had another idea which was *Song of Solomon*. When I finished *Song of Solomon*, I didn't have another idea for *Tar Baby* but by then I knew that it arrives or it doesn't arrive and I'm not terrified of a block, of what people call a block. I think when you hit a place where you can't write, you probably should be still for a while because it's not there yet.

GN: Even a block with an idea itself? That doesn't frighten you?

TM: It doesn't bother me. And that brings me to the book that I'm writing now called *Beloved*. I had an idea that I didn't know was a book idea, but I do remember being obsessed by two or three little fragments of stories that I heard from different places. One was a newspaper clipping about a woman named Margaret Garner in 1851. It said that the Abolitionists made a great deal out of her case because she had escaped from Kentucky, I think, with her four children. She lived in a little neighborhood just outside of Cincinnati and she had killed her children. She succeeded in killing one; she tried to kill two others. She hit them in the head with a shovel and

they were wounded but they didn't die. And there was a smaller one
that she had at her breast. The interesting thing, in addition to that,
was the interviews that she gave. She was a young woman. In the
inked pictures of her she seemed a very quiet, very serene-looking
woman and everyone who interviewed her remarked about her
serenity and tranquility. She said, "I will not let those children live
how I have lived." She had run off into a little woodshed right
outside her house to kill them because she had been caught as a
fugitive. And she had made up her mind that they would not suffer
the way that she had and it was better for them to die. And her
mother-in-law was in the house at the same time and she said, "I
watched her and I neither encouraged her nor discouraged her."
They put her in jail for a little while and I'm not even sure what the
denouement is of her story. But that moment, that decision was a
piece, a tail of something that was always around, and it didn't get
clear for me until I was thinking of another story that I had read in a
book that Camille Billops published, a collection of pictures by Van
der Zee, called *The Harlem Book of the Dead*. Van der Zee was very
lucid. He remembered everybody he had photographed. There was
this fashion of photographing beloved, departed people in full dress
in coffins or in your arms. You know, many parents were holding
their children beautifully dressed in their arms and they were affectionate photographs taken for affectionate reasons. In one picture,
there was a young girl lying in a coffin and he says that she was
eighteen years old and she had gone to a party and that she was
dancing and suddenly she slumped and they noticed there was blood
on her and they said, "What happened to you?" And she said, "I'll
tell you tomorrow. I'll tell you tomorrow." That's all she would say.
And apparently her ex-boyfriend or somebody who was jealous had
come into the party with a gun and a silencer and shot her. And
she kept saying, "I'll tell you tomorrow" because she wanted him to
get away. And he did, I guess; anyway, she died. Now what made
those stories connect, I can't explain, but I do know that, in both
instances, something seemed clear to me. A woman loved something
other than herself so much. She had placed all of the value of her
life in something outside herself. That the woman who killed her
children loved her children so much; they were the best part of her
and she would not see them sullied. She would not see them hurt.

She would rather kill them, have them die. You know what that means?

GN: I do, yes.

TM: And that this woman had loved a man or had such affection for a man that she would postpone her own medical care or go ahead and die to give him time to get away so that, more valuable than her life, was not just his life but something else connected with his life. Now both of those incidents seem to me, at least on the surface, very noble, you know, in that old-fashioned sense, noble things, generous, wide-spirited, love beyond the call of . . .

GN: . . . of a very traditional kind of female . . .

TM: That's right. Always. It's peculiar to women. And I thought, it's interesting because the best thing that is in us is also the thing that makes us sabotage ourselves, sabotage in the sense that our life is not as worthy, or our perception of the best part of ourselves. I had about fifteen or twenty questions that occurred to me with those two stories in terms of what it is that really compels a good woman to displace the self, her self. So what I started doing and thinking about for a year was to project the self not into the way we say "yourself," but to put a space between those words, as though the self were really a *twin* or a thirst or a friend or something that sits right next to you and watches you, which is what I was talking about when I said "the dead girl." So I had just projected her out into the earth. So how to do that? How to do that without being absolutely lunatic and talking about some medical students that nobody wants to hear about. So I just imagined the life of a dead girl which was the girl that Margaret Garner killed, the baby girl that she killed.

GN: How old was the child?

TM: Less than two. I just imagined her remembering what happened to her, being someplace else and returning, knowing what happened to her. And I call her Beloved so that I can filter all these confrontations and questions that she has in that situation, which is 1851, and then to extend her life, you know, her search, her quest, all the way through as long as I care to go, into the twenties where it switches to this other girl. Therefore, I have a New York uptown-Harlem milieu in which to put this love story, but Beloved will be there also.

GN: Always Beloved being the twin self to whatever woman shows up throughout the work.

TM: She will be the mirror, so to speak. I don't know, I'm just gonna write and see what happens to it. I have about 250 pages and it's overwhelming me. There's a lot of danger for me in writing it, which is what I am very excited about. The effort, the responsibility as well as the effort, the effort of being worth it, that's not quite it. The responsibility that I feel for the woman I'm calling Sethe, and for all of these people; these unburied, or at least unceremoniously buried, people made literate in art. But the inner tension, the artistic inner tension those people create in me; the fear of not properly, artistically, burying them, is extraordinary. I feel this enormous responsibility in exactly the way you describe the ferocity you felt when somebody was tampering with a situation that was gonna hurt . . .

GN: My people . . .

TM: Your people. Exactly. I have to have now very overt conversations with these people. Before I could sort of let it disguise itself as the artist's monologue with herself but there's no time for that foolishness now. Now I have to call them by their names and ask them to reappear and tell me something or leave me alone even. But it does mean that I feel exactly the way you do about this. They are such special company that it is very difficult to focus on other people. There is a temptation to draw away from living people, people who are extremely important to you and who are real. They're in competition a great deal with this collection of imagined characters. But these are demands that I can meet, and I know I can because they would not have spoken to me had I not been the one.

GN: Had you not been somehow worthy. I consider it being worthy to be used as that medium.

TM: They won't talk to you otherwise.

GN: No, I understand. Just before the women who lived on Brewster Place had faded back to from wherever they came, I had gotten a bound copy of the book—which I really call a tombstone because that's what it represents, at least for my part of the experience—and those women wrote me a little epigraph which I recorded in the front of the book. They told me that I must always remember them, remember how they came to be, because they were the ones who

were real to me and they were the ones I had to worry about. They
wanted me to know that they cared about me and that they understood that I had cared deeply about them. And having said that, they
just sort of faded on off. . . . A lot of people don't think that our
characters become that tangible to us.

TM: Some people are embarrassed about it; they both fear and
distrust it also; they don't solidify and recreate the means by which
one enters into that place where those people are. I think the more
black women write, the more easily one will be able to talk about
those things. Because I have almost never found anyone whose work
I respected or who took their work that seriously, who did not talk in
the vocabulary that you and I are using; it's not the vocabulary of
literary criticism.

GN: No, it's not.

TM: And it's not taught. People speak, of course, of the muse and
there are other words for this. But to make it as graphic a presence or
a collection of presences as I find it absolutely to be, it's not even a
question of trying to make it that way—that's the way that it appears.
There are not a lot of people to whom one speaks that way. But I
know that that's what it is. It isn't a question of searching it out. It's
a question of my perceptions and in that area, I know.

GN: They become so tangible that not only do you deal with them
affectionately, but sometimes you deal with them very irately.
Listening to you talking about the self, I can remember with *Linden
Hills* the woman who was imprisoned in that basement. I actually
invented a mirror, if you will, for her after she had gone through all
her experiences. After she had dug up the remnants of the other
Nedeed women, I created a way for her to see her own reflection in a
pan of water because she had no self up until that moment. And
when she realized that she had a face, then maybe she had other
things going for her as well, and she could take her destiny in her
own hands. But the point of all that was what was going to happen
step by step once she discovered herself—she was going to barge up
out of that basement, etc.—and I had *my* ending all set. But when
this character who had lived with me now for two years finally
discovered her face in that pan of water, she decided that she liked
being what she was. She liked being a wife and a mother and she was
going upstairs and claim that identity. And I said, "Oh, Lord,

woman, don't you know what the end of this book has got to be? You've gotta tear that whole house down to the ground, or my book won't make any sense." Obviously, she didn't care. And I was angry with her for a good week—I just stopped writing and ran around the house cursing her. But then again that was *her* life and her decision. So the ball was thrown back into my lap—my job was to figure out a way for this woman to live her life and for me to end that book the way I wanted to.

TM: Break her arm and make her . . .

GN: Exactly. But it's marvelous, Toni. There's something so wonderful about being and even grappling with those things and being in the midst of just watching them coming to fruition.

TM: Oh, yes.

GN: You know, when I finished *Linden Hills,* I said to myself, of course, the first day or two days after, "Never again! I must have been crazy!"

TM: "This had been too hard!"

GN: And just last week, I was thinking, "God, you know, that was fun!" Truly! And I can see it reflected in your eyes—the fun of it, now the challenge of it.

TM: It's truly amazing. And the wonderful thing is when I go and sit down and try to write—maybe I need a color, I need the smell, I need something, and I don't have it. And as soon as I get concave, a small thing comes and when I pick up that yellow lined tablet, Gloria, it is always there; not necessarily when you call it, not even when you want it, but always when you need it. And, as they say, "right on time."

GN: But do you ever wonder, since we have no control over when it comes, if we have no control over when it will leave—forever?

TM: Well, I thought after *Tar Baby* I would just quit. I had written four books. You know, I would just stop and do nothing and then I got involved in filming them which I had always stayed away from. I don't want to see it in another form; besides, I can't think that way. But then little by little, some people whom I respect bought *Tar Baby* and I got involved in producing *Song of Solomon*, and in both instances there were people who wanted fidelity, wanted faithfulness in the film to the book. As I got more involved in that, I had some conflict with the novel I've just described. But what happened was that—you see, the mercy of these people is incredible because when you get in their lives, other things happen also so you don't have to decide *whether* you'll do the novel—all of it surfaced at the same time. One idea shot up another and another and another. So I didn't find these projects in competition with each other. But I think, at the moment, that I won't write anything after *Beloved.*

GN: I know you said that before.

TM: That's exactly what I said. But I thought that about each book so no one pays any attention to me on that score. This is the one. This is it. Maybe I'll write a play or maybe I'll write a short story. Maybe I won't. At any rate, what's gratifying is that—see, this is going to sound very arrogant, but when I wrote *The Bluest Eye*, I was under the distinct impression, which was erroneous, that it was on me, you know, that nobody else was writing like that, nobody, and nobody was going to.

GN: Well, you were right about that. Yes, you were!

TM: And I thought, "No one is ever going to read this until I'm dead. No one's going to do this." I really felt that—you know, I kept it sort of tight, but I thought, "Nobody's going to write about these people that way."

GN: That's not arrogant. That's the truth.

TM: They're going to make them into some little comic relief or they're going to sap it up. No one is going to see what I saw which was this complex poetic life. And it was as grand and as intricate and as profound as anybody had walked this earth. That's what I thought. And no one is going to write from the inside with that kind of gentleness, not romanticizing them, but knowing that whatever happened to them, there was that heartbeat, that love, that understanding. That's what I thought.

GN: Also, because your unique signature would have to be on that since the story was filtered through you. Whatever may have happened in the past and future . . .

TM: Well, I don't feel that way anymore.

GN: You don't feel that . . . no, I don't think—it could have, yes, the subject matter; I don't want to argue with you. I think the subject matter could have been tackled and, if we go back, we can look at it having been tackled in various ways. Wallace Thurman, *The Blacker the Berry.* Same subject matter, two different texts. The sensibilities were different. No, you're saying that no one could have done it that way, quite true. Arrogance would be to say no one could have done it that well and that's up to us to say that, that's not up to you to say that. Not well, but that way.

TM: But now I feel that, thank God, some things are done now. I used to think it was like a plateau; now there are these valleys, if you will, full of people who are entering this terrain, and they're doing extraordinary things with novels and short stories about black women and that's not going to stop; that's not going to ever stop.

GN: No, no, because one is built on another.

TM: And there won't be these huge gaps, either, between them. It's possible to look at the world now and find oneself properly spoken of in it.

GN: Because oneself spoke up for oneself.

TM: That's the point. It wasn't anybody else's job. I'm sitting around wondering why A, B, or C didn't tell my story. That's ridiculous, you know. This is *our* work and I know that it is ours because I have done it and you know it is because you've done it. And you will do it again and again and again. I don't know. It's a marvelous beginning. It's a real renaissance. You know, we have spoken of renaissances before. But this one is ours, not somebody else's.

GN: But being the pioneer of that renaissance within the contemporary time period, how do you feel about that, about watching the black women writers who have now come up after you. In a sense, Toni, you were the first widely accepted black woman writer.

TM: No. Paule Marshall, whom I had not read at that time, had written that incredible book before me.

GN: *Brown Girl, Brown Stones.*

TM: Yes, stunning, in the fifties. And, of course, there was Zora Neale Hurston and, you know, there were women before, so that's what I meant when I said—I was just ill-read, that's all, because I had gone to those schools where . . .

GN: Ill-taught.

TM: Ill-taught. And they didn't have those books in my libraries so it was a long time before I had a thrill of being introduced to such women. It was a double thrill for me because I was introduced to them after I had written, you see. And many people who are trying

to show certain kinds of connections between myself and Zora Neale
Hurston are always dismayed and disappointed in me because I
hadn't read Zora Neale Hurston except for one little short story
before I began to write. I hadn't read her until after I had written. In
their efforts to establish a tradition, that bothers them a little bit. And
I said, "No, no, you should be happy about that." Because the fact
that I had never read Zora Neale Hurston and wrote *The Bluest
Eye* and *Sula* anyway means that the tradition really exists. You
know, if I had read her, then you could say that I consciously was
following in the footsteps of her, but the fact that I never read her
and still there may be whatever they're finding, similarities and
dissimilarities, whatever such critics do, makes the cheese more
binding, not less, because it means that the world as perceived by
black women at certain times does exist, however they treat it and
whatever they select out of it to record, there is that. I hadn't read
Jean Toomer either. I didn't read him until I came into publishing and
was . . . well, that was the time when there was the sort of flurry of
reprints so people could get things. I was reading African novels and
things like that, but, you know, all sorts of things that were just
unavailable to me. They weren't at Cornell and they certainly
weren't at Howard University in the days that I was there.

But your question about how I felt—it's like, there's nothing quite
like seeing, for me there's nothing like reading a really, really fine
book; I don't care who wrote it. You work with one facet of a prism,
you know, just one side, or maybe this side, and it has millions of
sides, and then you read a book and there is somebody who is a
black woman who has this sensibility and this power and this talent
and she's over here writing about that side of this huge sort of
diamond thing that I see, and then you read another book and
somebody has written about another side. And you know that eventually that whole thing will be lit—all of these planes and all of the
facets. But it's all one diamond, it's all one diamond. I claim this
little part, you did this one, but there's so much room, oh, my God.
You haven't even begun and there's so much room and each one is
another facet, another face of this incredible stone, this fantastic
jewel that throws back light constantly and is constantly changing
because even the face that I may have cleaned or cleared or dealt
with will change. It looked like it was saffron light to me, but maybe

twenty years later it looks blue. That's the way I feel about it.
Geometrically all those things touch in a way, but each person has
his own space, his own side of the diamond to work on. That's so
gratifying, so exciting. That eliminates the feeling I had at the beginning—that of solitude. That my work doesn't have anything to do
with life as it goes on, but as though there were something secret in
my head when I was writing the book.

Is that so? Is that the way it was? I read the conversation between
Gloria Naylor and me again; remember it again; listen to tapes of it.
It's all there—not so orderly or so exact, but right nevertheless. Still,
is that so? What am I missing and why do I care? It's okay to print
whatever in any newspaper, magazine, or journal from the college
weekly to *Vogue,* from *Il Tempo* to the Cleveland *Plain Dealer.* I
never comment on the interview; never write letters correcting errors
or impressions. I am content to read proof and content not to see
proof at all. So what's missing from this one that made me want to
add to it and made Gloria want to preface it? Neither of us wanted an
interview and we hope this is not one. An interview is my trying to
get to the end of it; an interview is my trying to help the reporter or
student fill in the blank spaces under the questions so she or he
will believe he or she has some information; it is my saying eight or
ten things eight or ten times into a tape recorder in precisely the
same way I've said them before. And my mind drifts so when I am
being interviewed that I hardly remember it. For while I am talking
(about my work, the state of one thing, the future of another), the
alert part of my mind is "interviewing" the interviewer: Who are
you? Why are you doing this? This is not the way to find out
anything; an hour? Why do you want to be good at it?
    I see them select or make up details to add to the fixed idea of me
they came in the door with—the thing or person they want me to be.
I sense it and, if I am feeling lazy, I play to it—if not I disappear—
shift into automatic and let them have any shadow to play with,
hoping my smoke will distract them into believing I am still there.
    Because an interview is not an important thing.
    But a conversation—well now—that's something. Rare and getting
more so. And this meeting between Gloria Naylor and me was going
to be that. Not one but *two* people present on the scene, talking the

kind of talk in which something of consequence is willing to be
revealed; some step forward is taken; some moment or phrase flares
like a lightning bug and both of us see it at the same time and will
remember it the same way. We didn't care how we "came off" or if
we said something useful or memorable to anybody else—or whether
what we said was good copy. In fact, we would use the good offices
of the *Southern Review* assignment to meet and see if we liked
each other or not. No observers.

She brought a tape recorder which we treated like a nuisance—
which it was—so much so we forgot to turn it on all morning. Until
the afternoon it lay on the table like an envelope addressed to
"Occupant" that we were going to get around to opening in a minute,
in a minute—when we had time. She had no list of questions; took
no notes. Whatever would be missing from the "piece"; that what-
was-so, we would provide. I would say what I was thinking when I
said _____ . What I thought when she said _____ .
When we laughed. Or were interrupted by telephone or one of my
children or something on the stove. But are these the things that
make up a conversation: What happens between and around what is
said? the silence after one word? the frown after another?

I meant to be ready, of course. She followed my directions and
arrived when she said she would. I have never found a reliable way to
be on time. Either I sit in airports two hours before flight time or
stand perspiring at gates whose little signs have been taken down.
But I meant to be dressed at least. I'd been up since five o'clock
getting all sorts of things done, none of which included putting on
shoes or street clothes. That tickled her and she laughed about it off
and on the whole day. That was good because her smile really is one,
and it's hard not to join in with one of your own.

She says my work was critical to her decision to write prose. She
believes that, but I know my work may have figured in *when* she
would write a novel but not *whether*.

She is troubled about political and/or vs. aesthetic responsibility;
about whether having children would hurt or derail her work; about
the limits of her obligations to the community.

She is amazed by the joy it gives her—writing. Fiercely attentive to
the respect it demands of her.

She is angry and hurt by deceptions in publishing—its absence of honor. She is amused by her self; pleased by her triumphs. In short, worried about all the right things. Pleased about all the real things.

I look at her and think for the thousandth time how fine it is now. So many like her and more coming. Eyes scrubbed clean with a Fuller brush, young black women walking around the world who can (and do) say "I write is what I do. I do this and that too—but write is what I *do*, hear?" Women who don't have to block what they know; keep secret what they feel; who welcome their own rage and love because it has voice, place, point and art—and the art is *hers*, not somebody else's. She wears on her head the "hat" she made—not one she bought made by somebody else.

She likes my chair. The river. The warm bread. "Do you ever leave this place? What for?"

I remind her of someone and she likes that. A link. I am not alien.

It was a conversation. I can tell, because I said something I didn't know I knew. About the "dead girl." That bit by bit I had been rescuing her from the grave of time and inattention. Her fingernails maybe in the first book; face and legs, perhaps, the second time. Little by little bringing her back into living life. So that now she comes running when called—walks freely around the house, sits down in a chair; looks at me, listens to Gloria Naylor and anybody else she wants to. She cannot lie. Doesn't know greed or vengeance. Will not fawn or pontificate. There is no room for pupils in her eyes. She is here now, alive. I have seen, named and claimed her— and oh what company she keeps.—TM

Toni Morrison Tries Her Hand at Playwriting

Margaret Croyden / 1985

From the *New York Times* 29 December 1985: H6, H16. Copyright © 1985 by the New York Times Company. Reprinted by permission.

When Toni Morrison, author of the best seller *Tar Baby* and winner of a National Book Critics award for *Song of Solomon*, accepted the Albert Schweitzer Professorship of the Humanities at the State University of New York at Albany, she expected to lead the proverbially quiet life of an academic—teaching writing and writing fiction. Instead she found herself deeply involved in the theater, as a playwright.

Her drama, *Dreaming Emmett*, commissioned by the New York State Writers Institute at SUNY-Albany and directed by Gilbert Moses, will have its world premiere Saturday at the Market Theater there. It will be produced, in conjunction with the Writers Institute and SUNY's Capital District Humanities Program, by the Capital Repertory Company, a resident theater founded by Peter Clough and Bruce Bouchard.

The theme of *Dreaming Emmett* derives from the case, notorious 30 years ago, of a black 14-year-old Mississippi youth named Emmett Till who apparently whistled or made remarks to a white woman that were interpreted as sexual insults. He was beaten and killed, and his alleged murderers, white men, were acquitted by an all-white jury. The case became a worldwide symbol of Southern racism, a spark that helped ignite the civil rights movement. The production will commemorate the first celebration of the Rev. Dr. Martin Luther King Jr.'s birthday as a national holiday.

This venture into theater is a brave act for a novelist, even for one so distinguished as Toni Morrison. Not only does any new play invite sharp scrutiny at a time when serious drama is in decline, but novelists turned dramatists have historically failed in their efforts to move from printed page to the boards.

Asked about this in a recent interview, Miss Morrison laughed and replied: "Oh, I'm aware of the situation all right. I know it's odd. I keep asking Bill Kennedy"—the Pulitzer Prize-winning author who created the Writers Institute—"to find one American who wrote novels first and then successful plays. Just one. And neither he nor I could come up with any one American. Even Henry James was a failure. He tried it three times and each time it was worse than the other. But I feel I have a strong point. I write good dialogue. It's theatrical. It moves. It just doesn't hang there. Besides I have Gilbert Moses. And I have great respect for him as a stage director."

Although she has been writing novels her entire adult life, Miss Morrison knows the world of theater and film. Several years ago she wrote the lyrics for a musical, *New Orleans*, which was done as a workshop production at the Public Theater in New York, and recently she completed a screenplay based on her novel *Tar Baby*. Much of her writing was accomplished during her 20 years as an editor for Random House, where she championed the work of some of the country's foremost black writers. She wrote her novels at night, after her two sons were in bed and household chores were done. Of late she has been involved in a new novel, *Beloved*, a project temporarily put aside during the work on *Dreaming Emmett*.

The idea for *Dreaming Emmett* came to Miss Morrison two years ago, before she went to Albany. It was conceived, she said, "not as a novel, or an essay, but as a play. I wanted to see a collision of three or four levels of time through the eyes of one person who could come back to life and seek vengeance. Emmett Till became that person." But the play remained unfinished. Only when Tom Smith, associate director of the Writers Institute, and Mr. Kennedy said they would pay for the commission to finish the play did she complete it.

The institute, originally funded from Mr. Kennedy's MacArthur Foundation award, recently achieved permanent support from New York State and thus had the resources to become a co-producer of *Dreaming Emmett* with the Capital Repertory Company. Mr. Kennedy and his colleagues at the institute are very concerned with playwriting, not just fiction, and they hope to establish an extensive theater program in the future.

What convinced them that Miss Morrison could come up with an effective play? "Sheer intuition," said Tom Smith. "There are two things. One is how theatrical she is when she reads from her works and gives lectures. In teaching her books to my students I had been reading them aloud in class and was stuck by how marvelous some of the scenes were as scenes, especially in *Song of Solomon*. And then she was here on campus." Mr. Smith is aware of the history of writers "trying to go from fiction to theater. So it seemed a risk, yes, but it was the kind of thing that we wanted to do, risk or no. I think it was the sheer presence of Toni herself that convinced us."

Bruce Bouchard and Peter Clough of the Capital Repertory Company agree. "It was funny the way it all happened," said Mr. Clough. "We were sitting around in a restaurant one night, Kennedy, Smith and ourselves, and Toni summarized the play. She talked for 45 minutes about how she would treat the story and how she imagined the dream . . . We had never become committed to anything that quickly before, but that night we did." Mr. Bouchard added: "Toni is like an actress. We fell under her spell. When she speaks, you listen."

In Miss Morrison's play, Emmett Till is intended to symbolize the plight of contemporary black urban youth—their disproportionately high rate of death by violence. Like many Americans, Miss Morrison is deeply perturbed by this tragedy of anonymous and wasted Emmett Tills.

"There are these young black men getting shot all over the country today, not because they were stealing but because they're black," she said. "And no one remembers how any of them looked. No one even remembers the facts of each case. Certain things were nagging at me for a long time—the contradictions of black people, the relationships between black men and women, between blacks and whites, the differences between 1955 and 1985.

"And what is this about anyhow, this whistling at a woman? Is it the rite of passage or what? Why was it such an important thing for the boy to do? He thought it was a male thing. The white men understood that, too. It was a male rite of passage that all men understand. But the interesting thing is that the men accused of the murder had a store right in the middle of the black area, and they prided themselves as having that ability to work with and among blacks, and they didn't want to lose that status. If this boy got away with this offense, then their reputation among white people as 'handling' blacks would be threatened."

These are among the questions Miss Morrison raises in her play in a complex nonnaturalistic form. The characters and the action shift back and forth in time and place, and there is a play within a play. The nonlinear story involves an anonymous black boy who was murdered. In a dream state he suffers the pain of remembering his death 30 years before. Seeking revenge and a place in history, he summons up the perpetrators of his murder, as well as his family and friends, all to be characters in his dream. But his ghosts refuse to be controlled by his imagination; all see the past in their own way, as the boy doggedly searches for a meaning to his death—and thereby his life. At one point he is challenged by a member of his imaginary audience, a black woman who rejects his dream and provokes a confrontation on sexual issues.

The play as a whole raises questions about history. Can the murder of a Mississippi boy 30 years ago be a shared collective nightmare of the American soul, black and white? Is the past too different from the present for any generation ever to perceive the past? Is history a "dream" that produces only ambiguity and forgetfulness?

No simple answers are suggested. "There are no good guys or bad guys," says Tom Smith. "They all have their own dreams. The text deals with layers of human experience in human terms rather than in philosophical or abstract terms."

Nor is the play political or factual; it is not a docudrama. "I like to make up stuff," says Miss Morrison. "I take scraps, the landscapes of something that happened, and make up the rest. I'm not interested in documentaries. I'm not sticking to the facts. What is interesting about the play is the contradiction of fact. *Dreaming Emmett* is really that. It's about dreaming up those characters."

William Kennedy considers Miss Morrison's conception "very original. It's poetry of a certain kind of violence. Toni has been able to take one of the toughest themes, child murder, and make it the subject of a retrospective history. It puts Till's death in a totally different context. By the time the play is over, everyone has a new perception about what the reality was; a great many revelations take place and a great many reversals."

The staging was entrusted to Gilbert Moses, a good friend of Miss

Morrison with whom she had long wanted to collaborate. The challenge for Mr. Moses—who had staged Amiri Baraka's *Slave Ship* and more recently two segments of the television series *Roots*—was to create an effective theatrical experience out of a script that suggested the strong imagery that is such a notable feature of Miss Morrison's novels, to find theatrical metaphors to express the painful themes and ambiance of the drama.

For the set, the designer Dale Johnson, in collaboration with Mr. Moses, created a nonrepresentational image of an abandoned cotton mill that is supposed to suggest malevolence. Portions of the stage will physically move "to allow for a change in perception," Mr. Moses explained. Actors will stand and talk on moving platforms, so that the central character "can control the stage when he controls his dream." At times actors wear masks to show how a face appears to a child or to the world. Props such as a vintage jukebox bring to mind black urban life in the 1950's in contrast to the 1985 language and sensibility of the main character. "The images are all indicated in Toni's writing," Mr. Moses said, "so that I could dream just what Toni dreamed and that would be my contribution to the dream."

Miss Morrison, who has been attending rehearsals, finds working in the theater intriguing, especially in comparison with writing fiction. "The play is both more and less," she said. "It's less in the setting of a mood and in manipulating the readers. In the novel one has control of everything. Giving that up in a play is not pleasant for me. But on the other hand, there is a thing that happens on the stage. After giving up control, you see the manifestation of the work through somebody else's mind . . . Like going to auditions. Everyone reads the lines in a different way. When I read the lines, I hear only my voice. When you hear the actresses and actors read they give new meanings to the lines and so the texture of the play changes. But in a novel, I only hear it one way, through my voice."

Toni Morrison's voice has been a powerful one in literature. Those working with her on *Dreaming Emmett* feel that she will now also be a powerful theatrical voice.

An Interview with Toni Morrison

Christina Davis / 1986

From *Presence Africaine: Revue Culturelle Du Monde / Cultural Review of the Negro World* 1145 (1988):141–50.

In 1986, Christina Davis met with Toni Morrison in Albany, New York. The interview that follows was carried out with the 30th Anniversary of the First International Conference of Black Writers and Artists (held at the Sorbonne in September 1956) in mind.

Toni Morrison was born in Lorain, Ohio, and studied at Howard University and Cornell University. She taught at Howard and other Universities before becoming the first black woman to hold the position of Senior Editor at Random House Publishing Company in New York. While there, she edited the work of Toni Cade Bambara, Angela Davis, Gayl Jones and Muhammad Ali, among others. She is currently Schweitzer Professor of the Humanities at the State University of New York at Albany.

While teaching at Howard, Toni Morrison began to write. Her first novel, *The Bluest Eye,* was published in 1970. It was followed by *Sula* (1973), *Song of Solomon* (1977), *Tar Baby* (1981) and *Beloved* (1987). In early 1986, the Capital Repertory Company in Albany performed *Dreaming Emmett,* Toni Morrison's first play, based on the lynching of 14-year-old Emmett Till in 1955. The author has received numerous awards for her work and was named Distinguished Writer of 1978 by the American Academy of Arts and Letters. Her novels have been translated into many foreign languages, including French.

She is an active member of organizations such as the National Council on the Arts, the Helsinki Watch Committee and the Board of Trustees of the New York Public Library. She is Chairperson of the New York State Education Department's Committee on Adult Illiteracy.

Christina Davis: September 1986 marks the 30th Anniversary of the First International Conference of Black Writers and Artists at the Sorbonne. Among the themes of the Conference was the need for *Africans* to discover and explore the historical truth about Africa. How has the discovery and affirmation of the truth about the black experience in the United States been a preoccupation of Black American writers?

Toni Morrison: I think it's the *only* preoccupation of Black American writers. The way in which they see the experience of course varies from time to time. Some energy was spent trying to persuade mainstream white America that the experience that most black people had was insufferable and changeable and that black people were worthy of their compassion (. . .) Some of the interest has been to find whatever cultural connections there were between Afro-Americans and Africans, but it's always been interesting to me that Africans are not interested in it at all.

My own preoccupations are quite different—or maybe they're not quite different, but what has interested me is the fact that those two descriptions I just gave you were geared toward educating or clarifying or stimulating something, some response in the white community—which is a legitimate pursuit on the face of it—and perhaps very little attention was given to addressing certain kinds of problems among the members of the black community in a way that was not pedagogical. There was a long period of pedagogy going on in fiction among black people. It seems to me that black people patronizing black people is as unfortunate as being patronized by white people . . .

I respect the emotional and intellectual intelligence of black people because I respect my own emotional intelligence, therefore I did not want to write books that had simple-minded points. I wanted to explore the imagination as well as the problems of black people and it seems to me that this is a more contemporary and perhaps more recent pursuit among black writers.

Christina Davis: When you talk about *"names that bore witness"* in *Song of Solomon,* would they be part of the historical experience of Blacks in the United States?

Toni Morrison: Yes, the reclamation of the history of black people in this country is paramount in its importance because while you can't really blame the conqueror for writing history his own way, you can certainly debate it. There's a great deal of obfuscation and distortion and erasure, so that the presence and the heartbeat of black people has been systematically annihilated in many, many ways and the job of recovery is ours. It's a serious responsibility and one single human being can only do a very very tiny part of that, but it seems to me to be both secular and non-secular work for a writer. You have to stake it out and identify those who have preceded you— resummoning them, acknowledging them is just one step in that process of reclamation—so that they are always there as the *confirmation* and the affirmation of the life that I personally have not lived but is the life of that organism to which I belong which is black people in this country.

Christina Davis: What do you feel are links between African and Afro-American literatures?

Toni Morrison: I'm only discovering those links in a large sense— that is, as a reader and as a scholar—and I'm not sure which ones are genuine and which ones are not. I know the impact that African authors have had on me as a reader, the doors that were opened for me by that contact through literature, because that's the only contact I had. I'm also aware of the vocabulary used to describe what we say as black people in this country—the scholarly vocabulary used in traditional texts to describe *how* we say and how we are is a code designed for destruction, so that one's job is to clear away the code and see what really is in the language and what are the connections.

When I first began to write, I would do no research in that area because I distrusted the sources of research, that is, the books that were available, whether they were religion or philosophy and so on. I would rely heavily and almost totally on my own recollections and, more important, on my own insight about those recollections, and in so doing was able to imagine and to recreate cultural linkages that were identified for me by Africans who had a more familiar, an overt recognition (of them). So much of what is true about Afro-Americans is not only the African but the American—we are very much that and trying to separate those things out can be very difficult, if you *want* to separate them out. We are a brand new human being in this country.

Christina Davis: I understand you dislike having your work described as ''magic realism''. Why is that?

Toni Morrison: I was once under the impression that that label ''magical realism'' was another one of those words that covered up

what was going on. I don't know when it began to be used but my
first awareness of it was when certain kinds of novels were being
described that had been written by Latin American men. It was a
way of *not* talking about the politics. It was a way of *not* talking
about what was in the books. If you could apply the word "magical"
then that *dilutes* the realism but it seemed legitimate because there
were these supernatural and unrealistic things, surreal things, going
on in the text. But for literary historians and literary critics it just
seemed to be a convenient way to skip again what was the truth in
the art of certain writers.

My own use of enchantment simply comes because that's the way
the world was for me and for the black people I knew. In addition
to the very shrewd, down-to-earth, efficient way in which they did
things and survived things, there was this other knowledge or perception, always discredited but nevertheless there, which informed their
sensibilities and clarified their activities. It formed a kind of cosmology that was perceptive as well as enchanting, and so it seemed
impossible for *me* to write about black people and eliminate that
simply because it was "unbelievable". It functioned as a raiment—
the body that was in the middle was something quite different—
and also it was part and parcel of this extraordinary language. The
metaphors and the perceptions came out of that world. So I have
become indifferent, I suppose, to the phrase "magical realism" but I
was very alert at the beginning when I heard it because when I would
read the articles about it, it always seemed to me that it was just
another evasive label.

Christina Davis: All the forces, spiritual forces and so on, are very
real in their own way, although they're different from what's usually
called realism, and they're promptly dismissed as magical.

Toni Morrison: Of course, that *is* the reality. I mean, it's not as
though it's a thing you do on Sunday morning in church, it's not a
tiny, entertaining aspect of one's life—it's what *informs* your sensibility. I grew up in a house in which people talked about their dreams
with the same authority that they talked about what "really" happened. They had visitations and did not find that fact shocking and
they had some sweet, intimate connection with things that were not
empirically verifiable. It not only made them for me the most interesting people in the world—it was an enormous resource for the

solution of certain kinds of problems. Without that, I think I would have been quite bereft because I would have been dependent on so-called scientific data to explain hopelessly unscientific things and also I would have relied on information that even subsequent objectivity has proved to be fraudulent, you see. But for my mother to decide that myself and my sister, when we were infants, would not go into a tuberculosis hospital as this doctor said we should because we had been exposed to tuberculosis was not based on scientific evidence. She simply saw that no one ever came out of those sanatoriums in the '30s and also she had visitations. It was interesting to me that they were treating tubercular patients at that time in a way that would kill them because they didn't *have* all of the right information.

Christina Davis: This of course is very similar to the African relationship with the ancestors and the passing from one state to another rather than death as the Western world knows it.

Toni Morrison: It's interesting—the concept of an ancestor not necessarily as a parent but as an abiding, interested, benevolent, guiding presence that is yours and is concerned about you, not quite like saints but having the same sort of access, none of which is new information. It's just that when it comes from discredited people it somehow has some other exotic attachment: thus the word "magic" I remember many people were very upset when some major journalistic work was done on my work and the heading was "Black Magic": that is to say, my work was black magic. It was a favorable heading to them but the implication was that there was no intelligence there, it was all sort of, you know, "the panther does not know he is graceful because it is his nature to leap that way."

Christina Davis: Another theme of the Sorbonne Conference was defining the unity of black people scattered all over the world. To what extent do you feel contemporary literature reflects that unity or disunity?

Toni Morrison: Well, certain questions have surfaced. There was a time when the literature that was being written, non-fiction as well as fiction, hammered away at the connections and it got very romantic, which I suppose was inevitable but was unfortunate. Then it took another turn in which it just got very interesting. Recent books seem to take either that connection for granted or to explore it in some way that is a little bit different from the sort of wonderful, illusory

connection that they thought existed. You know, it was easy for
Black Americans, Afro-Americans—some of them—to think about
Africa almost the way the conquistadors thought about it, or as one
big continent full of everybody in their neighborhood, instead of very
distinct, very different, very specific, widely divergent people and
what connected them *perhaps* was their skin, but not really that. So
that the *enormous* differences are more interesting to me than the
similarities because it's too easy to get into the trap of the monolithic
black person, you know, the classic, "uni" person.

Christina Davis: Would you like to mention a few of the differences
that you find interesting among Africans or among Africans and
Afro-Americans, as far as literature is concerned?

Toni Morrison: Well, I think there are certain things that have come
through, rained down on us in America, that don't seem to have
happened in Africa. Color—skin color, the privileges of skin in this
country are different. I don't mean they don't exist in Africa, they
must. Concept of beauty. License, sexual license in this country
versus sexual license in African literature. *Enormous* differences in
gender, you know: the expectations of one gender of another, what
black women in America expect of black men and what black men in
America expect of black women, and differences there. And then just
the impact of the white world on an African country—the difference
between Kenya and South Africa. I mean it's *huge* differences, you
see. And what the similarities are between the impact of the white
world on a black human being in Boston versus that same impact in
South Carolina and Mississippi. Those things leaped up at me.
Reading Camara Laye, for example—*The Radiance of The King*—
was an important thing for me. Just being in that position and watching that man stripped as it were, going farther and farther and farther
back and the complex array of people that he met, Africans that he
met or who came into his purview, was for me an extraordinary
thing: a very narcotic kind of experience, a journey for me that was
overwhelming, quite.

Christina Davis: I wanted to ask if there's an African writer or
African writers that you feel particularly akin to or whose work you
feel especially close to?

Toni Morrison: Well, neither akin nor close but certainly a real
education for me. Chinua Achebe was a *real* education for me, a real

education. And certainly the plays of Soyinka and *The Beautyful Ones Are Not Yet Born* of Ayi Kwei Armah—those things were at that time real, and they're the kinds of books that one can re-read with enormous discoveries subsequently.

Christina Davis: We've been talking about literature but I'd like to ask what you feel that Afro-American and African *writers* have in common *as writers?* Or, on the contrary, what separates them in their respective positions?

Toni Morrison: The major thing that binds us—there may be others because I don't dwell on it quite that much—is the clear identification of what the enemy forces are, not this person or that person and so on, but the acknowledgment of a way of life dreamed up for us by some other people who are at the moment in power, and knowing the ways in which it can be subverted. That *is* a connection: we know who he is. What separates us are the things that separate all people, one of which is the way you identify what the problems are and the disguises in which they appear.

This country is so full of material things. There's a great deal of freedom in terms of movement in one sense or in terms of ability to acquire *things*. It can hide misery and pain enormously and also can imprison you in a way, you know, because you have your things but you have to take care of them. And that's a real problem for Black Americans, it's a real problem for all Americans, but it's a serious problem for Black Americans who envision success in certain ways and have difficulty manipulating power once it's in their hands. Because the definitions of success and the ways in which one acquires and therefore *holds* power are quite different in a *totally* capitalistic country. And it can be a dead weight, you know: it can be just heavy shoes that you're walking around in so that certain spiritual things get lost or defrauded in a way. Sometimes people from other countries come here and are quite overwhelmed by the variety of things that are easily found, a wide variety, and its size, and they think how marvelous it all is and I suppose in relative terms it is.

I was fascinated to hear some South Africans on the radio once who were measuring the freedom of black people here against their own and being very curious about what black people were complaining about. They didn't understand it and why should they understand it, because they are relative things. They were sitting in New York in the U.N. so maybe . . . I mean the conversation was there.

Interesting things have happened since that time—the awareness of just the basic hell, the outlines of a basic hell are much more obvious among Black Americans now. There are organizations that are quite serious and there's a movement afoot now that at the moment is concentrated on relief, but it will not stop there.

Christina Davis: Is there anything of all this similarity or difference among the writers that's particular to women writers, African women writers and Afro-American women writers?

Toni Morrison: I think there's something very special about women writers, black women writers in America and those that I know of in any real sense in Africa—Bessie Head, for example, in Africa or Gloria Naylor here. There's a gaze that women writers seem to have that is quite fascinating to me because they tend not to be interested in confrontations with white men—the confrontation between black women and white men is not very important, it doesn't center the text. There are more important ones for them and their look, their gaze of the text is unblinking and wide and very steady. It's not narrow, it's very probing and it does not flinch. And it doesn't have these funny little axes to grind. There's something really marvelous about that.

Christina Davis: I'm sure I'm not the first person who has remarked on the similarity between your speaking or reading voice and your written voice. How did you find your voice as a writer?

Toni Morrison: Tell me what you mean: my speaking voice and my written voice?

Christina Davis: The only way I can describe it to you is to tell you that I've heard other writers read and found a cleavage between the voice that comes off the page and the voice that comes into the ear.

Toni Morrison: Ah well, that may mean that my efforts to make aural literature—A-U-R-A-L—work because I do hear it. It has to read in silence and that's just one phase of the work but it also has to *sound* and if it doesn't *sound* right . . . Even though I don't speak it when I'm writing it, I have this interior piece, I guess, in my head that reads, so that the way I hear it is the way I write it and I guess that's the way I would read it aloud. The point is not to need the adverbs to say how it sounds but to have the sound of it in the sentence, and if it needs a lot of footnotes or editorial remarks or description in order to say how it sounded, then there's something wrong with it.

So I do a lot of revision when I write in order to clean away the parts of the book that can *only* work as print, but it also must work as a total story because that is one of the major characteristics of black literature as far as I'm concerned—it's not just having black people *in* it or having it be written by a black person, but it has to have certain kinds of fundamental characteristics (one of) which is the participation of the *other,* that is, the audience, the reader, and that you can do with a spoken story.

You have to learn how much information to give and how much to keep out and when you need color and when you need a metaphor and when you don't, so that two people are busy making the story. One is me and one is you and together we do that, we invent it together and I just hold your hand while you're in the process of going there and hearing it and sharing it, and being appalled by this and amused by that and happy about this and chagrined about that and scared of this and grateful for that. An artist, for me, a black artist for me, is not a solitary person who has no responsibility to the community. It's a totally communal experience where I would feel unhappy if there was no controversy or no debate or no anything—no *passion* that accompanied the experience of the work. I want somebody to say amen!

Christina Davis: Ruth and Pilate in *Song of Solomon* are very different women, yet each has her particular strengths and, on occasion, they join forces. In both *Song of Solomon* and *Sula,* three generations of women live together. Do your women characters have a special role to play in your work?

Toni Morrison (laughs): Well, in the beginning I was just interested in *finally* placing black women center stage in the text, and not as the all-knowing, infallible black matriarch but as a flawed here, triumphant there, mean, nice, complicated woman, and some of them win and some of them lose. I'm very interested in why and how that happens, but here was this vacancy in the literature that I had any familiarity with and the vacancy was me, or the women that I knew. So that preoccupied me a great deal in the beginning. It still does, except now I'm interested also in the relationships of black men and black women and the axes on which those relationships frequently turn, and how they complement each other, fulfill one another or hurt one another and are made whole or prevented from wholeness by things that they have incorporated into their psyche.

Christina Davis: At the end of *Song of Solomon* we leave Milkman flying through the air. And we don't know what ultimately happens to Son in *Tar Baby* either. Why do you end your novels ambiguously?

Toni Morrison (laughs): Well, I can't shut the door at a moment when the point of the book was the availability of choices and Milkman in *Song of Solomon:* the quality of his life has improved so much and he is so complete and capable that the length of it is irrelevant really. It's not about dying or not dying, it's just that this marvelous epiphany has taken place and, if I close the door, then it would be misleading to say one thing or the other.

For Son, his lament was that he had no choice in this matter, he really was stuck, and he was then provided with one by a woman, but I couldn't make the choice *for* him. I just had to show what the two possibilities were: you join the twentieth century with all of its terror or you abandon the twentieth century and live in some mythological world in private, and which is the briar patch? The reader had to figure that out for him- or herself and that is also part of ending stories. You don't end a story in the oral tradition—you can have the little message at the end, your little moral, but the ambiguity is deliberate because it doesn't end, it's an ongoing thing and the reader or the listener is in it and you have to THINK *(laughs)*. That's what I mean by participating—you have to think what do you want it to be: you want him to live, you want him to die, you want him to go with Jadine, you want him to join the men, you want him to kill Guitar, you want Guitar to kill him or what? You're there, you really are, and I just cannot pass out these little pieces of paper with these messages on them telling people who I respect "this is the way it is" and close the door, because I don't want anybody to do that to me *(laughs)*.

Christina Davis: That really disturbs people—to be made to think.

Toni Morrison: Well, I know. We do read books quite differently. I mean we're taught to read them like you open a medicine cabinet and get out an aspirin and your headache is gone. Or people are looking for the "how-to" book—you know, thirty days and you'll have a flat stomach, or three days as the case may be. So that they are looking for easy, passive, uninvolved and disengaged experiences—television experiences, and I won't, I won't do that.

Christina Davis: I've been impressed by the seriousness with which you prepare your participation in round-tables and panels—the fact that when you come to participate you have something to say that you've obviously thought about, and you're not waiting for somebody to ask you some kind of leading question. This is not true of every writer, unfortunately. Would you have a comment on that?

Toni Morrison: I don't go anywhere because I'm asked, just as I don't write anything just because I can. I have to have something to say, if for no other reason that to stay awake! So that if I do agree to lecture or discuss any topic with somebody else it's something that I'm interested in—what I think about it or what other people think about it—and want to articulate it. So I don't take any of that casually and, also, I think I have something to say or some questions to ask anyway. If I don't have the right answers, sometimes I just have the right questions.

Christina Davis: In your opinion, have these past thirty years been important for the renaissance and growth of black culture?

Toni Morrison: I think so, in a very special way, because I'm not sure that the other Renaissance, the Harlem one, was really ours. I think in some ways it was but in some ways it was somebody else's interest in it that made it exist. This one is interesting because it may have started out as a fashionable thing to do because of the Civil Rights Movement and so on, but it ended up as . . . we snatched it! *(laughs)*. So maybe this is really *our* Renaissance for the moment, rather than entertaining or being interesting to the Other.

Christina Davis: I'd like to end the formal interview here and thank you.

Talk with Toni Morrison

Elsie B. Washington / 1987

From *Essence* October 1987: 58, 136–37.

Toni Morrison enters a room quietly. And when she speaks, the cadence is tempered by Ohio, by Kentucky and other points south. Morrison's voice recalls the rich sound of our best preachers. She is, by turns, warm or wry as she reflects on the wonder of it all. Her conversation is rich in imagery and humor, peppered with words that send you to a dictionary: eleemosynary, denouement. When the subject approaches the art of writing, or family, or community, her words come gift-wrapped in firmness, love and hope. She is sister, teacher, aunt.

She speaks with wisdom. And we *know* she can write. First there was *The Bluest Eye* (1970), then *Sula* (1974). Morrison wrote both while working as an editor at Random House and raising her two sons alone. During this period she also developed a reputation for nurturing and publishing Black writers, among them Toni Cade Bambara and Gayl Jones. *Song of Solomon* was published in 1977 and won Morrison the prestigious National Book Critics' Circle Award for fiction. In 1981 she published *Tar Baby*. Since then she has held the distinguished Albert Schweitzer Chair at the State University of New York at Albany and has done some playwriting. (*Dreaming Emmett*, whose title refers to young Emmet Till, lynched in Mississippi in 1955, was produced last year in Albany.)

From 1982 to the end of 1986, Morrison also crafted another novel, a kind of epic prose poem, exquisitely rendered, about Black love and life and survival in the era of slavery and its aftermath. Titled *Beloved*, it was published last month (Alfred A. Knopf; hardcover, $18.95). It is fair to call this new novel long-awaited—six years *is* long for those of us who love Morrison's work. The wait was worth it.

Recently the author, who lives in Rockland County, New York, shared with *Essence* some of her thoughts about her work, her life and the resilience of Black people.

Essence: If you were writing the book-jacket copy for *Beloved*, how would you describe it?

Morrison: I would have enormous difficulty describing it in any terms that would make it simple. If I could understand it in a hundred words or less, I probably wouldn't have written a book. With hindsight, I think what's important about it is the process by which we construct and deconstruct reality in order to be able to function in it. I'm trying to explore how a people—in this case one individual or a small group of individuals—absorbs and rejects information on a very personal level about something [slavery] that is undigestible and unabsorbable, completely. Something that has no precedent in the history of the world, in terms of length of time and the nature and specificity of its devastation. If Hitler had won the war and established his thousand-year Reich, at some point he would have stopped killing people, the ones he didn't want around, because he would have needed some to do the labor for nothing. And the first 200 years of that Reich would have been exactly what that period was in this country for Black people. It would have been just like that. Not for five years, not for ten years, but for 200 years or more.

So the central action of *Beloved* posed the perfect dilemma, for me as a writer, from which to explore things I wanted to understand about that period of slavery and about women loving things that are important to them.

Essence: What did you come to understand about those women, those people?

Morrison: Those people could not live without value. They had prices, but no value in the white world, so they made their own, and they decided what was valuable. It was usually eleemosynary [charitable], usually something they were doing for somebody else. Nobody in the novel, no adult Black person, survives by self-regard, narcissism, selfishness. They took the sense of community for granted. It never occurred to them they could live outside of it. There was no life out there, and they wouldn't have chosen it anyway. Those were the days of Black people who really loved the company of other Black people.

Essence: We seem to have lost that.

Morrison: We're just distracted, that's all. Black people live all over the world and in all sorts of neighborhoods, but when they think about comfort and joy, they think about one another. That is the vestige of the days when we thought about staying alive, when we thought about one another.

In some ways those were the most complicated of times, in some ways they were not. Now people choose their identities. Now people choose to be Black. They used to be *born* Black. That's not true anymore. You can be Black genetically and choose not to be. You just change your mind or your eyes, change anything. It's just a mind-set.

In my work, what I want to do is present the consequences of certain kinds of choices and the risks and the benefits. *Beloved* is an incredible story about those choices.

Essence: It took you four years to write the book. Do you write every day?

Morrison: I write every day if I have something to say every day.

Essence: Have you found any new, young Black women writers recently?

Morrison: Sure. I've seen quite a few who are really good.

Essence: What's different about writing now than, say, 15 years ago? Do you see a direction that Black women's fiction is going in?

Morrison: There are certain preliminary, editorial, explanatory steps these women don't have to take. The nice thing about it is that their work is not harangue and it's without apology. They don't have to grind any axes. Fifteen years ago Paule Marshall, Maya Angelou, Alice Walker and Toni Cade Bambara were already writing, and they still are. The amazing thing to me is that among all the Black women writing, there's this incredible range; no one is like the other. Nobody has exhausted the range. It may be generation after generation before someone does, or it may not be then. But Jamaica Kincaid and Toni Cade Bambara are not so different that they don't belong in the same bookstore.

Essence: What do you make of the discussion about Black men writers versus Black women writers? A lot of people are saying that because Black women are being published, publishers won't look at Black men writers anymore.

Morrison: I don't know if the facts support that. My feeling, based on the people I've published, is that there were as many men as there were women. I didn't find any reluctance to publish men. In fact, I think, if you count Black women writers, maybe there are a hundred.

That's not a thousand. I mean that's nothing. If there are ten Black women who have published two novels each, it's amazing. A few years ago, there was the first collection ever published of political essays written by a Black woman—June Jordan. Think about that. It's amazing there are so few.

You have to realize that the publishing industry is a commercial one, and they will promote whatever they think will sell. In the 1970's a certain kind of confrontational Black-man-on-white-man thing could get published. But the fashion, as well as the ideology, has changed. That exacts an unfair price from Black writers and is a serious problem to address. Those who complain are right. The problem *I'm* having is: Why does there have to be a victim or villain in this piece, and why is that villain *me*?

The issue that Black men writers raise is part of a larger issue, and that can't be dismissed. Some part of what they're saying is true. But it's not because Black women writers are doing anything that shouldn't be done or that is counterproductive or counterrevolutionary.

Essence: Others have criticized the portrayal of Black men by women writers.

Morrison: First of all, no one should tell any writer what to write, at all, ever. No more than you would tell Roberta Flack what to sing, or Miles Davis what to play. I thought one of the goals of the whole business of liberation was to make it possible for us not to be silenced, no matter what we said.

Essence: You were married, divorced and have two grown sons. How did you find the time to write and edit *and* raise your children as a single mother?

Morrison: I don't think I did any of that very well. I did it ad hoc, like any working mother does. Every woman who's got a household knows exactly what I did. I did it on a minute-to-minute basis. Trying to plan for certain things, but not always being able to, and failing in many ways. But I don't go anywhere. I don't have any elaborate social life. I don't go anywhere to be happy, I don't go on vacations, I don't ski. I don't do any of the so-called fun things in life. Writing is what I do, for me that is where it is—where the vacation is, the fun is, the danger, the excitement—all of that is in my work.

Essence: What about kids' needs? You can choose not to go out, but can you choose not to comfort a crying child?

Morrison: No, you can't. You have to be interrupted. There was never a place I worked, or a time I worked, that my children did not interrupt me, not matter how trivial—because it was never trivial to them. The writing could never take precedence over them. Which is why I had to write under duress, and in a state of siege and with a lot of compulsion. I couldn't count on any sustained period of free time to write. I couldn't write the way writers write, I had to write the way a woman with children writes. That means that you have to have immense powers of concentration. I would never tell a child, "Leave me alone, I'm writing." That doesn't mean anything to a child. What they deserve and need, in-house, is a mother. They do not need and cannot use a writer.

Essence: You talk a lot in your works about grandparents and ancestors. Why is it so important to keep them in mind?

Morrison: It's DNA, it's where you get your information, your cultural information. Also it's your protection, it's your education. They were so responsible *for* us, and we have to be responsible *to* them. Knowing as a child how to care for my grandfather, being told what to do for him, gave me a lot of information about growing old, respecting people. It's payback—for all those times he played the violin for us and drew pictures for us. I remember reading the Bible to my grandmother when she was dying; she used to take our hands and dance us around the kitchen table. You can't just *take*. Our ancestors are part of that circle, an everwidening circle, one hopes. And if you ignore that, you put yourself in a spiritually dangerous position of being self-sufficient, having no group that you're dependent on.

Essence: What can we look for next from Toni Morrison?

Morrison: I've started my next book, as well as the one after.

Essence: You once said, "A novel should be unquestionably political and irrevocably beautiful." I think *Beloved* fulfilled that.

Morrison: Thank you. The word *novel* means "new." A novel ought to confront important ideas, call them historical or political, it's the same thing. But is has another requirement, and that is its art. And that should be a beautiful thing. That's the way I feel.

Author Toni Morrison Discusses Her Latest Novel *Beloved*

Gail Caldwell / 1987

From the *Boston Globe* 6 October 1987: 67–68. Reprinted cour-
tesy of the *Boston Globe*.

A brutal rain has just swept in over midtown Manhattan, and Toni
Morrison is taking refuge under the umbrella of her lunch date,
whom she has known about 10 minutes. Without any hesitation she
puts one arm around me and grasps my wrist with her free hand, a
gesture of such familiarity that, to passers-by, we must look more
like old friends than amicable strangers. It is pure Toni Morrison, and
a glimmer of the portrait that emerges over the next few hours:
Warm and sometimes infectiously funny, this small woman with
graying hair—wearing boots, skirt and sweater, and large gold hoop
earrings—has a magnetism that rivals the spirit of her fiction.

Undaunted by the staccato rainstorm or the cabs swerving through
noon-hour traffic, Morrison keeps up a nonstop conversation all the
way to a French restaurant on East 50th Street, where she makes a
quick study of the menu, ordering swordfish steak and, for dessert,
raspberries with *creme anglais* and coffee. That settled, she leans
back against the booth with a relieved smile. "This is the first time all
week they've let me have lunch," she says. "Usually, they bring me
cottage cheese."

"They" are Morrison's well-intentioned publicity crew at Alfred
A. Knopf, who are trying against all odds to cram a month's worth of
national book promotion into five days in New York. Morrison, who
holds the Schweitzer Chair at the State University of New York in
Albany, is on her way to the University of California at Berkeley for
four weeks as a visiting professor in creative writing and Afro-
American studies. The engagement dovetails coincidentally with
Knopf's September release of her new novel: *Beloved*. When she
made the Berkeley commitment a year ago, Morrison had no way of
knowing the book would hit the New York Times Best-Seller List the
same week as its official publication date. In three subsequent weeks,

it has climbed to No. 3, a rare ascent for a work of serious fiction. With an initial run of 100,000 copies, the novel is already in its third printing.

Although the legions of faithful have grown steadily since her first novel, *The Bluest Eye*, was published in 1970, Morrison is not accustomed to this kind of reception. And in spite of a radiance that causes waiters to turn back to her and smile, she confesses to being tired. "The exhaustion I'm feeling now is quite new," she says, "because I used to be able to do this quite well—I felt I had to work hard to call attention to my books. I almost felt this missionary zeal, because 15 years ago a black woman novelist was 'novel.' I thought if they [the public] got accustomed to the idea, then other black women writers wouldn't have to break brand new ground. So I used to plow the soil, so to speak. This time I thought, well, that's not necessary anymore."

Not for Morrison, at any rate. If *The Bluest Eye* and her next novel, *Sula* found eager audiences, *Song of Solomon*, published in 1977, found an exuberant one, going on to win the National Book Critics Circle Award in 1978. *Tar Baby* followed in 1981; by then, Morrison had been at the crest of a new wave of Afro-American literature for more than a decade. An editor at Random House since 1967, she resigned in 1983 to write full time; at 56, she lives in Rockland County, N.Y., with the younger of her two sons.

Morrison spent two years thinking about the story of *Beloved* and another three writing it; she says now that she was so frightened by the effort that she hit a writing impasse in 1985. She had conceived of the novel as a three-volume work; when she gave the manuscript to her editor, Bob Gottlieb (formerly of Knopf, now of the *New Yorker*), she was already convinced that she had failed.

"I had decided that I was never going to meet the deadline, and I would just have to live with it. But I gave Bob what I had, and said, 'I'm sorry, because I really and truly have only a third of a book.'

"And he read it and said, 'Whatever else you're doing, do it, but this *is* a book.' I said, 'Are you sure?' "

Morrison laughs. "I was happy that, after all these years, what I had done could be published. I was not sure for a long time. I mean,

I trust Bob a lot, but I kept saying, 'What do you think?' Not
meaning, 'is it any good?' but 'are you sure this is IT?' ''

This was most certainly it, as Gottlieb realized immediately, for
Morrison had given him "Beloved" in its entirety, save the page-and-
a-half coda at the end. The novel is extraordinary, even by Morrison
standards, with a lyricism equal to the sadnesses it plumbs. Set in
Ohio in 1873, *Beloved* tells the story of Sethe, an ex-slave who fled
the South with her children 18 years earlier. She now lives alone with
her youngest daughter, Denver, but their isolation is threatened by a
presence in the house: the ghost of her other girl, Beloved, who was
murdered as an infant. How that tragedy came about—and just who
was responsible—is the mystery at the center of *Beloved,* which is as
much about the mother-daughter bond as it is the crimes of slavery.

Morrison says she works from the ground up, conceiving of "the
smaller details, the images," before the entire architecture of a novel
appears. But unlike her four previous books, the idea for the plot of
Beloved came from an actual event—gleaned from a 19th-century
newspaper story she'd discovered while editing *The Black Book* (an
overview of black American history) at Random House. The woman
in the news story became Sethe, and Morrison began to write.

"What was on my mind," says Morrison, "was the way in which
women are so vulnerable to displacing themselves, into something
other than themselves. And how now, in the modern and contemporary world, women had a lot of choices and didn't have to do that
anymore. But nevertheless, there's still an enormous amount of
misery and self-sabotage, and we're still shooting ourselves in the
foot.

"It occurred to me that I'd read these stories about black women
. . . because we were at the forefront of making certain kinds of
decisions, modern decisions that hadn't been made in 1873.

"The past, until you confront it, until you live through it, keeps
coming back in other forms. The shapes redesign themselves in other
constellations, until you get a chance to play it over again."

Morrison still views *Beloved* as the first of three works, and that,
she says, has helped counteract the melancholy that usually accom-
panies a book's completion. The struggles she encountered along the
way paid off: *Beloved* is driven by a voice so pure that it half-seems
as though its narrators are gathered around the reader's kitchen

table. Its shifting narration builds to a crescendo of voices at the end
of the novel, particularly that of Beloved—who has come back as a
young woman looking to reclaim her past.

"I couldn't get Beloved's voice," says Morrison, "I just couldn't
get there. I wrote around it: She was there, but she couldn't say
anything . . . I could get Denver's and Sethe's voices, but I just
couldn't get that girl to say where she had been."

Paul D, the former slave from Sethe's past, has his own way of
saying where he's been, a poetry of lament that seems written from
the inside looking out. "I'll tell you," says Morrison about capturing
his voice, "you know how actresses do? You just get in there, and
see what the world looks like in there. I can even write dialogue
when he's talking and I'm inside him, and then I have to come out
and get in the other person. Rewriting was that constant shifting, and
trying to do him justice. I don't want to shortchange anybody. It has
something to do with honorably rendering another life.

"Paul D's like a lot of other black men I used to know, and listen
to—my father, my uncles, and the way they used to talk."

It's not the only time Morrison's family had a hand in *Beloved*. As
a child, she listened to the ghost stories her parents told; all her
novels are rich with supernatural lore; from the dream imagery of
Sula to the flying metaphors of *Song of Solomon*. When Beloved's
flesh-and-blood manifestation shows up at Sethe's house one day—
no lines on her palms and no history to speak of—her presence
seems as ordinary as an afternoon visit from the local preacher.

"As a child, everybody knew there were ghosts," says Morrison.
"You didn't put your hand under the bed when you slept at night.
It's that place that you go to [in *Beloved*], right away . . . a shared
human response to the world. And that's where I had to go to, with
Beloved's voice, because I couldn't confuse it with my own." Morri-
son laughs. "It starts getting crazy, you know, trying to do that."

With its lush, Gauguin-like imagery and commonplace mysticism,
Beloved draws from a wellspring not unlike that of the Latin American fabulists. Morrison nods at the comparison between black
American folklore and magic realism, though she says she was well
into *Song of Solomon* before she discovered Gabriel Garcia Marquez.

"Their stuff was so readily available to them—that mixture of

Indian and Spanish. Whereas I felt the preachers, the storytelling, the folklore, the music was very accessible to me, but I felt almost alone. It wasn't only mine, but I didn't have any literary precedent for what I was trying to do with the magic.

"So I thought, boy, those guys—they've got it. Everybody understood the sources of their magic right away. Whereas mine was discredited, because it was held by discredited people. 'Folklorists!' Now it's sort of a little subject in the academy, but it did not have any currency . . . it's perceived of as illiterate.

"People give a lot of credence to the intelligence, the concentration, the imagination necessary for listening to music, but never for listening to stories. That somehow seems like a dumb thing that people who can't read do. And I know how hard it is to listen, and what's engaged when you listen."

If Morrison's early work quickly became required reading in Afro-American literature courses around the country, it was lists of standard English courses, Afro-American or otherwise. Still, the embrace of "ethnic" and "women's" literature in the last 15 years—read: nonwhite-male—is viewed by some as a ghettoization of literature, more stifling than liberating. And while Morrison herself has received superlative-laden praise for her work, the words "black" and "female" almost always preface such claims.

"Well, I get unnerved by all of it," says Morrison. "When they say I'm a great American novelist, I say, 'Ha! They're trying to say I'm not black.' When they say I'm a wonderful woman novelist, I think, 'Aha, they think I don't belong.' So I've just insisted—insisted!—upon being called a black woman novelist. And *I* decided what that meant—in terms of this big world that has become broader and deeper through the process of reclamation, because I have claimed it. I have claimed what I know. As a black and a woman, I have had access to a range of emotions and perceptions that were unavailable to people who were neither.

"So I say, 'Yes, I'm a black woman writer.' And if I write well enough, then maybe in about five years—or 10, or 15—it'll be like, 'Do you write for the Russians, or do you write for the French?' I mean, that kind of question, you can't put to anyone other than women and blacks."

Morrison laughs. "I've always had a secret desire to write reviews of white people's books from that point of view, and make all these observations. I think that would be a scream. I'd say, 'This is a better book because that's the way white people *really are*. I mean, what does that mean?''

The color and gender demarcations of contemporary fiction have begun to blur in the last decade, in part due to writers such as Morrison, whose contributions stand tall against any literary standard. And while she underplays her own participation in that change, she says she's witnessed its effects, particularly in the schools and universities.

"The black kids [where I lectured], when they would ask questions, they used to say—vis a vis *Song of Solomon* or *Sula*—they'd say, 'I don't know anybody like that.' Or, 'wear shoes.'

"And I would say, 'I don't know anybody like that either.'

"They were always disassociating themselves from the class of blacks to which they did not belong. And they weren't talking to me anyway; they were talking to their fellow [white] students, All of the time, at least one person would make sure that I understood that a wine-maker like Pilate [in *Song of Solomon*] they loved, but that was not part of *their* experience.

"They were at great pains to let me know that they were literate. That doesn't happen anymore.

"Painful as it is, there was a void before, and now there's something in it. And you know, I'm not the first black writer. So that it means that the cumulative effect of all those writers who went before—the Zoras [Neale Hurston] and the [Ralph] Ellisons—in its real sense, it means it is there now.''

The difficulties Morrison encountered with *Beloved* came from the heights and depths she tried to conquer: The girl Beloved's voice at the end of the novel is wrenching testimony, not just her private suffering but of all the ravages of slavery. For Morrison, it was more than a personal triumph.

"When I had problems, I thought: If they can live it, I can write about it. I refuse to believe that that period, or that thing [slavery] is beyond art. Because the consequences of practically everything we do, art alone can stand up to. It's not the historians' job to do that— you know what I'm saying? You will get some truth out of it that is not just the province of the natural or social sciences.

"I said, then the slaveholders have won if this experience is beyond my imagination and my powers. It's like humor: You have to take the authority back; you realign where the power is. So I wanted to *take* the power. They were very inventive and imaginative with cruelty, so I have to take it back—in a way that I can tell it. And that is the satisfaction."

In the Realm of Responsibility: A Conversation with Toni Morrison

Marsha Darling / 1988

From the *Women's Review of Books* 5(March 1978):5–6.

As I thought about the significance of the themes and questions that flow from *Beloved*, I remembered being repeatedly reminded as a child that "what goes around must also come around": everything we create in thought and action we keep the original of. Sooner or later, this lesson in accountability went, we must own not only our intentions, our goals, but also their consequences—our actions—which may not have been consistent with the intentions and values they sprang from. I read *Beloved* as a story about living consciously and accountably in our many worlds; and I began to want to hear directly what Toni Morrison had to say about these themes and issues as they emerge from the levels of intimacy the characters in her book convey.

One evening we began talking by telephone about the historical and spiritual contours of *Beloved*. We talked about the existence of the spirit world as a complement to the human one. In establishing an overarching frame of reference for the novel, Toni immediately brought up the issue of restlessness amongst ancestor spirits. These are spirits which have been largely unacknowledged and unaccounted for, as the dislocation of African peoples and individuals—the diaspora—has swallowed the memory of their existence. As Toni spoke of the African doctrine of last things, I heard a call to Black peoples to close the gap in our understanding of our links with the One Life Force abiding in many forms.

MD: What are our responsibilities to the living and the dead? What are the boundaries between the living and the dead? For instance, who—what—brings the baby spirit Beloved to 124 Bluestone Road? Is she summoned? Does she come because of some higher law that has not been reckoned with? Reading *Beloved* got me thinking about

246

cause, effect—what are those boundaries, whose responsibilities? Do you want to suggest that it is Sethe accounting to herself that summons the spirit? Does Beloved bring herself? Does Sethe bring Beloved?

TM: I will describe to you the levels on which I wanted Beloved to function. That may answer the question in part. She is a spirit on one hand, literally she is what Sethe thinks she is, her child returned to her from the dead. And she must function like that in the text. She is also another kind of dead which is not spiritual but flesh, which is, a survivor from the true, factual slave ship. She speaks the language, a traumatized language, of her own experience, which blends beautifully in her questions and answers, her preoccupations, with the desires of Denver and Sethe. So that when they say "What was it like over there?" they may mean—they do mean—"What was it like being dead?" She tells them what is was like being where she was on that ship as a child. Both things are possible, and there's evidence in the text so that both things could be approached, because the language of both experiences—death and the Middle Passage—is the same. Her yearning would be the same, the love and yearning for that face that was going to smile at her.

The gap between Africa and Afro-America and the gap between the living and the dead and the gap between the past and the present does not exist. It's bridged for us by our assuming responsibility for people no one's ever assumed responsibility for. They are those that died en route. Nobody knows their names, and nobody thinks about them. In addition to that, they never survived in the lore; there are no songs or dances or tales of these people. The people who arrived—there is lore about them. But nothing survives about . . . that.

I suspect the reason is that it was not possible to survive on certain levels and dwell on it. People who did dwell on it, it probably killed them, and the people who did not dwell on it probably went forward. They tried to make a life. I think Afro-Americans in rushing away from slavery, which was important to do—it meant rushing out of bondage into freedom—also rushed away from the slaves because it was painful to dwell there, and they may have abandoned some responsibilities in so doing. It was a double-edged sword, if you understand me.

There is a necessity for remembering the horror, but of course there's a necessity for remembering it in a manner in which it can be digested, in a manner in which the memory is not destructive. The act of writing the book, in a way, is a way of confronting it and making it possible to remember.

MD: One of my questions was going to be—and I think you've just answered it—where's the healing? There's healing in the memory and the re-memory. Yes, each character tells her or his story, and through that there are confrontations with each other; there are a lot of things that go on, yet there's a healing in bringing it into 1873.

TM: And no one speaks, no one tells the story about himself or herself unless forced. They don't want to talk, they don't want to remember, they don't want to say it, because they're afraid of it—which is human. But when they do say it, and hear it, and look at it, and share it, they are not only one, they're two, and three, and four, you know? The collective sharing of that information heals the individual—and the collective.

MD: Toni, I've read one or two other articles where people have interviewed you, and you talk about doing research for the book, and how to cast Margaret Garner in a way so as to create Sethe. So some of it you clearly sat down and thought about, did some research about. But there are parts of the book that I am astounded by. For instance: there are sections of the book where you have people thinking to one another telepathically—or at least that's how I'm interpreting it. Beloved has an extra-human quality about her which for anyone who is psychic is *real*. When I say it's an extraordinary book, that's the level that I'm talking about. This led me to want to ask you, were parts of this book channeled?

TM: I did research about a lot of things in this book in order to narrow it, to make it narrow and deep, but I did not do much research on Margaret Garner other than the obvious stuff, because I wanted to invent her life, which is a way of saying I wanted to be accessible to anything the characters had to say about it. Recording her life as lived would not interest me, and would not make me available to anything that might be pertinent. I got to a point where in asking myself who could judge Sethe adequately, since I couldn't, and nobody else that knew her could, really, I felt the only person who could judge her would be the daughter she killed. And from there Beloved inserted herself into the text . . .

I didn't start out thinking that would be what would happen in the book. So that when you say "channeling" I'm taking that to mean part of what writing is for me, which is to have an idea and to know that it's alive, that things may happen to it if I am available to a character or a presence or some information that does not come out of any research that I've done.

MD: There are times in the book where Beloved speaks and there are times when she thinks. So are you also talking about two different levels of communication?

TM: There are times when she says things, what she's thinking, when she's asking something, responding to somebody. The section in which the women finally go home and close up and begin to fulfil their desires begins with each one's thoughts in her language, and then moves into a kind of threnody in which they exchange thoughts like a dialogue, or a three-way conversation, but unspoken—I mean unuttered. Yet the intimacy of those three women—illusory though it may be—is such that they would not have to *say* it.

MD: How is Beloved pregnant?

TM: Paul D.

MD: (laughing) I know. If she is a human being I could easily comprehend that. That part of the story also forced me to stretch— really stretch.

TM: (laughing) Nobody likes that part. I know that a couple of people to whom I have said what I just said to you, said "I don't want to know that," so I thought, "okay." But there is a moment somewhere in time in which that's what you have to know. That is, ghosts or spirits are real and I don't mean . . .

MD: . . . just as a thought.

TM: That's right. And the purpose of making her real is making history possible, making memory real—somebody walks in the door and sits down at the table so you have to think about it, whatever they may be. And also it was clear to me that it was not at all a violation of African religion and philosophy; it's very easy for a son or parent or a neighbor to appear in a child or in another person.

MD: Does she teach Paul D to call her name, to summon her? She asks him, "Call me by my name."

TM: She tells him that's what he has to do—so he does. (Laughing) He's sunk.

MD: I like the men in *Beloved*. I think I experience Paul D as a healer.

TM: Very much, yes.

MD: Of course we hear his story through his words, but Halle we know by his works, by his deeds, and yet he's so important to these four children, to Sethe, to Baby Suggs, And we don't meet him. You obviously were very deliberate about that. Here is a part of the nuclear family in the book and we know him only by his works.

TM: Well, that's the carnage. It can't be abstract. The loss of that man to his mother, to his wife, to his children, to his friends, is a serious loss and the reader has to feel it, you can't feel it if he's in there. He has to *not* be there.

I was sitting in a radio station somewhere and the man who was interviewing me said, "What are you saying about Black women in this book, when Sethe survives and gets across the river and her husband doesn't?" And I said, "What do you mean?" And he said, "Are you saying that the women are stronger?" I said, "They're not stronger. What about Halle? You couldn't ask for a stronger man. He sold his life so that the women and the children could be free." This man wanted to engage me in a fake argument, a divisive controversy. I said, "Sethe makes it, she's tough, but some things are beyond endurance and you need some help. So she has some finally from the women and then from Paul D."

The notion of the devastation of those families is real, and you can't communicate how serious it is without indicating that at some point the system will stop you. I don't want to suggest that slavery was a terrible thing but with a little luck and endurance it was all right. Usually it's an abstract concept—but I and the reader have to yearn for their company, for the people who are gone, to know what slavery did.

MD: I found myself wondering what difference it would have made if Halle had been there the day that the white men came across the yard to get Sethe, in what was free territory. What difference would his physical presence have made to Sethe's sense of the possible?

TM: In fact it didn't make a difference, because in fact Margaret Garner escaped with her husband and two other men and was returned to slavery.

MD: Despite the fact that she killed the child, she was returned?

TM: Well, she wasn't tried for killing her child. She was tried for a *real* crime, which was running away—although the abolitionists were trying very hard to get her tried for murder because they wanted the Fugitive Slave Law to be unconstitutional. They did not want her tried on those grounds, so they tried to switch it to murder as a kind of success story. They thought that they could make it impossible for Ohio, as a free state, to acknowledge the right of a slave-owner to come get those people. In fact, the sanctuary movement now is exactly the same. But they all went back to Boone County and apparently the man who took them back—the man she was going to kill herself and her children to get away from—he sold her down river, which was as bad as was being separated from each other. But apparently the boat hit a sandbar or something, and she fell or jumped with her daughter, her baby, into the water. It is not clear whether she fell or jumped, but they rescued her and I guess she went on down to New Orleans and I don't know what happened after that. The point of all this being that my story, my invention, is much, much happier than what really happened.

MD: That's real clear to me. Sethe lives in a world where she gets to be with the man she loves. And she gets to have four children that are by him and she is nineteen, fleeing, running away. And if things look bad, things have not been miserably intolerable . . .

TM: . . . not a total dead end, where only death would relieve her. And she gets to have a second shot.

MD: Right. If anything, the fact that she just won't let all of that be undone, for me, did say something about her being able to pull together over time a sense of her self and a taste of freedom.

TM: Yes, she does have a taste of freedom. And therefore she is able to scratch out something and then maybe more and maybe more. So she can consider the possibility of an individual pride, of a real self which says "you're your best thing." Just to begin to think of herself as a proper name—she's always thought of herself as a mother, as her role.

MD: I wanted to ask you about your sense of Sethe as mother, woman. There is a way that she loves that is intense. And I'm not sure where I see you locate her *self*. She tells us at one point that she is not separate from these children; she is these children and these children are her. Could you talk some about that? That is a real

powerful part of the book and very controversial, in that she takes
responsibility for the very breath in their bodies.

TM: Under those theatrical circumstances of slavery, if you made
that claim, an unheard-of claim, which is that you are the mother of
these children—that's an outrageous claim for a slave woman. She
just *became* a mother, which is becoming a human being in a situation which is earnestly dependent on your not being one. That's who
she is. So to claim responsibility for children, to say something about
what happens to them means that you claim all of it, not part of it.
Not till they're five or till they are six, but *all* of it. Therefore when
she is away from her husband she merges into that role, and it's
unleashed and it's fierce. She almost steps over into what she was
terrified of being regarded as, which is an animal. It's an excess of
maternal feeling, a total surrender to that commitment, and, you
know, such excesses are not good. She has stepped across the line,
so to speak. It's understandable, but it is excessive. This is what the
townspeople in Cincinnati respond to, not her grief, but her arrogance.

MD: Is that why they shun her? They go away, they leave, they
just abandon her.

TM: They abandon her because of what they felt was her pride.
Her statement about what is valuable to her—in a sense it damns
what they think is valuable to them. They have had losses too. In her
unwillingness to apologize or bend . . . she would kill her child again
is what they know. That is what separates her from the rest of her
community.

MD: And what they punish her for.

TM: Oh, very much.

MD: I actually like that part of the book. I know Black people like
that.

TM: Sure.

One of the things that's important to me is the powerful imaginative way in which we deconstructed and reconstructed reality in
order to get through. The act of will, of going to work every day—
something is going on in the mind and the spirit that is not at all the
mind or the spirit of a robotized or automaton people. Whether it
is color for Baby Suggs, the changing of his name for Stamp Paid,
each character has a set of things their imagination works rather

constantly at, and it's very individualistic, although they share
something in common. So it's important to me that the interior life of
each of those characters be one that you could trust, one that felt like
it was a real interior life; and also be distinct one from the other, in
order to give them—not "personalities," but an interior life of people
that have been reduced to some great lump called slaves.

MD: I had started reading *Beloved* a long time ago, maybe two and
a half months ago, and it got to the point where Beloved and Sethe
would enter my dreams and I knew that part of the reason was that I
was being so in earnest about the book, reading it at such close
attention, because I was going to review it. But I also thought that it
had to do with the clarity and the intensity of how I could experience
them as characters.

TM: That's good. Because the whole point is to have those characters, and any that I do, if they're successful, move off the page and
inhabit the imagination of whoever has opened herself or himself to
them. I don't want to write books that you can close (laughing)
and walk on off and read another one right away—like a television
show, you know, where you just flick the channel. It's very important to be as discreet as possible, that the writing be as understated
and as quiet as possible, and as clean as possible and as lean as
possible in order to make a complex and rich response come from the
reader.

They always say that my writing is rich. It's not—what's rich, if
there is any richness, is what the reader gets and brings him or
herself. That's part of the way in which the tale is told. The folk tales
are told in such a way that whoever is listening is in it and can shape
it and figure it out. It's not over just because it stops. It lingers and
it's passed on. It's passed on and somebody else can alter it later.
You can even end it if you want. It has a moment beyond which
it doesn't go, but the ending is never like in a Western folktale where
they all drop dead or live happily ever after.

MD: Toni, the women characters you create are intense, strong,
active presences. In this novel they talk to us from the nineteenth
century. But you are obviously saying things about the here and now
and about women here and now. Could you elaborate on that?

TM: The story seemed to me to yield up a persistent struggle by
women, Black women, in negotiating something very difficult. The

whole problem was trying to do two things: to love something bigger than yourself, to nurture something; and also not to sabotage yourself, not to murder yourself.

MD: In terms of decisions, choices we make?

TM: Yes. I'll say it this way. This story is about, among other things, the tension between being yourself, one's own Beloved, and being a mother. The next story has to do with the tension between being one's own Beloved and the lover. One of the nicest things women do is nurture other people, but it can be done in such a way that we surrender anything like a self. You can surrender yourself to a man and think that you cannot live or be without that man; you have no existence. And you can do the same thing with children.

It seemed that slavery presented an ideal situation to discuss the problem. That was the situation in which Black women were denied motherhood, so they would be interested in it—everybody would be interested in making, holding, keeping a family as large and as productive as it could be. Even though there are greater choices now, an infinite variety of choices, the propensity for self-dramatizing seems to me to be just as great. I'm curious about it, that's all. For me it's just an examination of what on earth is going on, what is all this about? And the thread that's running through the work I'm doing now is this question—*who is the Beloved?*

The Pain of Being Black:
An Interview with Toni Morrison
Bonnie Angelo / 1989

From *Time* 133.21 (22 May 1989): 120–23. Copyright © 1989 Time Inc. Reprinted by permission.

Q: In your contemporary novels you portray harsh confrontation between black and white. In *Tar Baby* a character says, "White folks and black folks should not sit down and eat together or do any of those personal things in life." It seems hopeless if we can't bridge the abysses you see between sexes, classes, races.

A: I feel personally sorrowful about black-white relations a lot of the time because black people have always been used as a buffer in this country between powers to prevent class war, to prevent other kinds of real conflagrations.

If there were no black people here in this country, it would have been Balkanized. The immigrants would have torn each other's throats out, as they have done everywhere else. But in becoming an American, from Europe, what one has in common with that other immigrant is contempt for *me*—it's nothing else but color. Wherever they were from, they would stand together. They could all say, "I am not *that*." So in that sense, becoming an American is based on an attitude: an exclusion of me.

It wasn't negative to them—it was unifying. When they got off the boat, the second word they learned was "nigger." Ask them—I grew up with them. I remember in the fifth grade a smart little boy who had just arrived and didn't speak any English. He sat next to me. I read well, and I taught him to read just by doing it. I remember the moment he found out that I was black—a nigger. It took him six months; he was told. And that's the moment when he belonged, that was his entrance. Every immigrant knew he would not come as the very bottom. He had to come above at least one group—and that was us.

Q: When you think about what the Jews did as leaders in the civil rights movement, in the forefront of trying to break the barriers, how do you account for the abrasiveness between blacks and Jews now?

A: For a long time I was convinced that the conflict between Jewish people and black people in this country was a media event. But everywhere I went in the world where there were black people, somebody said, What about the blacks and Asians? What do you think about the blacks and the Mexicans? Or, in New York at one time, blacks and Puerto Ricans? The only common denominator is blacks.

I thought, "Something is disguised, what is it?" What I find is a lot of black people who believe that Jews in this country, by and large, have become white. They behave like white people rather than Jewish people.

Q: Hasn't the rift been brought about partly by the anti-Semitic rhetoric of black Muslims like Louis Farrakhan?

A: Farrakhan is one person, one black person. Why is it that no black person seems to be rabid about Meir Kahane? Farrakhan is rejected by a lot of black people who wouldn't go near that man. It's not an equal standard—one black person is all black people.

Q: But sometimes whites feel that all white people are being similarly equated, when in fact attitudes among whites range from the Ku Klux Klan right over to the saints.

A: Black people have always known that. We've had to distinguish among you because our lives depended on it. I'm always annoyed about why black people have to bear the brunt of everybody else's contempt. If we are not totally understanding and smiling, suddenly we're demons.

Q: You've said that you didn't like the idea of writing about slavery. Yet *Beloved*, your most celebrated book, is set in slavery and its aftermath.

A: I had this terrible reluctance about dwelling on that era. Then I realized I didn't know anything about it, really. And I was over-whelmed by how long it was. Suddenly the time—300 years—began to drown me.

Three hundred years—think about that. Now, that's not a war, that's generation after generation. And they were expendable. True, they had the status of good horses, and nobody wanted to kill their stock. And, of course, they had the advantage of reproducing without cost.

Q: *Beloved* is dedicated to the 60 million who died as a result of slavery. A staggering number—is this proved historically.

A: Some historians told me 200 million died. The smallest number I got from anybody was 60 million. There were travel accounts of people who were in the Congo—that's a wide river—saying, "We could not get the boat through the river, it was choked with bodies." That's like a logjam. A lot of people died. Half of them died in those ships.

Slave trade was like cocaine is now—even though it was against the law, that didn't stop anybody. Imagine getting $1,000 for a human being. That's a lot of money. There are fortunes in this country that were made that way.

I thought this has got to be the least read of all the books I'd written because it is about something that the characters don't want to remember, I don't want to remember, black people don't want to remember, white people won't want to remember. I mean, it's national amnesia.

Q: You gave new insight into the daily struggle of slaves.

A: I was trying to make it a personal experience. The book was not about the institution—Slavery with a capital S. It was about these anonymous people called slaves. What they do to keep on, how they make a life, what they're willing to risk, however long it lasts in order to relate to one another—that was incredible to me.

For me, the torturous restraining devices became a hook on which to say what it was like in personal terms. I knew about them because slaves who wrote about their lives mentioned them, and white people wrote about them. There's a wonderful diary of the Burr family in which he talks about his daily life and says, "Put the bit on Jenny today." He says that about 19 times in six months—and he was presumably an enlightened slave owner. Slave-ship captains also wrote a lot of memoirs, so it's heavily documented.

There was a description of a woman who had to wear a bell contraption so when she moved they always knew where she was. There were masks slaves wore when they cut cane. They had holes in them, but it was so hot inside that when they took them off, the skin would come off. Presumably, these things were to keep them from eating the sugar cane. What is interesting is that these things were not restraining tools, like in the torture chamber. They were things you wore while you were doing the work. Amazing. It seemed to me that the humiliation was the key to what the experience was like.

There was this ad hoc nature of everyday life. For black people, anybody might do anything at any moment. Two miles in any direction, you may run into Quakers who feed you or Klansmen who kill you—you don't know. When you leave the plantation, you are leaving not only what you know, you are leaving your family.

Q: Have you any specific proposals for improving the present-day racial climate in America?

A: It is a question of education, because racism is a scholarly pursuit. It's all over the world, I am convinced. But that's not the way people were born to live. I'm talking about racism that is taught, institutionalized. Everybody remembers the first time they were taught that part of the human race was Other. That's a trauma. It's as though I told you that your left hand is not part of your body.

How to breach those things? There is a very, very serious problem of education and leadership. But we don't have the structure for the education we need. Nobody has done it. Black literature is taught as sociology, as tolerance, not as a serious, rigorous art form.

I saw on television some black children screaming and crying about the violence in their school. But what do we do about that?

Q: But there is violence in schools that are all black, black against black.

A: Black people are victims of an enormous amount of violence. I don't have any answers other than what to do about violence generally. None of those things can take place, you know, without the complicity of the people who run the schools and the city.

Q: That's a strong condemnation. Complicity suggests that these conditions are seen as O.K.

A: Human beings can change things. Schools must stop being holding pens to keep energetic young people off the job market and off the streets. They are real threats because they may know more, they may have more energy, and they may take your job. So we stretch puberty out a long, long time.

There is nothing of any consequence in education, in the economy, in city planning, in social policy that does not concern black people.

That's where the problem is. Are you going to build a city to
accommodate more black people? Why? They don't pay taxes. Are
you going to build a school system to accommodate the children of
poor black people? Why? They'll want your job. They don't pay
taxes.

Q: Many people are deeply concerned that these young black
students are dropping out.

A: They don't care about these kids. I don't mean that there are
not people who care. But when this wonderful "they" we always
blame for anything say we've got to fix the schools, or we have got to
legalize drugs, what they care about is their personal well-being: Am
I going to get mugged? Are the homeless going to be in my neighborhood?

Q: You don't think there is great concern out there that American
society has things seriously wrong with it? Not just because "I can't
walk down the street"?

A: Yes, but I do not see vigorous attack on the wrongness. I see
what I call comic-book solutions to really major problems. Of course,
a new President can make a difference—he can reassemble the
legislation of the past 20 years that has been taken apart and put it
back. They said it didn't work. It's like building a bridge a quarter of
the way across the river and saying, "You can't get there from
here." Twenty years! It never had a generation to complete the work.
Somebody has to take responsibility for being a leader.

Q: In one of your books you described young black men who say,
"We have found the whole business of being black and men at the
same time too difficult." You said that they then turned their interest
to flashy clothing and to being hip and abandoned the responsibility
of trying to be black and male.

A: I said they took their testicles and put them on their chest. I
don't know what their responsibility is anymore. They're not given
the opportunity to choose what their responsibilities are. There's
60% unemployment for black teenagers in this city. What kind
of choice is that?

Q: This leads to the problem of the depressingly large number of
single-parent households and the crisis in unwed teenage pregnancies. Do you see a way out of that set of worsening circumstances
and statistics?

A: Well, neither of those things seems to me a debility. I don't think a female running a house is a problem, a broken family. It's perceived as one because of the notion that a head is a man.

Two parents can't raise a child any more than one. You need a whole community—everybody—to raise a child. The notion that the head is the one who brings in the most money is a patriarchal notion, that a woman—and I have raised two children, alone—is somehow lesser than a male head. Or that I am incomplete without the male. This is not true. And the little nuclear family is a paradigm that just doesn't work. It doesn't work for white people or for black people. Why we are hanging onto it. I don't know. It isolates people into little units—people need a larger unit.

Q: And teenage pregnancies?

A: Everybody's grandmother was a teenager when they got pregnant. Whether they were 15 or 16, they ran a house, a farm, they went to work, they raised their children.

Q: But everybody's grandmother didn't have the potential for living a different kind of life. These teenagers—16, 15—haven't had time to find out if they have special abilities, talents. They're babies having babies.

A: The child's not going to hurt them. Of course, it is absolutely time consuming. But who cares about the schedule? What is this business that you have to finish school at 18? They're not babies. We have decided that puberty extends to what—30? When do people stop being kids? The body is ready to have babies, that's why they are in a passion to do it. Nature wants it done then, when the body can handle it, not after 40, when the income can handle it.

Q: You don't feel that these girls will never know whether they could have been teachers, or whatever?

A: They can be teachers. They can be brain surgeons. We have to help them become brain surgeons. That's my job. I want to take them all in my arms and say, "Your baby is beautiful and so are you and, honey, you can do it. And when you want to be a brain surgeon, call me—I will take care of your baby." That's the attitude you have to have about human life. But we don't want to pay for it.

I don't think anybody cares about unwed mothers unless they're black—or poor. The question is not morality, the question is money.

That's what we're upset about. We don't care whether they have babies or not.

Q: How do you break the cycle of poverty? You can't just hand out money.

A: Why not? Everybody gets everything handed to them. The rich get it handed—they inherit it. I don't mean just inheritance of money. I mean what people take for granted among the middle and upper classes, which is nepotism, the old-boy network. That's shared bounty of class.

A Conversation with Toni Morrison

Bill Moyers / 1989

From *A World of Ideas II*. Ed. Andie Tucher. Garden City: Doubleday, 1990. Copyright © 1989 by Public Affairs Television, Inc. Used by permission of Doubleday, a division of Bantam Doubleday Dell Publishing Group, Inc.

Moyers: You said recently that it's a great relief to you that terms like "white" and "race" are now discussable in literature. How so?

Morrison: Because a language has been developed and has still some sovereignty in which we mean "white," and we mean "black," or we mean ethnic, but we say something else. There's an enormous amount of confusion. It's difficult to understand the literature of the country if you can't say "white" and you can't say "black" and you can't say "race." Now, at last, we can look clearly, for example, at Herman Melville, at Edgar Allan Poe, at Willa Cather, at real issues that were affecting founding American writers.

Moyers: The public rhetoric of our time has been filled with "race" and "white" and "black." It seems a surprise to hear you say, "Well, now at least we can discuss those in literature." You're saying that they weren't a part of our tradition of story-telling?

Morrison: Not in the critiques. Not in the discourse. Not in the reviews. Not in the scholarship around these works. It was not a subject to be discussed; race was not considered worthy of discussion. Not only that, there was an assumption that the master narrative could not encompass all of these things. The silence was absolutely important. The silence of the black person.

Moyers: The silence. His voice is never heard.

Morrison: Never heard. Blacks don't speak for themselves in the texts. And since they were not permitted to say their own things, history and the academy can't really permit them to take center stage in the discourse of the text in art, in literature.

But in public discourse, when we talk about neighborhoods, or policy, or schools, or welfare, or practically anything, the real subject is race or class. We may call it "disadvantaged," or "undeveloped," or "remedial," or all these euphemisms for poor people and/or black people, and/or any nonwhite person in this country. That is the subject of practically all of the political discourse there is. But it has been kept out of the art world.

This country is seething with the presence of black people. But it was always necessary to deny that presence when we discussed our literature. I read all those books in undergraduate school, as everybody did. We never talked about what was really going on. We talked about Huck Finn and Jim, and we thought about how wonderful the innocence of this radical child was as a paradigm for the American coming of age.

Moyers: The white American . . .

Morrison: The white American coming of age, because the story is about the construction of a white male. But Huck grows up and becomes a moral person because of his association with Jim, a black slave who is called a boy, never a man. To Mark Twain's credit, he provides the extraordinary scene where you realize that Jim has a wife and a child. He's trying to get home to them. Huck's trying to get out to the wild territory, while Jim is trying to get home. Jim tells Huck a terrible story about a time when he told his daughter to shut the door, and she didn't do it. He told her again, and she didn't do it. And he got annoyed and he hit her, and then later realized that while she had been sick recently, she had lost her hearing. And suddenly there's this man who has a context.

Moyers: A family and emotions.

Morrison: It's an overwhelming thing for Huck to say, these black people think about children the same way "we" do. It's a revelation to him. The question is, why is it a revelation?

Moyers: The artist is supposed to carry our moral imagination. Yet in the 1840s and '50s, on the eve of the Civil War, in the period of traumatic conflict over abolition and slavery, the American novelists were not dealing with those issues. Hawthorne was writing European gothics with ruins and ghosts and the supernatural. James Fenimore Cooper was writing adventure stories set in primeval forests. The best-selling novels on the eve of the Civil War, in fact, were soppy stories written by women about courageous orphans. Your people never show up in the novels of that time. How do you explain that?

Morrison: Well, they do. They do show up. They're everywhere. They're in Hawthorne's preoccupation with blackness. They're in all the dark symbols. They're in the haunting one senses in his fiction. What's he haunted by? What is the guilt? What is the real sin that is really worrying Hawthorne all his life? They're there. They're in Fenimore Cooper. They're in Melville. They're everywhere in Poe. I don't care where they find their story; writers are informed by the major currents of the world.

Moyers: But blacks don't emerge in these stories as people with context, with family, with emotions.

Morrison: No. The characters are discredited and ridiculed and purged. But the idea of those characters, the construction of them as an outside representation of anarchy, collapse, illicit sexuality—all of these negative things that white Americans feared are projected onto this presence, so that you find these extraordinary gaps and evasions and destabilizations. The chances of getting a truly complex human black person in an American book in the nineteenth century were minimal. Melville came probably very close with classic complexities, but not real flesh and blood people.

Moyers: He used them as symbols.

Morrison: Each one of the white men in *Moby-Dick* has a black brother. They're paired together. Fedallah is the shadow of Ahab. Queequeg is the shadow of Ishmael. They all have them, and they work together in tandem all through the book. What I'm saying is that while there is no realistic representation, the subtextual information is powerful. It's all self-reflective. It's all about the fabrication of a white male American.

Moyers: What is it in our makeup that just does not want to confront the reality of race? We didn't want to deal with it in the era of our founding. We just tried to act as if it wasn't there. It took a bloody and last-minute Civil War to cope with slavery itself, and then immediately after that war was over, the waters closed around and it was as if the war hadn't been. Even today, our political system seems such a complex evasion of race that we don't have to face it.

Morrison: Learning how to be an adult is very hard. So much has to be disassembled. The past has to be revised. The way one thinks about things has to change. Now, many people are not only willing to do it, they're eager to do it. They are tired of this sort of Kafka nightmare world that we're living in. But many other people cannot bear the thought of having to revise their own concept of themselves, their own neuroses, their own sense of the past. There's something else, though, that I am becoming convinced of. In some quarters, racism really feels good.

Moyers: Everybody needs somebody to look down on.

Morrison: I was looking at a television show recently in which somebody was roaming around South Africa talking about the imminent release of Nelson Mandela. Some of the white people were very upset by this and wanted apartheid to become even purer. They felt so strongly about it that they are willing to go off and establish their own little counties. They were so determined not to have any black people there that they decided on an extraordinary thing: to do their own work: They would allow no black laborers. They would plow their own land, empty their own slop jars, and so on. Now some of these people were twenty, twenty-five years old.

This sort of attitude is not a conversation; this is not dialogue. This is nothing. This is madness. This is scraping around in the bottom of the barrel of cliché in order to support the habit. The habit of disdain. So their racism is wasteful. It doesn't help. It's not economical, it's not profitable. You don't get anything for it. It has no reason for being. It has no scientific proof, no basis, nothing. Ever. Everybody knows that now. So why is it around?

Moyers: Is it conceivable that you could write a novel in which blacks are not center stage?

Morrison: Absolutely.

Moyers: Do you think the public would let you? Since you've achieved such fame by writing about black people, does the public now expect you to write only about black people?

Morrison: I will, but I won't identify them as such. That's the difference. There are two moments in *Beloved* when I tried to do just that. I set up a situation in which two people are talking—two black people—and some other people enter the scene. They're never identified as either black or white, but the reader knows instantly, and not because I use the traditional language of stereotype. One moment comes when Paul D and Sethe are walking down the street, and he touches her shoulder to lead her off the sidewalk onto the ground because three women are walking this way. That's all. But you know who they are.

There's another moment when he's in despair, talking to a friend, and a man rides up on a horse and says, "Where is Judy?" He calls the woman by her first name. You can tell by the reactions of the black man who the rider is, but I don't have to say it.

What I really want to do, and expect to do, is not identify my characters by race. But I won't be writing about white people. I'll be writing about black people. It will be part of my job to make sure my readers aren't confused. But can you think what it would mean for me and my relationship to language and to texts to be able to write without having to always specify to the reader the race of the characters?

Moyers: What does it do for us to talk about this now?

Morrison: I think it's liberating. You can see what it is that has destabilized you. You know what has gone down beneath the cracks. I think racism feels crazy. I think people who really and truly are staunch, steady racists—the ones for whom it feels good, it's right and they know it, which is why they invent documentation from biblical sources and all sorts of odd places—I think at the same time there's a part of them that knows it's truly psychotic. Racism doesn't work intellectually. I think it was Robert Penn Warren who wrote about an incident when some black students were jailed for taking part in a sit-in demonstration. The sheriff who jailed them was furious about these demonstrations, and furious that they wanted to sit at whites-only lunch counters. Then he said, "But you know, I was raised by a black woman." With tears running down his face he said, "I loved her." His rage was at the students he had to lock up. But there was another rage: that he had to stop loving that woman. He really did love her. And the craziness was of having to say to her, "You don't belong to me; I can't love you anymore. It's over." Racism makes you deny the real world of your emotions.

Moyers: There is such a gulf between the "inner city" today and the rest of the country in both imagination and reality, in politics and literature. If you were writing for the rest of the country about the "inner city" today, what metaphor would you use?

Morrison: Love. We have to embrace ourselves. Self-regard. James Baldwin once said, "You've already been bought and paid for. Your ancestors already gave it up for you. You don't have to do that anymore. Now you can love yourself. It's already possible."

I have a feeling of admiration and respect and love for these black people in the "inner city" who *are* intervening. Some of them are going in and saying, "You four girls—you come to my house every Thursday and we're going to eat, or I'm going to take you out." These are professional women who become companions to these children. I love those men I heard about in Chicago—black professional men—who went every lunch hour to the playgrounds in Chicago's south side to talk to children. Not to be authoritarian, but just to get to know them, without the bureaucracy, without the agencies. They simply became their own agency. Or some woman told me a couple of weeks ago that black men were going into shelters and spending time holding crack babies. Just holding them. Now I'm sure it does something for the baby, but think what it does for that man to actually give up some time and hold a baby. There are organizations, of course, there are still agencies, but there are also these individuals who do care for children—the caretakers, the lovers. That has to be the most glorious thing that is going on.

Moyers: The love you're talking about is the love inspired by moral imagination that takes us beyond blood.

Morrison: Absolutely.

Moyers: A critic once said, "Toni Morrison writes about places where even love found its way with an ice pick." You say love is the metaphor. When I go back through your novels, love is there in so many different ways and forms. The women in your novels particularly do extraordinary things for love. There's a grandmother who has her leg amputated so that her insurance policy will buy a house and take care of her children as they grow up. There's Sethe, who is willing to kill her children before the slave catchers can come and seize them. What kind of love is that?

Morrison: Some of it's very fierce. Powerful. Distorted. The duress they work under is so overwhelming. But I think they believed, as I do, that when people say, "I didn't ask to be born," they are wrong. I think we *did*. That's why we're here. We have to do something nurturing that we respect before we go. We must. It is more interesting, more complicated, more intellectually demanding and more morally demanding to love somebody. To take care of somebody. To make one other person feel good.

Now the dangers of that are the dangers of setting one's self up as a martyr, or as the one without whom nothing could be done. But like the acquisitions of knowledge, that's what the mind does. I mean, it may not get the knowledge you want it to have, but it's busy all the time.

Moyers: In your novel *Beloved,* Paul D says to Sethe, "Your love is too thick." Is that what you're talking about?

Morrison: It can be excessive.

Moyers: How do we know when our love is too thick?

Morrison: We don't. We really don't. That's a big problem. We don't know when to stop. When is it too much and when is it not enough? That is the problem of the human mind and the soul. But we have to try. Not trying is so poor for the self. It's so poor for the mind. It's so uninteresting to live without love. Life has no risk. Love just seems to make life not just livable, but a gallant, gallant event.

Moyers: But I have a sense in so many of the love stories in your novels that love is destined to be doomed by the world.

Morrison: In the stories, I place the characters on a cliff. I push them as far as I can to see what they are made of. I say to them, "You really think you're in love? Well, let me see what it's like under these circumstances. You think this is important; what about this?" I place them in that tragic mode so I can get at what those emotions really are. What is interesting to me is that under the circumstances in which the people in my books live there is this press toward love. They triumph in that sense. Which is not to say they don't get sick and die—everyone does. I mean, the decay is already out there somewhere because we're mortal. We really are mortal. That's what it means. The point is what is the process while you are here?

Moyers: What about Ella in *Beloved* who says, "If anybody was to ask me I'd say, 'Don't love nothing' "?

Morrison: I've heard that said many times. "Don't love nothing. Save it." You see, that was one of the devastating things in the experience of black people in this country, the effort to prevent full expression of their love. And the sentiment that Ella has is conservative. If you want to hang on to your sanity or hang on to yourself, don't love anything; it'll hurt. The next time they break its back, you'll have a little love left over. You kind of husband it. You hold it back. And of course that's true not just of African-Americans, it's true of all sorts of people. It's so risky. People don't want to get hurt; they don't want to be left; they don't want to be abandoned. It's as though love is always some present you're giving somebody else. It's really a present you're giving yourself.

Moyers: On the other hand, there's Pilate, your character who reminds me of my aunt Mildred. In *Song of Solomon* she says, "I wish I'd a knowed more people. I would of loved them all. If I'd a knowed more, I would a loved more." There are people like that, too.

Morrison: That's a totally generous free woman. She's fearless. She's not afraid of anything. She has very few material things. She has a little self-supportive skill that she performs. She doesn't run anybody's life. She's available for almost infinite love. If you need her—she'll deliver. And she has complete clarity about who she is.

Moyers: Did you know people like that?

Morrison: Yes, in my family there are women who presented themselves to me that way. They are just absolutely clear and absolutely reliable. They have this sort of intimate relationship with God and death and all sorts of things that strike fear into the modern heart. They have a language for it. They have a blessedness maybe. But they seem not to be fearful.

It's to those women that I really feel an enormous responsibility. Whenever I answer questions such as the ones you put to me about how terrible it all is and how it's all going down the drain, I think about my great-grandmother and her daughter and her daughter and all those women. Incredible things happened to those people. They never knew from one day to the next about anything, but they believed in their dignity. They believed they were people of value, and they had to pass that on. And they did it. So when I confront these little twentieth-century problems—

Moyers: Well, you also created a twentieth-century woman in *Sula*. She's out there, independent, uncontained, and uncontainable, you said. You called her the New World black woman. Why?

Morrison: Well, she's experimental. She's sort of an outlaw: she's not going to take it anymore. She's available to her own imagination.

Other people's stories, other people's definitions are not hers. The thing about Sula is that she makes you do your own defining for yourself.

I think one of the interesting things about feminine intelligence is that it can look at the world as though we can do two things or three things at once—the personality is more fluid, more receptive. The boundaries are not quite so defined. I think that's part of what modernism is. And I think that we're probably in a very good position to do that as black women. I mean we're managing households and other people's children and two jobs and listening to everybody and at the same time creating, singing, holding, bearing, transferring the culture for generations. We've been walking on water for four hundred years.

Moyers: Have these women you created taught you anything?

Morrison: Oh yes. All the books are questions for me. I write them because I don't know something. In *Tar Baby,* for instance, there was something in there I really did not understand: what is the problem between a pair of lovers who really love one another but are culturally different? What is the battle about? Culture? Class? When Son and Jadine can't speak to one another, they're both a little right, but nobody will give—nobody will say, "Okay, I'll give you this little bit." What have they learned? How can you manage to love another person under these circumstances if your culture, your class, your education are that different? All the while I wrote that book I was eager for them to make it. You know, end up and get married and go to the seashore.

Moyers: And yet?

Morrison: They didn't. They each had to learn something else, I think, before that could happen. With *Beloved,* I began to think about motherhood. It's not the all-encompassing role for women now, it can be a secondary role, or you don't have to choose it. But on the other hand, there was something so valuable about what happened when one became a mother. For me it was the most liberating thing that ever happened to me.

Moyers: Liberating? Isn't every mother a hostage to love?

Morrison: Liberating because the demands that children make are not the demands of a normal "other." The children's demands on me were things that nobody else ever asked me to do. To be a good

manager. To have a sense of humor. To deliver something that
somebody could use. And they were not interested in all the things
that other people were interested in, like what I was wearing or if
I were sensual. All of that went by. You've seen the eyes of your
children. They don't want to hear it. They want to know what you
are going to do now—today? Somehow all of the baggage that I had
accumulated as a person about what was valuable just fell away. I
could not only be me—whatever that was—but somebody actually
needed me to be that.

It's different from being a daughter. It's different from being a
sister. If you listen to your children and look at them, they make
demands that you can live up to. They don't need all that overwhelming love either. I mean, that's just you being vain about it. If you
listen to them, somehow you are able to free yourself from baggage
and vanity and all sorts of things, and deliver a better self, one that
you like. The person that was in me that I liked best was the one my
children seemed to want. Not the one that frowned when they walked
in the room and said, "Pull your socks up." Also, you could begin to
see the world through their eyes again—which are your eyes. I found
that extraordinary.

Moyers: You raised them by yourself, didn't you?

Morrison: Yes.

Moyers: Would you have liked to have had the help of a compan-
ion?

Morrison: Yes. It would have been nice to have somebody else to
think things through with you. The more the merrier. I needed a
lot of help.

Moyers: As I listen to you talk about the liberation of motherhood
and love, I find all the more incredible Sethe's willingness to kill
her daughter, Beloved, rather than let the slave trader kidnap her.

Morrison: That was Margaret Garner's story. She was a slave
woman who escaped from Kentucky and arrived in Cincinnati to live
with her mother-in-law. Right after she got there the man who owned
her found her. She ran out into the shed and tried to kill all her
children. Just like that. She was about to bang the head of one up
against the wall when they stopped her.

She became a *cause célèbre* for the abolitionists because they were
attempting to get her tried for murder. That would have been a big

coup because it would have assumed she had some responsibility over those children. But the abolitionists were unsuccessful. She was tried for the "real" crime, which was stolen property, and convicted and returned to that same man.

I didn't want to know a great deal about her story because there would be no space for me to invent, but what struck me was that when they interviewed her she was not a mad-dog killer. She was very calm. All she said was, "They will not live like that. They will not live like that." Her mother-in-law, who was a preacher, said, "I watched her do it. And I neither encouraged her nor discouraged her." So for them, it was a dilemma. Shall I permit my children, who are my best thing, to live like I have lived, when I know that's terrible? So she decided to kill them and kill herself. That was noble. She was saying, "I'm a human being. These are my children. This script I am writing."

Moyers: Did you ever put yourself in her position and ask, "Could I have done that to my two sons?"

Morrison: I ask it a lot. As a matter of fact, the reason the character Beloved enters the novel is because I couldn't answer it. I didn't know whether I would do it or not. You hear stories of that in slavery and Holocaust situations, where women have got to figure it out—fast, really fast. But the only person I felt had the right to ask her that question was Beloved, the child she killed. She could ask Sethe, "What'd you do that for? Is this better? What do you know?" For me it was an impossible decision. Someone gave me the line for it at one time which I have found useful. "It was the right thing to do, but she had no right to do it."

Moyers: And you've never answered it in your own case. "Could I do it?"

Morrison: I've asked. I don't know. I really don't know. There are some things that I could imagine as the fate of my children, particularly when they were young, that I'd have to think very carefully about. Would I be willing to let certain things happen? There are terrible things in the world. Suppose you knew for sure, as some people have learned later, that your children have been sold to child pornographers?

Moyers: What do you think is the primary role of the novel? Is it to illuminate social reality, or is it to stretch our imagination?

Morrison: The latter. It really is about stretching. But in that way you have to bear witness to what *is*. The fear of collapse, of meaning-lessness, of disorder, of anarchy—there's a certain protection that art can provide in the guise, not even of truth, but just a kind of linguistic shape of a life or a group of lives. Through that encounter, when you brush up against that, if it's any good, or it touches you in some way, it does really rub off. It enhances. It makes one or two things possible in one's own life, personally. You see something. Somebody takes a cataract away from your eye, or somehow your ear gets unplugged. You feel larger, connected. Something of sub-stance you have encountered connects with another experience.

Novelists can do that. Art can do it in a number of ways. But it certainly should stretch. I don't want to read a book that simply reinforces all my prejudices and ignorances and things I half-know. I want one that says, "Oh, I'd forgotten—but that is exactly the way it looks," or "Oh, that's what that feeling is."

Moyers: That's what you've done for so many others. The paradox to me is that I grew up in a small Southern town in the 1930s and '40s and '50s—twenty-two thousand people, half black, half white. It wasn't until I read your novels and the novels of people writing, as you do, about the past that I really knew what the folks on the other side of the tracks were thinking and feeling and experiencing.

Morrison: That's important if a book can do that.

Moyers: If only a book could do it now, for people who are in our circle of the present. Why do we have to wait so long for reconcilia-tion?

Morrison: You were ready for the information. You were available to the book. Some people are not available to the book, to that information. I'm sure there are books that I am just not ready to hear. It's not that the novel batters you down and gets rid of barri-cades or opens doors. The person inside you has to be accessible. There has to be a little crack in there already, some curiosity. Some willingness, you know, to know about it. Some moment when you really don't have the blinders on. We know people who just zip their eyes shut, who are totally enclosed in the neurotic and frequently psychotic prison of racism. But if ever any chinks can be made from the inside or outside, then they become accessible to certain kinds of information.

Moyers: Are you aware when you're writing that you're going to invade my imagination? That you're going to subvert my perception? Were you intentionally trying to do that?

Morrison: Totally. I want the reader to feel, first of all, that he trusts me. I'm never going to do anything so bad that he can't handle it. But at the same time, I want him to see things he has never seen before. I want him to work with me in the book. I can rely on some things that I know you know. For instance, I know you don't believe in ghosts, none of us do, but—

Moyers: I wouldn't go too far in that assumption.

Morrison: Well, we were all children. We all knew that we did not sleep with our hands hanging outside the bed. To this day if you wake up and your hand is hanging out there you move it back in. So I can rely on readers to know those things. But I do want to penetrate the readerly subconsciousness so that the response is, on the one hand, an intellectual one to what I have problematized in the text, but at the same time very somatic, visceral, a physical response so that you really think you see it or you can smell it or you can hear it, without my overdoing it. Because it has to be yours.

I don't describe Pilate a lot in *Song of Solomon*. She's tall and she wears this ear thing and she says less than people think. But I felt that I saw her so clearly, I wanted to communicate the clarity, not of my vision, but of a vision so that she belongs to whoever's envisioning her in the text. And people can say, "Oh, I know her. I know who that is. She is . . ." and they fill in the blank because they have invented her.

An Inspired Life: Toni Morrison Writes and a Generation Listens

Dana Micucci / 1992

From the *Chicago Tribune* 31 May 1992: sec 6.3. Reprinted with the permission of Dana Micucci and the *Chicago Tribune*'s "Womenews."

NEW YORK—"It's always the same sort of compulsion and delight," says novelist Toni Morrison of her writing. Her voice is soft and lulling, punctuated frequently by an exuberant laugh that hints of a warm and ready generosity.

Morrison, 61, hailed by critics as one of the most important African-American female writers of our generation who has become a voice for a culture, has just published her sixth novel, *Jazz*. Her first book since winning the Pulitzer Prize for *Beloved* in 1988, *Jazz* tells the story of a love triangle while evoking the pulsating tempo of Harlem in the 1920s.

"I wanted to show how ordinary people lived and viewed that period in history," Morrison says.

"Jazz itself is one of the most vital artistic forms in the world. It symbolizes an incredible kind of improvisation, a freedom in which a great deal of risk is involved."

Her parents' stories about the 1920s of their youth partly inspired *Jazz*, says Morrison, who recalls the "gleaming terms of excitement and attraction" they used to describe that era.

"Everything is great for the writer's mill," she says.

Morrison was born Chloe Anthony Wofford to parents who had migrated from Georgia and Alabama and settled in Lorain, Ohio, just west of Cleveland. She is the second-oldest of four children. Her late father, George Wofford, worked in a steel mill. Her mother, Ramah Willis, who still lives in Lorain, sang jazz and opera.

"We played music in the house all the time," says Morrison, who describes her family as "joyful, high-spirited people" whose story-telling tradition influenced her writing.

"People talked more back then and had a tendency to recount their

275

lives in large narrative gestures," she says. "It was a form of entertainment."

Morrison recalls being "utterly devoted" to her father and vying
for his attention with her older sister. (Morrison also has two younger
brothers.)

"Being in the second-girl position is about as anonymous as you
can get," she says. "I felt I had no pride of place. I started reading
when I was 4 and read all the time. I found comfort and solace in
other people's narratives."

But she is also a product of her parents' strong-willed characters,
Morrison says.

"They could always do something about a difficult situation," she
says, "They never tucked tail. I felt much endowed by their tenacity.
My father always took it for granted that I could do anything, and
my mother and grandmother never entertained fragility or vulnerability."

" 'After all, look what we did,' they'd say about their escape from
life-threatening situations in the racially tense South."

She recalled hearing stories about "white boys" threatening her
grandmother's family on her farm in Greenville, Ala.

Morrison, who says she never set out to be a writer but always
wanted to teach, graduated from Howard University in Washington,
in 1953 with a degree in English literature and classics.

The first woman in her family to attend college, she earned her
master's degree in English as Cornell University two years later and
went on to teach English at Texas Southern University in 1956 and
1957. While teaching at Howard University from 1958 to 1963, she
began writing.

At the time she was a member of an informal writing group, for
which she wrote a "little story" that in 1970 became her first novel,
The Bluest Eye, an account of racial tensions in Lorain, Ohio.

"Writing was something I did privately at night like women with
families who use their off hours for creative projects," Morrison
says. "I didn't call myself a writer. I just did it to pass the time, and I
enjoyed it."

"But once I began *The Bluest Eye* it was such an energizing
experience, I felt bored with what was out there. Suddenly I wanted

to move from what other people thought and imagined to what I thought and imagined."

It wasn't as effortless as it sounds, however. In 1963, Morrison separated from and eventually divorced her husband, an architect she had met in Washington. (Morrison is guarded about her personal life and refuses to discuss the marriage further. She only will say that she raised two sons, Ford, now 30, and Slade, now 26, on her own.)

"It was a little bleak at that time," she says. "My back was up against the wall, and I didn't want the easy route, which was to live at home with my family or to be in another dependent situation. I wanted to find out who I was and whether I was tough enough."

After Morrison left her teaching post at Howard, she worked as a textbook editor at L. W. Singer, a division of Random House Publishers in Syracuse, N.Y. for two years. She then moved to New York and continued as an editor for Random House for the next 20 years.

She also managed to teach English on Fridays at Rutgers and Yale Universities until she was offered the Albert E. Schweitzer Humanities Chair at the State University of New York in Albany. She held that post from 1984 to 1989, when she moved to Princeton University, where she is Robert F. Goheen Professor, Council of the Humanities.

"I was partly drawn to teaching because I didn't know what to do with a master's in English," Morrison says. "Once I got into it, I really enjoyed it. Now my students ask me how they can become writers, and I tell them to go out and get a [paying] job!"

Throughout her teaching and editing careers, Morrison says she found the time and courage to continue writing.

After some favorable reviews and modest sales for her first book, Morrison's second novel, *Sula*, which is about friendship between women, was published in 1974 to much critical acclaim.

Then followed *Song of Solomon*, winner of the National Book Critics Circle Award in 1977; *Tar Baby*; and *Beloved*, which was based on an 1850s newspaper account of Margaret Garner, a runaway slave who killed her 2-year-old daughter to save her from slavery.

Morrison downplays the Pulitzer Prize she won for *Beloved*, saying she was surprised and flattered but that it didn't alter her life significantly.

Her motivation to write is more personal, she says. All of her

novels pose questions, says Morrison, who has become known for
exploring issues of gender and race in ways few others have success-
fully attempted.

"I'm interested in how men are educated, how women relate to
each other, how we are able to love, how we balance political and
personal forces, who survives in certain situations and who doesn't
and, specifically, how these and other universal issues relate to
African-Americans," she says. "The search for love and identity
runs through most everything I write."

Writing is the place where she can be courageous, says Morrison,
where she can "think the unthinkable."

"It's an exploration of the possibilities of self and being human in
the world, and it allows me to stretch and grow deeper. I always
wanted to have some teeth in my work."

She had planned to stop writing after her fourth book, but something kept pushing her, she says. "Every now and then some incredi-
bly compelling idea comes up and poses itself as a question. Then I
find myself formulating characters who can work out answers to the
questions."

In lyrical, rhythmic prose, *Jazz* tells the story of Joe Trace, a
middle-aged door-to-door cosmetics salesman; his wife, Violet, a
beautician; and Joe's 18-year-old lover, Dorcas—a love triangle with
a tragic end that serves as a starting point for Morrison's exploration
of her characters' sorrows, secrets and violent pasts.

Expressing Violet's rage at her husband's adultery, Morrison
writes: ". . . her hand, the one that wasn't holding the glass shaped
like a flower, was under the table drumming out the rhythm on the
inside of his thigh, his thigh, his thigh, thigh, thigh, and he bought
her underwear with stitching done to look like rosebuds and violets,
VIOLETS, don't you know, and she wore it for him thin as it was
. . . while I was where? Sliding on ice trying to get to somebody's
kitchen to do their hair?"

Morrison hardly seems ready to lay down her pen, having just
published, in addition to *Jazz*, a collection of critical essays. *Playing
in the Dark* is an inquiry into the significance of African-Americans
in American literature and the imaginative ways in which white
writers appropriated the lives and language of blacks.

"Black characters were used to represent endless love, like Jim in

Huckleberry Finn, for example," Morrison says. "The response of writers like Twain, Melville, Faulkner and Hawthorne toward blacks hadn't been recognized by critics in a formal study, she says."

Morrison, who has become a role model for African-American women and women in general, views that responsibility with seriousness and humility.

"My rank in terms of writing is of no interest to me. The truth is that you have to face blank paper, and labels don't help you much."

"I am happy if I can serve as an inspiration to others and to women who want to write. But it's not right for people to transfer their own internal responsibilities to a role model."

"My job is to be a morally responsible human being. And that's a private struggle."

Morrison's public struggles, however, have been similar to those faced by all women, she says.

"Whether it was in the university or the corporation, there was always that sense of dismissal, easy contempt and patronage. There's always a barrier to break down. Each profession has a territory reserved for women that one woman will eventually challenge."

As a single mother trying to keep career and family intact, she admits to having made "a lot of mistakes."

"It was very difficult writing and rearing children because they deserve all your time, and you don't have it," says Morrison, who has not remarried.

"It's easy to overestimate and underestimate your ability to do both. I regret having had to work alone and raise children. But the other choices were unacceptable to me. I had to see if it was possible to be on my own."

One thing she doesn't regret was "putting writing at the center" of her life.

"You just shift priorities. And if you want to do it badly enough you'll find the time. You'll be so eager to get to it that it won't be a burden. Women shouldn't wait for someone to give them permission to write."

All That Jazz

Betty Fussell / 1992

From *Lear's* 5.8 (1 October 1992): 68. Reprinted by permission of the author and the Watkins/Loomis Agency.

As I walk across the Princeton University campus toward Dickinson Hall, everything looks as I imagine it did when Scott Fitzgerald danced across the lawns: the grass as green, the ivy as thick, the Gothic as faux. So little seems to have changed this side of paradise that the face framed by mullioned windows across McCosh Court is startling. It's not the face of some golden preppie or tweedy prof, but of Aïda, performed by Leontyne Price: a face of strong brows, carved lips, and iron-gray hair piled in a bun. Up close, Toni Morrison, like the characters in her novels, seems larger than life—a phrase she scorns: "There isn't anything bigger than life," she has said. Still, some lives, like Morrison's, are bigger and richer than others.

When she stands to greet me in her office, I am shocked to see how short she is. Height, though, has nothing to do with the powerful way she fixes you in her gaze or transfixes you with her voice. I was warned that she can be prickly, but she wraps me in a cocoon of warmth and laughter so intimate and spontaneous that I'm unaware, at first, of how skillfully she is playing me. Toni Morrison does not so much give an interview as perform one, in a silken voice that can purr like a saxophone or erupt like brass.

At 61 she is more famous than ever (she won the Pulitzer Prize in 1988 and there is talk of a Nobel) and in some ways more elusive. But the public Toni Morrison has been very much on view of late. Last spring, her sixth novel, *Jazz*, and her volume of critical essays, *Playing in the Dark*, both made the best-seller list of *The New York Times*; this month, Pantheon Books will publish a collection of essays that she edited on the Clarence Thomas–Anita Hill debate. Called *Re-Racing Justice, En-Gendering Power*, it includes a provocative introductory piece by Morrison herself. She also lectures frequently and seems increasingly inclined to air her views on the culture and politics of race.

Wherever she appears, whether in person or on the printed page, her performance is of a piece. With warmth, humor, flamboyance, and passion, she grabs your imagination and hauls you into her mythic world, where the supernatural is common and the ordinary strange, where the earthly and unearthly meet in city streets and country pastures and hearts of darkness.

If her vision and ambition are on the grand scale, her manner is easy and personal. Immediately she creates a link between us by talking about her two grown sons, aged 30 and 26. The older one, Ford, is a flutist, guitar player, and sound engineer, a musician like Morrison's mother. The younger one, Slade, is a budding architect whose graduation present from his mother is a year abroad, "the year none of us had and always wanted, the year we missed," she says, figuring we share Depression memories and motherhood, knowing I'll respond when she adds, "It's good when your children come back to you grown."

Toni Morrison has been a teacher for nearly 40 years—in the 1960s, Stokely Carmichael and Claude Brown were among her students at Howard University—and she is at home in academe. Still, her worldly aura is slightly out of sync in Princeton. The casual cottons she wears today are accented by an outside gold-and-diamond ring. Her standard campus office is guarded by a personal secretary who has an office of her own. Morrison has a comfortable house near Lake Carnegie but often retreats to a second home up the Hudson in New York. She is immensely popular on campus, I'm told, but some of her colleagues envy the wealth she's amassed, both from books and from lectures, for which she is reportedly paid $10,000 a pop. And some Princeton hostesses resent the distance she keeps from the local social scene.

There are even those who think her talents are wasted on the undergraduates she teaches here: As one colleague puts it, "It's like asking a Rolls Royce mechanic to work on a Fiat." But Morrison, who believes that teaching, like writing, is a powerful way to alter the imagination, seems challenged by her Princeton students.: "They are incredible," she says, adding with pleasure that they "fly, absolutely fly" with her interpretation of American literature through mythologies of race. "For some, it's as though literature has been given back to them."

By tradition, Princeton has been the most parochial and southern of the Ivies; as late as Fitzgerald's day, rich boys arrived with polo ponies and body servants, quartering them in what is still a black community not far from campus. But under Harold Shapiro, Princeton's first Jewish president, the university has changed the face of its curriculum along with its structure of power. Over the last few years, Shapiro has recruited a group of stellar Afro-American scholars for whom Morrison is the artistic and spiritual mentor, including Cornel West, director of Afro-American studies; Arnold Rampersad, director of American studies; and Albert Raboteau, new dean of Princeton's graduate programs. (Princeton had also tried to get Henry Louis Gates, Jr., whom Harvard recently hired to renew its moribund Afro-American studies program). All of them are redefining American history and the place of Afro-American culture within it. And because they all bridge departments, there's a potent cross-fertilization. "I don't think Princeton's old boys realize just how strong they are," one alum and longtime faculty member says with a laugh.

Morrison holds a double appointment at Princeton—she is also a tenured professor in the creative writing department, along with two other prominent novelists, Joyce Carol Oates and Russell Banks. With stars of this order, there's some crowding onstage, but Banks, for one, relishes the scene. "When you think of it, neither Toni, Joyce, nor I could have gone to Princeton, because of gender, class, or race," he says. "So it's kind of remarkable."

Morrison's combination of "serious scholarship, creative imagination, and connectedness to the larger world," as Banks puts it, gives her a moral authority many writers long for but few achieve. She is using that authority now to express overtly the political views that have been implicit in her novels from the beginning. Indeed, her new essay collection is bound to elicit the kind of controversy she welcomes in spelling out the politics of race, sex, and power.

What angered Morrison about the Thomas hearings was a public voyeurism fueled by what she calls "mythologies of blackness." "Black people, as a group, are used to signify the polar opposites of love and repulsion," she writes in her essay. To achieve Supreme

Court status, Thomas bleached his blackness, pretended to "raceless-
ness" by displaying his white bride. Hill's charges were intolerable
because they "re-raced" him, blackened his image, and for that she
became the guilty one. In a typical metaphoric leap, Morrison titled
her essay "Friday on the Potomac," to link the Senate's hearings on
an October Friday in 1991 with Daniel Dafoe's *Robinson Crusoe*
and his man Friday in 1719. In order to survive, the island savage
whom Crusoe named Friday was compelled to learn his master's
language, but in the process he lost his native tongue, and with it his
identity. Clarence Thomas lost no less, Morrison claims.

Her vision is strong, even heroic, and like James Joyce, she explodes institutionalized mythologies to invent her own. While she
attacks racial and sexual stereotypes, she reserves her full anger for
those who would deny they exist. "In a wholly racialized society,
there is no escape from racially inflected language," she asserts, and
to reclaim that language, to make felt "the dark, abiding, Afro-
American presence" that has been haunting America from its incep-
tion, to explore what shaped the American imagination and to change
the way America imagines itself—that is the task Morrison has set
herself.

She was born Chloe Anthony Wofford, the second of four children,
in 1931. Her parents had migrated from the south to the small
midwestern steel town of Lorain, Ohio. It was a place that didn't
have the luxury of strict segregation because the town was filled with
so many kinds of immigrants—Mexicans, Italians, southern whites,
Eastern Europeans—all looking for work. "I never lived in a black
neighborhood," she says now. Wherever her family lived, whether
"tentatively in little apartments over grocery stores" or in somewhat
better circumstances, "there was always a mix of races and nationali-
ties." Her father was the one who was racist, she believes: He felt
that all black people were superior to whites.

George Wofford had come north from Georgia at 16 and eventually
found work as a welder in the shipyards on the rim of Lake Erie.
Her mother, Ramah Willis, had come from Kentucky, where her
family had moved after they lost their land in Alabama at the turn of
the century and were forced to become sharecroppers. Her mother's
family were all musicians; her grandfather was a violinist, and her
mother had played piano in silent-movie theaters. But what her

mother mostly did, as she went about her chores, was sing, in a gorgeous voice, all day, all kinds of things: "My mother sang opera, she sang sentimental Victorian songs, she sang arias from *Carmen*, she sang jazz, and she sang blues, she sang what Ella Fitzgerald sang, and she sang 'Ave Maria.' " Music is what Morrison's novels are about "because music was everywhere and all around."

Morrison's family valued reading as much as music. "They thought it was a powerfully enabling thing to read," she says, and although her grandfather John Solomon Willis had no formal schooling—he went to school for only one day, to tell the teacher he wouldn't be back—he was known as a man who'd read the Bible three times through. Always a good student, Morrison read through the European and English classics, the great Russians, Shakespeare, Twain.

She was lucky in learning two languages, she says, one from books and the other from family talk at the mass gatherings that always took place when somebody came up from the South. Those communal memories gave her a rich world to draw on in her novels. Although her mother never once went back South to visit because her experience of it had been so bad, "she talked about it as though it were heaven, absolute heaven."

Morrison has good memories of her own childhood in Lorain, where she reveled in the rhythms and metaphors that knit communities together, in the ghost stories her parents told, and in the dream book her grandmother kept and played the numbers by. Even so, Morrison dreamed not of becoming a writer but a dancer, like Maria Tallchief. She didn't begin to write until she was 30, long after she'd acquired a B.A. from Howard and the nickname Toni from her classmates, had gotten an M.A. from Cornell, had taught English at Texas Southern and Howard universities, and had married and divorced a Jamaican architect, Harold Morrison. If she'd stayed married, she might never have begun to write, she told an interviewer earlier in her career. When the marriage ended after six years, she had a three-year-old and a baby on the way. She returned home to Lorain for a year, then got a job editing textbooks in a Syracuse subsidiary of Random House. She soon moved to New York and eventually became a senior editor at Random House, but she was nearly 40 before her years of writing at night after the children were put to bed culminated in her first novel. Published in 1970, *The Bluest Eye* is the story of a pathetically ugly child in Lorain who is raped by her drunken father. The book did not take the world by storm, but it provided a glimpse of what was to come. Not until she wrote her third novel, *Song of Solomon* (published in 1977), did her career begin to fly.

"The remarkable thing about Toni," says Erroll McDonald, the black editor who heads Pantheon Books, "is that with every book since *Song of Solomon* she has increased her readership substantially"—and the commercial rewards that go with it. Her critical and popular success, however, has not gone unpunished. Many accuse her of a racist agenda that interferes with both scholarship and art. Her essays have been criticized as political stump speeches and her novels as portentous and gushy. *The New Yorker* described *Tar Baby* as toppling "into dreadful pits of bombast"; and even an admirer finds that "her weak suit is always that self-romanticizing lyrical voice, that mythic stuff that gets to be a fancy dodge." Other critics, such as John Leonard, revel in that very sound, "as if Ellington had gone baroque. . . . Jazz, yes,; but also Mozart."

She's not one of those writers who pretends never to read her reviews. "I read them all—twice," she once told Dick Cavett. "She jokes about them," says a friend, "but I believe her when she says 'I don't want to hear it's a great book, I want to hear it's the greatest.' " She took a lot of flak from academics for venturing into literary criticism with *Playing in the Dark*, and she's annoyed. "I am frequently called upon to defend not what I say in criticism," she maintains, "but why I dared to enter that field." She's outraged by a publisher's ad for the volume, which describes her work as "an examination of the black experience in white literature." "It has nothing to do with with black experience, nothing at all," she says. "It has to do with the way classic American writers interpreted, imagined, and recorded an other, who was black, which had nothing to do with the way they really were."

In her novels, Morrison seeks to restore the oral language of black people, the mix of blues and jazz and gossip and tales; she also wants to tell her stories in a voice that can incorporate high culture and low, Greek tragic choruses and gospel songs, so "you don't feel the jumps"—as when her mother would smoothly shift from *Carmen* to hymns to blues. Morrison has involved herself in music more directly: She wrote the book and lyrics for a musical, *New Orleans*, about Storyville in 1917 (it has yet to be produced), as well as the lyrics for *Honey and Rue*, a song cycle performed by Kathleen Battle, with music by André Previn.

But while she has songs in her head, Toni Morrison is not a musician. Her instruments are words, not notes. She remembers that when she and her sister were small they were sent out to take piano lessons: "We thought we were somehow crippled, because everybody else just sat down and played and we couldn't." What she could do, she learned, was to write novels that read like operas on the page. Words came to Morrison in arias and choruses; she constructs tragic scenes of love and violent death while pushing her characters "toward the abyss somewhere to see what is remarkable, because that's the way I find out what is heroic."

Confronting the abyss that separates races, sexes, and classes gives power to her political utterances, even as she challenges conventional political wisdom. *The New Republic* ridiculed what it referred to as "Morrison's baby sitting service" after she defended teenage pregnancies in a 1989 interview in *Time*. And in discussing abortion, she alludes to the fact that blacks may have their own reasons to be distrustful of it. But her phrasing "When does the community own your egg?" deftly invokes slavery. There are many kinds of enslavement, she says in a voice soft as butter. Slavery is when people for centuries rebreed your children and slavery is when you legislate and govern women's bodies.

In *Beloved*, her fifth and possibly finest novel, a mother kills her baby to prevent the baby's enslavement. Murdering as part of mothering, the perversions of nurturing, the violence of love—these are issues she will continue to explore in her new novel, this time focusing on what she calls "the absolute violence" that women, endowed with all the riches of the '60s, '70s, and '80s, do to each other.

Not many writers today risk the cremation of so layered, so large, and so committed a world as Morrison's, but that daring has made her central to American writing, according to Russell Banks, because, like Melville's, her world is "grounded in the earth and manages to connect to the heavens as well." Adds Errol McDonald,

"In its sense of terror and sublimity," Morrison's world "hearkens back ultimately to Romantic literature, a sense of knowing there are things out there too high to get over, too low to get under, a sense of heaven and hell.'

My glimpse of Aïda in the Gothic windows of Dickinson Hall was prophetic; Aïda, the enslaved Ethiopian queen, both feared and beloved, whose heroic love-death is redeemed by song. When the curtain falls on our interview, I feel as if I've joined the chorus in a world like Verdi's that is bigger, richer, freer than before. The campus is the same when I walk back through the dappled shade of McCosh Court. But I am not.

Index